❧ Participant Observation ❧

❧ Participant Observation ❧

A Guide for Fieldworkers

Second Edition

Kathleen M. DeWalt and Billie R. DeWalt

ALTAMIRA
PRESS

A division of
ROWMAN & LITTLEFIELD PUBLISHERS, INC.
Lanham • *New York* • *Toronto* • *Plymouth, UK*

Published by AltaMira Press
A division of Rowman & Littlefield Publishers, Inc.
A wholly owned subsidary of The Rowman & Littlefield Publishing Group, Inc.
4501 Forbes Boulevard, Suite 200, Lanham, Maryland 20706
http://www.altamirapress.com

Estover Road, Plymouth PL6 7PY, United Kingdom

British Library Cataloguing in Publication Information Available

Library of Congress Cataloging-in-Publication Data

DeWalt, Kathleen Musante.
    Participant observation : a guide for fieldworkers / Kathleen M. DeWalt and Billie R. DeWalt.
       p. cm.
    Includes bibliographical references and index.
    ISBN 978-0-7591-1926-0 (cloth : alk. paper) —
    ISBN 978-0-7591-1927-7 (pbk. : alk. paper) —
    ISBN 978-0-7591-1928-4 (electronic)
    1. Participant observation. 2. Ethnology—Fieldwork. 3. Sociology—Fieldwork. 4. Social sciences—Fieldwork. I. DeWalt, Billie R. II. Title.
    GN346.4.D48 2011
    305.8001—dc22
                                            2010032385

Printed in the United States of America

✂ Contents ✂

❧ Preface ❧

As with the first edition of this book, we have written this volume with two audiences in mind. This book is meant to serve as a basic primer for the beginning researcher who is about to embark on a career that will employ the use of qualitative research and ethnographic approaches. At the same time, this work should be a useful reference and guide for experienced researchers who wish to re-examine their own skills and abilities in light of best practices of participant observation.

Participant observation is accepted almost universally as the central and defining method in cultural anthropology but in the late twentieth and early twenty-first centuries has become a common feature of qualitative research in a number of disciplines. Qualitative research in such diverse areas as sociology, education, nursing, and medical research draws on the insights gained through the use of participant observation for gaining greater understanding of phenomena from the point of view of participants. Participant observation has been used to develop this kind of insight in every cultural setting imaginable, from non-Western cultures little understood by Western social science, to ethnic and subcultural groups with North American and European settings, and to "virtual communities" that now congregate through electronic media.

In writing about participant observation as a method, we were immediately confronted with a problem that is also an issue in the analysis of data collected through the method. A good part of what makes up the method of participant observation, both the collection of information and analysis, is difficult to put into words. In part, it is because this is a method in which *control* of the research situation is less in the hands of the investigator than in other methods, even other qualitative methods. The investigator is reacting to and interacting with others in the events and situations that unfold before him or her. At the same time, investigators are bringing their own unique background and experience into the situation. Therefore, any discussion of "how to do it" must necessarily be abstract. There is no way to anticipate more than a small proportion of the situations in which investigators will find themselves. Just as learning about a new social or cultural context is experiential and, to an extent unspoken or tacit, so is learning to use participant observation effectively.

Since the first edition of this book appeared, participant observation as a tool for research on the internet has become common. We have incorporated some of the newer approaches to online research and included the work of several ethnographers who use computer-mediated communication or participation in massive multiplayer online role playing games in their research. We have also expanded our discussion of the use of participant observation in participatory and rapid research. In addition, we have reviewed some of the conventions of data management and analysis common in qualitative research that uses participant observation in the health professions and education. In this edition we have been able to draw on and learn from the work of a host of new researchers exploring new settings and addressing new questions. However, the basic message remains the same.

The beginning researcher is urged to experience field work at every opportunity and to practice the specific skills that we discuss in this book—active looking and listening, improving memory, informal interviewing, writing detailed field notes, and perhaps most importantly, patience. Beginners and experienced researchers should realize that every ethnographer and participant observer makes mistakes, and these are rarely fatal either to the individual or the research enterprise. We also believe, however, that the processes of learning how to be an effective participant observer can be enhanced and improved by an introduction to the work and thinking of more seasoned researchers. We believe that there are a number of basic principles that can be distilled from the experiences and mistakes of others.

Our original inspiration for tackling this book continues to come from our own mentors, Pertti (Bert) J. Pelto and Gretel H. Pelto, who helped us to come to appreciate and share their enthusiasm and love for doing field research. As pioneers in writing about anthropological methods, they have contributed substantially to making ethnographic research less of a mystical process. H. Russell Bernard continues to address new issues in the development of our methodological toolkit. Speaking of "toolkits," the series **The Ethnographer's Toolkit**, edited by Jean J. Schensul and Margaret LeCompte, has also provided inspiration. Mitch Allen, then at AltaMira, encouraged us to turn an earlier chapter into the first edition of this book. Since then, Rosalie Robertson and Jack Meinhardt, both formerly at AltaMira, encouraged us to take on the writing of a second edition. Bert Pelto's keen insights and cogent comments on the draft of the first edition of the book were, as always, key to our improving the manuscript.

We would also like to thank the many students with whom we have worked over the years. Their success in becoming anthropologists who are making real contributions to the discipline, to the institutions in which they are working, and especially to the people they study, is a great source of satisfaction to us. We hope that we have successfully captured some of what we taught them (as well as what they have taught us!) and that this volume will assist others in following in their footsteps to becoming contributing professionals. Our departments and centers at the Universities of Kentucky and Pittsburgh have been supportive of our research and have tolerated our long periods of time doing active field work.

Parts of the first edition were prepared while the authors were at the Rockefeller Foundation Study and Conference Center in Bellagio, Italy where Kathleen was a scholar in residence for April 2000. We would like to thank the Rockefeller Foundation and in particular the staff of the Bellagio Center (most especially Gianna Celli) for their support and wonderful accommodations during that time.

Most importantly, we would like to thank the many people with whom we have done field research during the past 40 years in a number of different settings—in Mexico, the people of Temascalcingo, Quebrantadero, El Porvenir, Derramaderos, Bateas, Alcalde, and communities along the Gulf of California; in Honduras, Pespire and many coastal communities around the Gulf of Fonseca; in Ecuador, people in the provinces of Cotopaxi, Carchi, Manabí, and Napo; in Kentucky, people from Red River Gorge, Central and Mountain Counties (pseudonyms), and Bourbon County; and the many other places in which we have worked for shorter periods of time. In each of these communities, people have welcomed us into their lives and communities, allowing us to participate and make observations about their lives and times. They taught us much and we hope that, in our published work, we have been able to reflect some small part of what we have learned from them.

On a personal level, we would like to thank our children, Saara and Gareth, for their forbearance in traveling with us or enduring our absences. Although our own partnership ended in 2002, we share the joy of seeing them thriving as successful professionals (a tropical biologist and attorney respectively). And, we delight in our two grandchildren, Owen Benjamin and Sasha Renée Ickes, to whom this volume is dedicated. We hope that the lives they have ahead of them are filled with as much enjoyment and excitement as we have experienced.

❧ 1 ❧

What Is Participant Observation?

Every one of us has had the experience of being a stranger in the midst of a new crowd. We walk into a room or join a large cluster of people all of whom seem to know and understand one another. As we nervously approach some part of the chattering crowd, we look for individuals to make eye contact or to shift their position to allow us to join the group. Our senses are on full alert. We observe the people present, how they are dressed, their relative age, who seems to be doing the most talking, and how each individual responds to what others are saying. We listen to conversations taking place to try to gauge the pace of the conversation, the degree of formality or informality of the language being used, and what it is that is being discussed. We look for ways in which we might begin to contribute to the dialogue. In such situations, each of us is engaging in something akin to ethnographic[1] fieldwork, and using the method that anthropologists call participant observation.

THE METHOD OF PARTICIPANT OBSERVATION

For anthropologists and social scientists, participant observation is a method in which a researcher takes part in the daily activities, rituals, inter-actions, and events of a group of people as one of the means of learning the explicit and tacit aspects of their life routines and their culture. Within this formal definition, "explicit" culture is a part of what people are able to ar-ticulate about themselves. "Explicit culture makes up part of what we know, a level of knowledge people can communicate about with relative ease" (Spradley, 1980:7). In contrast, "tacit" aspects of culture largely remain

1

outside our awareness or consciousness. It is the feeling of discomfort we have, for example, when someone stands too close to us or touches us in a way that seems too familiar.[2]

Participant observation is accepted almost universally as the central and defining method of research in cultural anthropology. Indeed, for writers such as McCall and Simmons (1969), Spradley (1980), Van Maanen (1988), Grills (1998), and Agar (1996), participant observation subsumes the bulk of what we call field research or, as it is more typically referred to in anthropology, fieldwork. Spradley (1980) used the term participant observation to refer to the general approach of fieldwork in ethnographic research, and Agar (1996) used participant observation as a cover term for all of the observation and formal and informal interviewing in which anthropologists engage.[3] Schensul, Schensul, and LeCompte (1999:91) write, "Participant observation represents the starting point in ethnographic research." They see participant observation as the foundation method for ethnographic research. For Bernard (2006) participant observation is a "strategic method" (343). That is, a method that comprises several methods at once. In Bernard's sense, one or more of the elements of a strategic method can be chosen depending on the question being asked. Participant observation "puts you where the action is and lets you collect data . . . any kind of data that you want, narratives or numbers."

In this book, in order to examine the specific issues in participating and observing in ethnographic research, we will take a somewhat more narrow view of participant observation. For us, participant observation is one of several methods that fit into the general category of qualitative research. Qualitative research has as its goal an understanding of the nature of phenomena, and is not necessarily interested in assessing the magnitude and distribution of phenomena (i.e., quantifying it). Participant observation is just one of a number of methods that are employed to achieve this kind of understanding. Other qualitative methods include structured and semi-structured interviewing, pure observation, and the collection and analysis of texts. The method of participant observation is a way to collect data in naturalistic settings by ethnographers who observe and/or take part in the common and uncommon activities of the people being studied.

We take this position because, while much of what we call fieldwork includes participating and observing the people and communities with whom we are working, the method of participant observation includes the use of the information gained from participating and observing through explicit recording and analysis. That is, all humans are participants and observers in all of their everyday interactions, but few individuals actually engage in the systematic use of this information for social scientific purposes. The method of participant observation requires a particular approach to the recording of observations (in field notes), and the perspective that the information collected through participation is as critical to social scientific analysis as information from more formal research techniques such as interviewing, structured observation, and the use of questionnaires and formal elicitation techniques. However, participant observation underlies much of the other techniques used in ethnographic fieldwork. It is a way of approaching the fieldwork experience, and gaining understanding of the most fundamental processes of social life. It provides context for sampling, open-ended interviewing, construction of interview guides and question-naires, and other more structured and more quantitative methods of data collection. It is rarely, if ever, the only technique used by a researcher conducting ethnographic research. In this volume we have separated the specific issues related to the collection, recording, and analysis of data from participant observation in order to discuss them more fully.

While anthropologists had carried out ethnographic fieldwork before him, Malinowski (1961 [1922], 1978 [1935]) is usually credited with developing "something novel" (Sanjek 1990b; Stocking Jr. 1983)—an approach to fieldwork that gradually became known as the method of participant observation. Firth (1985) also notes that Malinowski did not invent long-term research, living with the subjects of research, or working in the vernacular. What Malinowski contributed was to "supply principles of systematic, intensive collection and interpretation of field data to a de-gree of sophistication not known before" (30). Or, as Tedlock (1991) has said, "Malinowski's invention lay in elevating the fieldwork method into a theory" (83).

However, original or not, Malinowski's discussion of his approach still serves as the fundamental description of the method:

> Soon after I had established myself in Omarkana Trobriand Islands, I began to take part, in a way, in the village life, to look forward to the important or festive events, to take personal interest in the gossip and the developments of the village occurrences; to wake up every morning to a new day, presenting itself to me more or less as it does to the natives. I would get out from under my mosquito net, to find around me the village life beginning to stir, or the people well advanced in their working day according to the hour or also the season, for they get up and begin their labors early or late, as work presses. As I went on my morning walk through the village, I could see intimate details of family life, of toilet, cooking, taking of meals; I could see the arrangements for the day's work, people starting on their errands, or groups of men and women busy at some manufacturing tasks. Quarrels, jokes, family scenes, events usu-ally trivial, sometimes dramatic but always significant, form the atmosphere of my daily life, as well as of theirs. It must be remembered that the natives saw me constantly every day, they ceased to be interested or alarmed, or made self-conscious by my presence, and I ceased to be a disturbing element in the tribal life which I was to study, altering it by my very approach, as always

happens with a newcomer to every savage community. In fact, as they knew
that I would thrust my nose into everything, even where a well-mannered
native would not dream of intruding, they finished by regarding me as a part
and parcel of their life, a necessary evil or nuisance, mitigated by donations of
tobacco. (1961:7–8)[4]

Malinowski's approach was distinguished from earlier forms of fieldwork
in that it included an emphasis on everyday interactions and observations
rather than on using directed inquiries into specific behaviors. And, Sanjek
notes, following others (Leach 1957), "As he observed, he also listened"
(1990b:211).

Writing more than 70 years later, Bourgois, who lived for more than four
years in the neighborhoods in which he worked, described his approach to
research in a more contemporary context in similar terms:

I spent hundreds of nights on the street and in crackhouses observing dealers
and addicts. I regularly tape-recorded their conversations and life histories.
Perhaps more important, I also visited their families, attending parties and
intimate reunions—from Thanksgiving dinners to New Year's Eve celebrations.
I interviewed, and in many cases befriended, the spouses, lovers, siblings,
mothers, grandmothers, and—when possible—the fathers and stepfathers of
the crack dealers featured in these pages. (1995:13)

Boellstorff (2010) created an avatar and participated fully in the mas-
sively multiplayer online role-playing game (MMORPG), *Second Life*. He
used many of the conventional methods associated with ethnographic
fieldwork (participant observation, interview, and focus groups) in his research. As a participant observer he (his avatar) set up a household, made
friends, participated in group activities, and engaged in informal (as well
as more formal) interviewing. He attended weddings and parties; went
to dance clubs and bars, dropped in on friends and hung out. He bought
things, sold things, and even chatted with other participants on the methodological issues of conducting research on a "virtual" society. Over the
course of several years he spent thousands of hours in *Second Life*.[5] His writing of field notes was facilitated by being able to archive the text of conversations, although he wrote field note descriptions of his activities as well.

To differing extents, each of these ethnographers practiced the method
of participant observation by living in the community, taking part in usual
and unusual activities, "hanging out," and conversing (as compared with
interviewing), while consciously observing and, ultimately, recording what
they observed. The participating observer seeks out opportunities to spend
time with and carry out activities with members of communities in which
he or she is working. Because enculturation[6] takes place (Schensul et al.
1999) at the same time (it is hard to avoid), we believe that a tacit understanding of the experience is also being developed. It is an understanding

that is not easily articulated or recorded, but that can be mobilized in subsequent analysis.

In addition to one of the first explicit descriptions of participant observation, another of Malinowski's major contributions to anthropology was the development of the functionalist theoretical perspective that assumed "that the total field of data under the observation of the fieldworker must somehow fit together and make sense" (Leach 1957:120). Sanjek (1990b) argues that Malinowski's particular approach to fieldwork resulted in the development of the functionalist theoretical approach. Holy (1984) argues that his theoretical perspective predated his fieldwork and influenced his method of collecting information. Wax (1971) suggests that Malinowski needed to invent functionalism in order to justify both his method and his promotion of that method following his return to academia after the war. Whatever the actual succession of events and intellectual development was, the method of participant observation was closely tied to functionalist theory from its beginning.

To sum up, the key elements of the method of participant observation as used by anthropologists usually involve the following.

- Living in the context for an extended period of time
- Learning and using local language and dialect
- Actively participating in a wide range of daily, routine, and extraordinary activities with people who are full participants in that context
- Using everyday conversation as an interview technique
- Informally observing during leisure activities (hanging out)
- Recording observations in field notes (usually organized chronologically)
- Using both tacit and explicit information in analysis and writing

In the chapters that follow, we will have more to say about each one of these.

HISTORY OF THE METHOD

While Malinowski may have been the first anthropologist to describe this approach as a research method, he was not the first person or the first anthropologist to practice it. Wax (1971) begins her discussion of the history of participant observation with the mention of Herodotus and other ancient writers, and, for later times, points to amateur writers such as Condrington, Callaway, and Bogoras, who spent extended time with the people they wrote about, spoke the languages, and described everyday life in the nineteenth century. While Atkinson and Hammersley (1994) see

participant observation as primarily twentieth-century phenomenon, they
trace the philosophical and methodological roots of participant observation in the historicism of the Renaissance; and, in the nineteenth century,
to the development of hermeneutics as an approach to understanding humans in different settings and time periods.

The first anthropologist to write about using something akin to participant observation appears to be Frank Hamilton Cushing. Cushing was
assigned by the Smithsonian Institution's Bureau of Ethnology to collect
information about Zuni Pueblo in the southwestern United States in 1879
(Hinsley 1983; Sanjek 1990b). His supervisor, Spencer Baird, expected him
to spend about three months in Zuni Pueblo but Cushing spent four and
one-half years. Sanjek reports that Cushing wrote Baird in 1879 saying:

> My *method* must succeed. I live among the Indians, I eat their food, and sleep
> in their houses. . . . On account of this, thank God, my notes will contain
> much that those of all other explorers have failed to communicate. (Green
> 1978:136–37)

Cushing learned to speak Zuni and was inducted into a Zuni Pueblo and
then the Bow priesthood (Green 1978; Green et al. 1990; Sanjek 1990b).
In 1881, after two years of time with the Zuni, Cushing wrote to Baird saying: "I would be willing to devote, say, a year or two more to it to study
for a period almost as great, from the *inside*, the life of the Zuni, as I have
from the outside." Cushing's insistence on an internal, holistic, and organic
understanding of Zuni life and culture born of long-term participation,
fluency in the language, and intuitive, even poetic, insight presage both
Malinowski's approach and more contemporary approaches to ethnography. However, either because of Cushing's personality or his approach, he
produced few publications from his Zuni work relative to the length of time
he spent with the Zuni. His successor and others criticized him for having
become too involved with Zuni culture to write analytically and objectively
about it and he was accused of having "gone native" (Hinsley 1983). However, Cushing left Zuni, married and, with only a brief return to Zuni, spent
the rest of his career in New England. Eakins's well-known, romanticized,
and controversial portrait of Cushing, for which Cushing posed in Eakins's
studio after leaving Zuni, shows Cushing dressed in, and surrounded by,
Zuni artifacts and clothing assembled from several sources. The 1881–1882
photo taken by John Hilliers is titled *Ethnologist Frank Hamilton Cushing during his years as a member of Zuni Pueblo, wearing a Native American costume of
his own design*. Both of these works suggest a more self-conscious adoption
of the trappings of Zuni culture than the kind of adoption of the culture
that "going native" might imply. Muller (2009) suggests that "the case of
Frank Cushing's Zuni-man identity ultimately sheds light on the means by

which the material culture of a subordinate group can, under unique circumstances, be used by an individual from a dominant culture to construct an identity that provides him with unusual power and privileges." The case of Frank Cushing does illustrate a persistent conflict in the method of participant observation, that is the interplay of power in and identity for the researcher who insets herself into the lives of the subjects of her research.

Another important figure who used participant observation was Beatrice Potter Webb. In her 1926 memoir, *My Apprenticeship,* Webb described her work as a researcher with Charles Booth in the 1880s. Although she was the daughter of a nineteenth-century British industrialist and was raised in privileged conditions, she had a life-long concern for the poor. In order to learn more about the conditions of London's poor, she sought to gain acceptance in London's working class neighborhoods and in 1883, with the aid of her mother's nurse, she disguised her identity and visited poor neighborhoods. Later, she took a job as a rent collector in public housing in order to be able to spend her days in the buildings and offices in which her subjects of research lived and sought services. In 1888 Webb took a position as a seamstress in a London sweatshop.

Her approach contained many of the elements characteristic of participant observation. Although she may have spent her days among the poor, she did not live in the neighborhoods in which she was working. She certainly observed, but the degree of participation was limited to that which a rent collector would have had. Also, it is not clear that she systematically recorded field notes, although the stories of individuals she encountered do appear in her writings. A description of her findings is included in the volume *Problems of Modern Industry* written with her husband, Sidney Webb (Webb and Webb 1902).

During these years, Webb was much influenced by social reformer and researcher Charles Booth. Booth developed a group of researchers who carried out qualitative research within the context of statistical studies. Wax (1971) argues that Booth may have been the first researcher to combine the analysis of statistical data with information derived from participant observation.

At about the same time that Malinowski was researching and writing his book on the Trobriands, Margaret Mead may have independently arrived at using a method quite similar to Malinowski's. Sanjek suggests that she had not read Malinowski's book *Argonauts of the Western Pacific* when she traveled to Samoa in 1925 to conduct her first research based on original fieldwork among the Manu'a. In this project she focused on the lives of adolescent girls, but also carried out a more general ethnographic study of Manu'an social organization. Mead's description of her approach, in the introduction of her ethnography of Manu'a, is similar in many ways to Malinowski's and she speaks of "speech in action" as the heart of the method:

My material comes not from half a dozen informants but from scores of individuals. With the exception of two informants, all work was done in the native language. . . .Very little of it was therefore gathered in formal interviews but was rather deviously extracted from the directed conversations of social groups, or at formal receptions which the chiefs of a village afforded me on account of my rank in the native social organization. . . . The concentration upon a small community and detailed observations of daily life provided me with a kind of field material rarely accessible to the field ethnographer. (Mead 1969 [1930]:5)

While a good deal of information was gathered through informal interviewing and conversation, Mead also undertook to learn the skills required of Manu'an girls.

A rather disproportionate amount of my knowledge about Samoan custom and style came through my exposing myself to teaching—both in matters of etiquette, dancing, recitation of *fa'alupenga*—the stylized courtesy phrases and the making of artifacts. . . . I felt it was necessary to actually labor through the specific tasks . . . which a Samoan girl had to perform.

I combined the learner or novice's point of view with that of the ethnographer, a more explicit interpretation of the term *"participant observation"*—a term that had not then been invented—than is usual, or even necessary, in any kind of field work. (1969 [1930]:xix)

Mead's use of the method of participant observation is even more remarkable in that it represented a dramatic break with the approach of her mentor Franz Boas and other students he was training. They were still focused on the collection of texts and historical materials to document the disappearing native cultures in North America. Unlike her mentor, Mead was focused on understanding contemporary, living cultures, rather than disappearing cultures. Mead's use of the method of participant observation was also important because, rather than being used to gain a comprehensive and holistic description of the "totality" of a culture as Malinowski had (Sanjek 1990a), her work was focused on a particular problem. By 1930, then, participant observation had been employed both as an approach to a holistic description of a culture and as an approach to a focused discussion of a particular aspect of social life.

In a somewhat revisionist frame of mind, Stocking (1983) pointed out that if we consider that the ethnographic method can be divided into three main modes—participation, observation, and interrogation—Malinowski relied more heavily on the second and third of these. It is clear from his diaries (Malinowski 1967) that he was often left on the beach while his informants went off on exchange expeditions. Also, Malinowski was clearly not approaching the Trobrianders on the basis of social parity. Stocking suggests that Malinowski's relationship with the Trobrianders was closer to that of "petty lordship" because his informants apparently treated him as one of high rank (Malinowski 1967; Stocking 1983). As Mead's description quoted above indicates, she also was accorded a privileged position in Samoan society and much of her data were also derived from observation and interrogation.[7]

It is not clear when the actual term "participant observation" came into use to describe the method. The earliest use we can find of "participant observation" is in a treatise on methods published in the early 1920s (Lindeman 1924). In this work, Lindeman attempted to standardize and make more "scientific" the conduct of social research. He argued that observation is a form of asking questions ("What is the individual doing?" (185)), and that asking questions is a form of observation. He was also an early advocate of what has become known as the emic/etic approach.[8] That is, he thought that the full answer to the question what is going on comes both from the point of view of the researcher and from the point of view of the participant. To this end then, he advocated the use of "participant-observers" in social research about groups of people. In using this term, however, Lindeman was referring to participants who have been trained to be observers—"cooperating observers" in his terminology (Lindeman 1924:191)—rather than investigators who have adopted a participant role among a group of people.[9]

By the mid-1920s, a number of papers and books reference Lindeman's concept of participant-observer. However, references to the method as described by Malinowski and Mead do not appear in the sociology literature until the 1930s. A 1933 list of research projects being conducted by sociologists notes a project being carried out by Robert Merton (Lundberg 1937). By 1940, the term participant observation was in wide use in both anthropology and sociology and was included in the titles of papers by Lohman (1937) and Kluckhohn (1940).

The nature of the "communities" in which social research takes place, and the purposes to which research is put, participant observation has taken on new subjects and forms. As we note later in this volume, forms of participant observation that retain some of the historically relevant aspects of the method have been adapted to short-term research in aid of program planning, implementation, and evaluation. Also, as the description of the work carried out by Boellstorff illustrates, as the communities in which research takes place have come to include virtual communities of many types based on computer mediated communication (CMC), participant observation in virtual communities has become commonplace (see Boellstorff 2010; Constable 2003; Hine 2000, 2005). In later chapters we will discuss the methodological and ethical issues that new forms of participant observation raise for researchers and the readers of ethnography.

WHY PARTICIPANT OBSERVATION IS IMPORTANT

Irrespective of the topic or principal methods used in doing social scientific studies, we believe that the practice of participant observation provides several advantages to research. First, it enhances the quality of the data obtained during fieldwork. Second, it enhances the quality of the interpretation of data, whether those data are collected through participant observation or by other methods. Participant observation is thus both a data collection and an analytic tool. Third, it encourages the formulation of new research questions and hypotheses grounded in on-the-scene observation.

ENHANCING THE QUALITY OF
DATA COLLECTION AND ANALYSIS

What does attempting to participate in the events and lives around one mean to data collection and analysis? Living, working, laughing, and crying with the people that one is trying to understand provides a sense of the self and the other that is not easily put into words. It is a tacit understanding that informs the form of research, the specific techniques of data collection, the recording of information, and the subsequent interpretation of materials collected.

In studying Yolmo healing, for example, Robert Desjarlais (1992) trained to become an apprentice Yolmo shaman. To do so, he found it necessary to learn how to move and to experience his body as a Yolmo. He argues that much of what ethnographers can learn regarding peoples' lives is tacit and at the level of the body. He notes that as he gained cultural knowledge, learned how to sip tea, caught the meaning of jokes, participated in the practice of everyday life, these interactions shaped his "understanding of local values, patterns of actions, ways of being, moving, feeling" (Desjarlais 1992:26). Desjarlais argues that his body incorporated the meanings and gave a greater understanding of the images he experienced in trances as part of his training as a shaman.

> Through time, experiencing the body in this manner (including the residual, intermingling effect it had on how I stepped through a village, climbed a hill, or approached others) influenced my understanding of Yolmo experiences; it hinted at new styles of behavior, ways of being and moving through space that I did not previously have access to. By using the body in different ways, I stumbled on (but never fully assimilated) practices distinct from my own. Touching head to heart merged thinking and feeling (two acts unsegregated in Yolmo society); a sense of the body as a vessel dynamically compact led me to see Yolmo forms as vital plenums of organ and icon; and my loose assemblage of bent knees and jointed bones contributed to the springboard

technology that gradually brought some force and ease to my shamanic "shaking." (Desjarlais 1992:27)

The process by which this might take place, while difficult to convey in words, comes as the result of sharing the lives of people over a significant amount of time. Part of what we know about life in rural Mexico (or other places in which we have worked) is tacit. It is embodied in the way we walk, move, and talk (imperfectly translated, of course, because everyone still knows we are not Mexicans). We note that the timbre of our voices changes in Spanish to approximate that of Temascalcingo voices, and that we are much more animated in our speech and bodily gestures. Similarly, reflecting on many years of field experience in many different places, Mead wrote:

> Pictures taken in the field show the extent to which I adapted to the style of the people with whom I was working. In photographs taken in Bali I look disassociated, sitting among a people each of whom was separated from the others. In Samoa the pictures show me dressed up, sitting and standing to display my Samoan costumes and rank; in Manus I am alert and tense, half strangled by a child clinging around my neck; in Arapesh I have become as soft and responsive as the people themselves. (1970b:320)

This embodiment of tacit cultural form also informs interpretation of meaning. In the most obvious ways, it allows us to understand nonverbal communication, to anticipate and understand responses. It shapes the way in which we interact with others and, in a more fundamental way, it shapes the way we interpret what we observe.

Desjarlais is one of many ethnographers who have apprenticed themselves in the field in order to gain new perspectives. Coy (1989) argued that the apprenticeship experience results in "ways of knowing" and "learning to see" that are distinct from less participatory approaches. He argues, like Desjarlais, that these ways of knowing are connected to the physical performance of the duties required in the role being examined. Singleton (1989) notes that the experience of an apprentice of any sort is parallel to that of the ethnographer because both learn through participation/observation. Tedlock argues that successful formal and informal apprenticeships are ways of undergoing intensive enculturation (1991:71). The fieldworker who does not attempt to experience the world of the observed through participant observation will find it much harder to critically examine research assumptions and beliefs, and themselves (see Clifford 1997:91). A part of this process is coming not only to understand, intellectually, the perspective of participants in the context in which the researcher is working, but to "feel" the point of view of the other (Grills 1998; Katz 1988).

The problems inherent in dealing with information that is tacit and embodied rather than explicit and intellectualized should be obvious. How do we incorporate tacit knowledge in our analysis and writing? How do we make the insights it affords explicit enough to approach it analytically? How do we convey to others the type of insight we have (without sounding like we have "gone native")? We will address this question in greater detail in the discussion of analysis, interpretation, and writing in chapter 8. The first step, however, is clearly to be aware at the start of fieldwork that tacit knowledge is important to the process and to continually try to make the tacit explicit in field notes and analytic notes. Desjarlais's apprenticeship provides a model, although we do not know if he anticipated this before beginning his fieldwork, or discovered it during analysis. When the experience is a formal apprenticeship, this may be an easier tact. However, few of us see our fieldwork as a formal apprenticeship, even though part of the fieldwork experience is enculturation—that is, an apprenticeship in the "culture" and social life of the communities in which we are working.

We should also note that participant observation may, in some cases, be the only viable approach to research. Researchers who have worked in "deviant subcultures" with such groups as drug dealers (Adler 1985; Bourgois 1995), bank robbers and gangsters (Katz 1988), gangs (Brymer 1998), and poachers (Brymer 1991) have often argued that long-term participation in the setting was the only possible way to gain enough of the trust of participants to carry out research. Furthermore, the use of more formal methods might have "put off" informants.

Patricia Adler (1985) recounts the events that led to her research among drug smugglers and dealers in a community in the Southwestern United States. She and her husband, Peter Adler, were drawn into the social life of drug smugglers and dealers by serendipity. They were simply being neighborly. After a time, the economic basis of their new friends' and acquaintances' life styles became clear and the Adlers began an ethnographic study of drug trafficking that lasted for a number of years. Adler discovered that this was not a world populated by "criminal syndicates" but by "individuals and a small set of wheeler-dealers" she called "disorganized crime." It was a social and economic scene into which the average person, or drug researcher, would rarely or ever gain entrance. Adler argues that she would have been unable to gain any information concerning this illicit subculture if she had not gained the trust of her informants. In fact, as we will discuss later when we discuss participant roles, Adler argues that she and her husband could not have carried out the research without actively participating in the consumption, if not the marketing, of the drugs involved.

In a similar vein, Philippe Bourgois (1995:1) writes: "I was forced into crack against my will." By this he means that, like the Adlers, the choice of a place to live placed him in a setting in which he had, in some measure, to take part in the culture—if not the behaviors—of crack dealing and use. The view of the barrio and the structure of crack dealing within it that

Bourgois presents could only have been made by someone who dedicated a long-term commitment to the research and the community. Unlike the Adlers, who conducted much of their study covertly, Bourgois made it very clear he was carrying out research. He often openly audiotaped events and conversations, and taped semistructured interviews. Even with the research intent explicit, however, he was able to gain the trust and confidence of participants in a highly illegal activity.

Brymer (1998) was able to use "long-term field research" and "long-term personal relationships" (which, in his description, fit the definition of participant observation) to gain insight into two very distinct subcultures known for their wariness of outsiders. These were Mexican American gangs in the Southwest, and hunters and poachers in North America. Brymer is convinced that he has a much more nuanced view and insight into gangs and gang members than other people have. This was possible because of his knowledge of a particular dialect of Spanish called *pachuco*, which he acquired growing up with Mexican cowboys working without documentation in the Southwestern United States; seven years of working in several cities studying Mexican-American gangs; "hanging out" with gang members; hauling them around in his 15-year-old station wagon; and his use of informal interviewing techniques. Conventional wisdom saw the gangs as large and territorially organized but Brymer writes "after two years in the field, however, I had never seen a gang" (1998:146). In fact he found that, in general, the young men with whom he was working were most frequently part of small social groupings (*palomillos*) that were not particularly violent and, on the street, were not considered gangs. After two years, beginning to doubt his worth as a researcher, he happened upon an event that revealed the potential violence of the larger "gang" grouping of which the smaller units were a part. This event changed his entire view of gang formation, activity, and its place in the neighborhood. Brymer argues that only long-term field work and the confidence of the *palomillo* would have given him the opportunity to observe the coalescing of the "gang" from smaller groups under particular circumstances. The work with gangs points out not only the importance of gaining trust, or rapport, under the circumstance of long-term participant observation and speaking the language, but also the need for long-term field work to reveal the nature of rare events, in this case preparation for an all-out intergang fight, which fortunately never actually took place.

In his work with poachers, Brymer (1998, 1991) makes the point that, in the absence of field research, much of our information concerning illicit behaviors and the social systems that surround them comes from the "failed deviants"—the individuals who are apprehended and appear in crime statistics, or, for example, in drug rehab and narcotics prisons. It was only through long-term participant observation that Brymer was able to

show that the most common form of poaching was small-scale local hunting, often to provide food. The "good 'ole boys" engaged in this activity
were much less likely to be apprehended than the clueless tourist hunters,
trophy hunters, or even commercial hunters.

Like Adler and Bourgois, Brymer's study of poaching was the result of
stumbling onto this activity after buying a piece of land frequently poached
by local groups. He notes that it took two years of "testing" him before
the locals incorporated him into the group (which, remember, was poaching on his land). The serendipitous and opportunistic flavor of the initial
period of these interesting field research experiences suggests that perhaps
once pulled into the experience of participant observation, the researcher
is never again fully a participant in any setting, but always part observer on
the lookout for a new project.

Tobias Hecht's (1998) study of street children in a city in Northeast
Brazil would not have had the insight and depth that it does if Hecht had
not spent 16 months hanging out with children on the streets of Olinda.
During his research time, he also worked for one of the organizations that
served the needs of street children in Olinda. He visited the shantytowns
from which the children had come. Hecht also used taped interviewing
extensively in his research. However, in the end he says that the best data
were obtained when he gave in to the kids and turned the tape recorder over
to them to interview each other.

Brymer's two examples noted above also point to the importance of long-
term field work in understanding rare events. While a good deal of ethnography is based on descriptions of rare events collected through systematic
interviews,[10] the insight gained from direct observation has often provided
a paradigm twisting experience for the researcher. In part, the observation
of rare events is a function of the length of time in field research. However, some events, like preparation for gang war, are rarer because special
knowledge is required to even know they exist or to identify the venue in
which they take place. Studies of secret societies are an obvious example.
However, access to even more mundane and common events, activity, and
knowledge may rest in large part on the development of trust from participant observation. While not as dramatic as the examples noted above,
ethnographers have long recognized that information about such activities
as sorcery, witchcraft, and shamanism is only gained after long-term participation in a setting.

Hine (2000) and Constable (2003) both discuss how participation in
the on-line communities, not only as lurkers,[11] but also as participants in
list serves, news groups, chat rooms, etc., allowed them to appreciate the
participant's point of view even as they pioneered CMC mediated research.
Researchers have been entering virtual worlds as cultural settings since the

1990s. MMORPGs such as *Second Life* have become the sites of studies of everything from virtual culture to virtual economics (e.g., Boellstorff 2010).

FORMULATING NEW RESEARCH QUESTIONS

Grounded theory approaches (Glaser and Strauss 1967; Strauss and Corbin 1990, 1998) have long stressed the role of qualitative research in the development of hypotheses and theory. However, even if a researcher does not take a grounded theory approach, qualitative research in general, and participant observation in particular, encourages the continual reassessment of initial research questions and hypotheses, and facilitates the development of new hypotheses and questions as new insights occur as a result of increasing familiarity with the context. In chapter 8 we will discuss the nature of analysis of materials from participant observation in more detail. However, it is important to note that the process of analysis is inherently iterative. The active, insightful investigator should continually be reviewing field notes and transcripts and continually tossing out old ideas and posing new questions for study during the fieldwork and post-fieldwork phases of research. "Being there" in the fullest sense means that our ideas and notions are continually challenged and "resisted" by the actions and words of those within the setting (paraphrasing Becker 1970; Grills 1998:4).

As we will discuss later, participant observation provides many moments in which the "scales fall from our eyes" and a new understanding or hypothesis presents itself. To come full circle in our discussion here, the tacit understandings gained during participant observation facilitate the intuitive moments when a selection of notes about events, people, and conversations comes together to provide us with a deeper insight and understanding of behavior. Living and participating in the research context forces us to place our particular focus of study within the wider context. As Picchi writes: "participant observation disallows selective learning about a people. Adjusting to a new culture provides on a daily basis many different types of experiences that prevent anthropologists from concentrating too assiduously on any one aspect of people's traditions" (1992:144). As Becker (1970) notes, "being there" forces our ideas and assumptions to be resisted and tested by the actions and words of those in the setting.

In this chapter, we have provided a general definition and discussion of the concept and method of participant observation. Although participant observation is the main method that all humans use to learn their own culture, anthropologists and other social scientists have sought to more clearly define and formalize the method as a means for doing social research. As we have seen, although the method had been used earlier in social research,

Malinowski, Mead, Lindeman, and others began to more systematically write about doing participant observation.

For some kinds of research, participant observation has been the sole or main method used by social scientists. For some kinds of research, it may be the only practical method to use. It is important to emphasize, however, that participant observation is only one of many kinds of qualitative and quantitative social science methods that can be used in studying human behavior. Participant observation is the foundation of ethnographic research design; it supports and complements the other types of data collection commonly used in most ethnographic studies. As we have shown, participant observation can enhance the quality of data obtained during field research, it can enhance the quality of interpretation of data, and it is especially useful in assisting us to formulate new research questions and hypotheses.

Like any other method, skills in participant observation can be taught, learned, improved, and enhanced. In the following chapters of this book, we will discuss how someone can learn to be a participant observer, the choices that are sometimes necessary to be made in terms of how much participation and observation is done, what anthropologists and other social researchers have learned in enhancing our utilization of participant observation, how participant observation can be most usefully incorporated into research design, and the ethical issues concerned with using the method.

NOTES

1. Marcus and Fischer (1986:18) define ethnography as "a research process in which the anthropologist closely observes, records, and engages in the daily life of another culture—an experience labeled as the fieldwork method—and then writes accounts of this culture, emphasizing descriptive detail."

2. We may find it difficult to articulate what it is that makes us feel uncomfortable because these aspects of cultural knowledge remain outside of our general consciousness. It is participation in the context around us that allows us to gain insight into the tacit.

3. For Agar, the interview is more important than the participation, and observation serves as the source of questions about which to interview. However, he sees participant observation as providing the context for the rest of the enterprise.

4. Malinowski goes on to insist on the need to live in the community and cautions against living in compounds apart from the people under investigation like other "white men" (sic) do.

5. His virtual fieldwork in *Second Life* was interspersed and overlapped with his actual field research on sexuality and HIV/AIDS in Indonesia.

6. Enculturation is "the social process by which culture is learned and transmitted across generations" (Kottak 1994:16).

7. We have preserved Stocking's use of the term interrogation despite the negative connotations of the term. We would prefer the term "questioning" or interviewing.

8. The terms emic and etic have been adopted in anthropology as the means for referring to, respectively, the perspective of the native informant and the observer. Following Harris, "Emic operations have as their hallmark the elevation of the native informant to the status of ultimate judge of the adequacy of the observer's description and analysis"; "Etic operations have as their hallmark the elevation of observers to the status of ultimate judges of the categories and concepts used in descriptions and analyses" (1979:32).

9. Lindeman's participant-observer is closer to what we now generally refer to as a key informant. The role of the participant-observer is to provide insight into the thinking of a group and the individuals that make it up. The role of the participant-observer is distinct from the role of the "outside observer," who is the researcher. In a later volume, Hader and Lindeman (1933) elaborate on the role of participant-observer, as compared with direct observation, carried out by an "outside observer," suggesting ways to identify and train participant-observers.

10. To take one well-known example, Roy Rappaport never actually observed the full 12-year cycle of warfare, truce, and pig feasting described in his book *Pigs for the Ancestors* (1984). He was able to construct his account through interviews with informants.

11. Hine (2000) defines a lurker as "someone who reads messages posted to a public forum such as a newsgroup, but does not respond to the group" (160).

❧2❧

Learning To Be a Participant Observer

Theoretical Issues

When we began graduate school in anthropology in the early 1970s, there was very little in the way of books or courses on anthropological methods. The unfortunate attitude, expressed explicitly by many anthropologists we knew, was that people were either good field researchers or they were not. Generations of graduate students were sent to the field by their advisors with the expectation that they would either sink or swim. Those who were destined to become anthropologists would prove their mettle by not only surviving fieldwork but also coming back with information they could analyze in theoretical terms.

We were fortunate that we began our graduate studies with two individuals who were among the pioneers of writing about and training students in anthropological methods. In addition to publishing one of the first texts on anthropological methods, Pertti and Gretel Pelto (Pelto 1970; Pelto and Pelto 1978) also believed in incorporating students into their research projects. Much of what we learned about participant observation and anthropological field research began during our apprenticeship with the Peltos.

The point is that there are skills that are necessary to be a participant observer and that these skills can be learned. The beginner must realize that every ethnographer makes mistakes, and these are rarely fatal either to the individual or to the research. We also believe, however, that the processes of learning how to be an effective participant observer can be enhanced by an introduction to experience and thinking of more experienced researchers. There are a number of basic principles that can be distilled from the experiences and mistakes of others. Further, a number of researchers have reflected carefully on their experiences and that thinking can be helpful to both new and experienced investigators. In the following pages, we use

recent theoretical work in anthropology to examine the nature of, and some
of the inherent contradictions of, participant observation. Chapters 3 and 4
focus on the practical skills of being a better participant and being a better
observer. There we will review key skills, summarize approaches to developing them that have been successful, and provide insights from the work of
ethnographers who have grappled with learning and perfecting these skills.

LEARNING TO BE A PARTICIPANT OBSERVER

In writing about participant observation as a method, we are immediately
confronted with a problem that is also an issue in the analysis of data collected through the method. A good part of what makes up the method,
both the collection of information and analysis of it, is difficult to put into
words. In part, this is because this is a method in which the research is less
in control of the research situation than when using other methods, even
other qualitative methods. The investigator is reacting to and interacting
with others in the events and situations that unfold before him or her.
Any discussion of "how to do it" must necessarily be abstract. There is no
way to anticipate more than a small proportion of the situations in which
investigators will find themselves.

In addition, the experience of fieldwork is often discussed as intensely
personal—again, difficult to put into words. In an essay in which he attempted to explore this personal experience in beginning study of the Semai of Malaya, Dentan articulates the dilemma well:

> Many cultural anthropologists tend to romanticize fieldwork to the point of
> making a fetish out of it, claiming that their field experience gives them in-
> sights into the nature of human society that no other discipline can provide.
> This insight, they contend, stems from the fact that anthropological fieldwork
> is an intensely personal experience. The difficulty they have in communicating
> the nature of this experience makes their colleagues in other fields rather suspi-
> cious of anthropology's claim to superior insight. I am suspicious of it myself.
> Nevertheless, I want to stress how intensely personal the fieldwork was for me
> and Ruth. (1970:87)[1]

Just as learning about a new social or cultural context is experiential, and
to an extent, tacit, so is learning to use participant observation effectively. The
method draws heavily on behavioral skills and already established social skills
wedded to a flexible approach to new social situations. Learning to participate
in a new context means acquiring a set of understandings and reactions, that,
in fact, we may not fully appreciate until we begin analysis. The beginning
researcher is urged to practice at every opportunity the specific skills that are
important in participant observation. Those skills include both learning to

be an observer and learning to be a participant. Among them are: fitting in, "active seeing," short-term memory, informal interviewing, recording detailed field notes, and, perhaps most importantly, patience. Margaret Mead (1970a) suggests that before the new fieldworker goes to the field he or she should make an inventory of his or her own talents and skills, strengths and weaknesses. Mead suggests that those skills that may be important might include:

> memory for faces, ability to reproduce nonsense material from memory, ability to reproduce sensible material from memory, relative memory for things seen and things heard, ability to write and observe simultaneously, width of vision, ability to predict what will happen behind one by the expression on the faces of those in front, tolerance for continuous observation of the same type—e.g., kneeling with smoke in one's eyes for four hours recording trance behavior . . . attention span inside which attention is of the same quality, ability to attend to an unpleasant situation, susceptibility to disqualifying disgust reactions, ability to resist the impulse to interrupt an unpleasant or disturbing sequence of behavior, tendency to identify in a partisan fashion with preferred individuals, etc. (1970a:249)

All of these skills are fundamental to the method of participant observation. However, Mead does not suggest that a particular strength or deficit in these skills and abilities qualifies or disqualifies the researcher as an effective participant observer, but that an honest accounting can be a guide in the selection of the most effective questions, venues, and recording techniques for any particular fieldworker. While some ethnographers come to participant observation with a better grounding in some of these skills compared with others, almost everyone can learn them or improve on existing skills. Before discussing these skills, it is useful to more carefully examine participant observation.

OBSERVATION AND PARTICIPATION

It is important to recognize that participant observation is a method that combines two somewhat different processes. Bernard (2006) has made the important point that participant observation should be distinguished from both pure observation and pure participation. Pure observation, as used by some sociologists and psychologists (see Adler and Adler 1994; Tonkin 1984), seeks, to the maximum extent possible, to remove the researcher from the actions and behaviors so that they are unable to influence them. There are many examples of the use of pure observation in social science research. These include cases in which researchers tape everyday interactions or behavior for later analysis, or where researchers observe some type of behavior from behind a one-way mirror.

   Pure participation has been described as "going native" and "becoming the phenomena" (see Jorgensen 1989). "Going native," when a researcher sheds the identity of investigator and adopts the identity of a full partici- pant in the culture, is generally associated with a loss of analytic interest and often results in the inability of the researcher to publish his/her ma- terials. In the previous chapter, we discussed the example of Cushing who worked with the Zuni in the 1880s. He is often used as an example of an anthropologist who had "gone native," although we question the extent to which this is true. However, he published much less than his successor with the Zuni project, Jesse Fewkes, even though Fewkes was criticized for never having achieved the holistic view of Zuni society that Cushing had (Hinsley 1983). Later in the book, we will talk about Kenneth Good (Good 1991) who lived with and increasingly identified with the Yanomama, eventually marrying a Yanomama woman. With a coauthor, he was able to write a moving personal narrative of this time. However, he is careful to note that it is not ethnography and he has not and does not wish to pub- lish his ethnographic materials. On the other hand, Curt Nimuendaú (Paul 1953) who lived for decades with indigenous groups in the Brazilian state of Pará, took a native name and eventually died there. He, however, wrote in-depth ethnography and came to be known as the leading expert on the area (Nimuendaú 1983, 1987, 1993).
   Within these two extremes, however, a review of the work of research- ers using participant observation from Webb and Cushing, to Malinowski and Mead, and through contemporary researchers such as Adler, Desjarlais, Bourgois, Hecht, and Johnson shows that successful researchers have em- ployed a wide variety of strategies that range between pure observation and full participation in a culture. Spradley developed a typology to describe a continuum in the "degree of participation" of researchers (1980:58–62). From our perspective, Spradley's categories seem to confound the degree of participation with the degree to which an ethnographer becomes emo- tionally involved with a community. While these are related, we believe that these can and should be separated. In the discussion below, we have modified Spradley's categories to focus only on the aspect of participation.
   For Spradley, *nonparticipation* occurs when cultural knowledge is acquired by observing phenomena from outside the research setting, for example by watching television, reading newspapers, or reading diaries, documents, or fiction. A good deal of information can be acquired in this way even though no active interaction with people is required or takes place.[2] The study of texts, for example, has always been part of research in social science. In recent decades the analysis and interpretation of texts and other media has been incorporated more centrally into the theoretical approach of some social sci- entists. As important as this approach is to social and cultural analysis, it does not employ the method of participant observation. Some of those "texts"

may be conversations and chats on Internet sites. There is a growing number of researchers who participate in blogs and chats as part of their research approach. While lurking on website suggests some important ethical questions about research (see chapter 11), some researchers act as lurkers, covertly observing interaction on websites and blogs without directly participating and without revealing that they are researchers, in the virtual equivalent of nonparticipation. Others, however, have lurked more openly, making it clear that they might incorporate material from chats and list serves into their research. Still others (e.g., Constable 2003) have become fuller participants, chatting openly with the subjects of online research. We place these styles in categories more fully associated with participant observation.

Passive participation exists when the researcher is on the spot, but acts as a pure observer. That is, the researcher does not interact with people. It is as though the researcher uses the site as an observation post. If there is any role in the setting, it is that of "spectator" or "bystander." In general, at this level of participation, those being observed may not even know that they are under observation. Spradley notes that he acted as a spectator in the Seattle Criminal Court System by merely observing court proceedings. Eventually other people in the courtroom setting began to recognize him and to engage him in conversation by asking "What are you doing here?" and his role began to change from that of a passive participant. He eventually took a more active role, interviewing other regulars in the courtroom setting (Spradley 1970). A great deal of information about a setting can be obtained by taking only a spectator's role.

Moderate participation occurs when the ethnographer is present at the scene of the action, is identifiable as a researcher, but does not actively participate or only occasionally interacts with people in it. This level of observation could include structured observation as well as very limited participation. For example, some educational researchers observe classrooms. They are in the classroom, but principally as observers, not as participants. The use of ethnographic techniques in health-related research has included household observations of health practices or food intake (e.g., Gittelsohn et al. 1997). In these cases, the researcher is in the scene but acting as an observer, often with a very structured observational framework. However, it can also include a somewhat higher level of participation. Many anthropologists, for example, will live in their own house among a group of people, or perhaps even in a larger community near the place being studied. They essentially "commute" to the field to question informants or to participate in only certain of the everyday activities of the community.[3] Many of us in new research settings in which we are not fluent in the language begin at the level of moderate participation until a more active role is possible.

Active participation is when the ethnographer engages in almost everything that other people are doing as a means of trying to learn the cultural rules for behavior. Good, for example, talks about his decision to move into the *shapono* (large, circular communal houses) of the Yanomama as an important step in learning about them. He reports: "Yanomama nights were an event, that first night and every night afterward. It wasn't as if the community just went to sleep, then woke up the next morning. No, a Ya-nomama night was like another day. All sorts of things went on" (Good 1991:67). In a house in which 75 people were sleeping together, babies cried, men laid plans for a hunt, shamans took drugs and chanted, big men made speeches, all without regard to the others who were sleeping. At first, this was difficult for Good: "When something got me up, I was up. I'd lie in the hammock for an hour trying to get back to sleep among all the nighttime noises of the *shapono*. Eventually I got used to this, too. Like the Yanomama, I'd spend eleven hours in my hammock at night to get seven or eight hours of actual sleep" (Good 1991:68–69).[4] Good has no doubt that the insight derived from living in the *shapono* was superior to what he would have learned if he maintained his own dwelling.

Finally, in *complete participation*, the ethnographer is or becomes a member of the group that is being studied. Examples of this include ethnographers who are and study jazz musicians, or researchers who become hobos or cab drivers for a time (see Riemer 1977). It is important to note that Spradley's category of complete participation is not the same as "going native." Spradley is referring to a temporary event in which the researcher suspends other roles, in order to more fully integrate with the phenomenon, but continues to record observations in field notes and adopts an analytical stance at least partially during the research period and more completely after the period of participation.

Adler and Adler (1987) developed a somewhat different categorization scheme that is related to the amount of participation. Writing from the point of view of American sociologists working in North American settings, their scheme focuses on the types of roles for those who seek to become members (participants) in the groups they are studying. The three categories they use are peripheral membership, active membership, and full membership. Table 2.1 shows the relationship between Spradley's continuum with Adler and Adler's categorization. As the table indicates, when there is nonparticipation or passive participation, there is generally no membership role for the researcher.

The lowest level of involvement is the role of peripheral member. For Adler and Adler, this role applies to individuals who hold back from central members in the groups with whom they are working. Peripheral-member researchers become part of the scene, or of one group within it, but keep themselves from being drawn completely into it. They interact frequently and intensively enough to be recognized by members as insiders and to acquire first-hand information and insight.

Table 2.1. Correspondence of Spradley's Continuum of Participation with Adler and Adler's Membership Roles

Continuum of Participation	Membership Roles
Nonparticipation	No membership role
Passive participation	No membership role
Moderate participation	Peripheral membership
Active participation	Active membership
Complete participation	Full membership

In active membership, the researcher takes on some or all of the roles of core members. Hecht (1998), for example, began to work for one of the agencies that served the need of the street children he was studying in Northeast Brazil. Jeffrey Johnson (Johnson 1983, 1998; Johnson, Avenarius, and Weatherford 2006) took a job as a boat carpenter in a fish camp in Alaska when carrying out participant observation of the Alaskan fishery. Cushing was initiated into the Bow priesthood while working with the Zuni. In full membership the researcher becomes immersed in the group, and takes on an identity of the group. In both the roles of active and full membership, the researcher takes on some or all of the core membership responsibilities and duties. These roles most closely resemble the role of the classic participant observer.

Johnson, Avenarius, and Weatherford (2006) discuss the advantages of what they term "active participation" in research, which is close to Spradley's notion of "complete participation" and Adler and Adler's category of "active membership." In a study of migratory commercial fishermen on the west coast of the United States, Johnson, took jobs as a boat carpenter, tender worker, bookkeeper, and commercial crewman over several seasons to better understand commercial fishing. Weatherford (1986) took a job as a night clerk in a pornography store during a study of the red light district of Washington DC. As part of larger study on how Chinese and Taiwanese migrants maintain social networks in California, Avenarius took a job as a part-time worker in a Chinese-owned optometry store. She also became a member of several ethnic community organizations including a choir, several dance groups, and church organizations. The three authors review the ways in which taking on an active role in research allowed each of them to develop relationships with research participants in which the participants treated them as insiders, and shared their own reactions with other researchers they did not accept as insiders.

For Johnson, Avenarius, and Weatherford, being treated as insiders opened up new levels of understanding for them. Indeed, the people of the communities in which they worked joked with them about the ineptness of other researchers who did not take active participation roles and were seen always as outsiders. However, they also note several problems with an active participation approach. It may become more difficult to disengage from the field and withdraw. An active participation role may also affect the ability of the researchers to approach her/his analysis reflexively. More importantly, this type of participation raises thorny ethical issues depending on the extent to which the active participant is overtly a researcher. Several of the projects described were conducted in the 1970s and the researchers did not explicitly make it clear that they were conducting research. This would not be considered ethical in current practice. However, they point out, and we agree, that if they had made their observer roles more explicit, it would probably have had little impact on the data they were able to collect.

Hine (2000) in her ethnographic investigation into the trial of Louise Woodward, based entirely on computer mediated communication (CMC), reflects on the different levels of participation in internet-based participant observation. She notes that with the archiving of chats and newsgroups the ethnographer and the participants "no longer need to share the same time frame" (23). However, she goes on to argue that this "collapsing" time frame limits the data and the understanding of the researcher. She strongly advocates for a true presence of participation in CMC-based research focusing on the critical importance of experiencing what the other participants in CMC experience:

> A more active form of ethnographic engagement in the field also requires the ethnographer, rather than lurking or downloading archives, to engage with participants. Making this shift from an analysis of passive discourse to being an active participant in its creation allows for a deeper sense of understanding of meaning creation. Instead of being a detached and invisible analyst, the ethnographer becomes visible and active with in the field setting. (Hine 2000:23)

Determining the degree of participation and level of membership is sometimes done by the researcher and sometimes done by the community. We are personally acquainted with several examples that illustrate how researchers have adopted and adjusted their fieldwork in relation to these categories.

Phyllis Kelly and Eleanor Swanson, colleagues working in two neighboring *barrios* of the town of Temascalcingo, Mexico, in the early 1970s were independently asked to join women's dance groups. Men's and women's dance groups perform at both secular and religious holidays in those communities. Participation in dance groups is one of the beginning steps of the civil religious hierarchy (cargo system) common in these communities. At the lower steps of these systems, dancers not only have the obligation to dance at events, but must also contribute to the costs of festivals, including providing a meal for those occupying positions further up the hierarchy. A commitment to a dance group usually lasts three to five years. When in the communities, both Kelly and Swanson danced and contributed by taking on an active membership role and participating fully in the groups. Like most ethnographers, however, they eventually left the community and returned home. Both were able to schedule short field trips in order to participate in dances on some occasions. When they were unable to participate, they adopted the strategy used by many community members who had begun migrating to the United States to work. Like other absent members of the community, both Kelly and Swanson took the available alternative of an increased monetary contribution, essentially paying someone to dance for them in those years in which they could not be in the community. By opting for full membership and active participation, however, both Kelly and Swanson gained an insight into the workings of these communities they would not otherwise have had. In addition, almost 40 years later (in a visit to Temascalcingo by Kathleen in 2010), both Swanson and Kelly are remembered as dancers and friends by members of the communities in which they carried out research.

Some researchers are forced to take a greater degree of participation than they anticipate. Sociologist of religion David Martin (2000) was directing a survey of religious participation in South America and expected to be a passive participant and not opt for any membership role. He was surprised to be asked to give a sermon during a church service. While Martin was concerned that his increased participation in the life of church might somehow taint the data, he also saw that he had some obligation to give as well as take in the research setting. So, just as he was asking the members of the church to tell their stories, he took the opportunity to tell his story in a sermon.

Anthropologist John van Willigen (1989) working in Ridge County, a rural community in Kentucky, relied heavily on participant observation as a research method. His use of participant observation involved moderate participation and peripheral membership and, as part of his research on aging in these communities, he was attending church services in the county as well as other church related events. He too was surprised when the minister and congregation of one of the churches asked him to preach at a service. He did so, but was even more surprised when they presented him with the collection (somewhat over $4.00) at the end of the service!

It should be emphasized that while both Spradley and Adler and Adler identify types or categories, the balance between observation and participation achieved by an individual researcher can fall anywhere along the continuum. The key point is that researchers should be aware of the compromises in access, objectivity, and community expectations that are being made at any particular place along the continuum. Further, in the writing of ethnography, the particular place of the researcher on this continuum should be made clear. Methodological notes, field notes, and diary entries (chapter 9) should report the level of involvement of the researcher in the community or group being studied, and the degree to which the researcher comes to identify with the community.

PARTICIPATION AND OBSERVATION: AN OXYMORON IN ACTION?

Over the years since Malinowski and Mead described the method that has come to be known as participant observation, a number of writers have commented on the oxymoronic nature of the term and the almost impossible methodological and personal tension that participant observation implies. Benjamin Paul anticipated some of the current debates when he noted that "Participation implies emotional involvement; observation requires detachment. It is a strain to try to sympathize with others and at the same time strive for scientific objectivity" (1953:69).

Barbara Tedlock has argued that exploring the dynamic tension between participation and observation is critically important. She noted that, in the past, when ethnographers wrote personalistic accounts of their field research, they did so using pseudonyms. This was done in order to maintain their reputations as professional ethnographers. From her perspective, however, these more personalistic accounts should be part of the data of anthropology. She argues that we should engage in the "observation of participation," an approach that she terms narrative ethnography. Narrative ethnography combines the approaches of writing a standard monograph about the people being studied (the Other) with an ethnographic memoir centering on the anthropologist (the Self) (Tedlock 1991:69). What is most valuable in the kinds of accounts that she is advocating is that they go a long way toward demystifying the process of doing ethnography. That is, by examining how other anthropologists have dealt with the "degree of participation" and with their emotional involvement, students can better appreciate the circumstances, emotions, and reactions they are likely to experience when they begin their own field research.

Behar (1996) also believes that participant observation is an oxymoron or a paradox. *Participant* observation is a paradox because the ethnographer seeks to understand the native's viewpoint, but NOT "go native."[5] When the grant runs out we go back to our desks. But, as Behar argues, the ethnographer as researcher and writer must be a "vulnerable observer," ready to include all of his or her pain and wounds in research and writing, because it is part of what he or she brings to the relationship. While the focus on a term that is, at its root, paradoxical can be seen as adding to the mystification of the work of ethnography, it also highlights what we believe to be the creative tension between the goal of documented observation and the critical goal of understanding the situated observer. Bernard (2006) puts it this way:

> Participant observation involves immersing yourself in a culture and learning to remove yourself every day from that immersion so you can intellectualize what you've seen and heard, put it into perspective, and write about it convincingly. When it's done right, participant observation turns fieldworkers into instruments of data collection and data analysis. (344)

Finnström (2008) draws on the work of Swedish anthropologist Kaj Arhem (1994), who describes the data collection of anthropologist as "participant reflection" rather than "participant observation." Speaking of the tension between participation and analysis Finnström writes:

> As anthropologists, we do our best to participate in the works, questions, joys, and sorrows of our informants' everyday life. Then we take a few steps back, to be able to reflect on what we have learnt and experienced, again to step forward and participate. This we do daily in the field work encounter. (27)

We see a positive trend in anthropological research as writers increasingly are making explicit the role, degree of participation, and point of view they have adopted in research and write-up (see Scheper-Hughes 1992, 1996).[6] Some researchers have combined this with an explicit discussion of their own emotional involvement in participant observation. Geertz (1995) commented about the process of learning through participant observation in this way: "You don't exactly penetrate another culture, as the masculinist image would have it. You put yourself in its way and it bodies forth and enmeshes you." Behar drew on this metaphor to ask: "Yes indeed. But just how far do you let that other culture enmesh you?" (1996:5). The degree of participation, the membership role, and the amount of emotional involvement that ethnographers bring to the field will have an important impact on the kinds of data collected and the sort of analysis that is possible.

While not all of us are ready to adopt the path of vulnerable observation, participating allows the ethnographer to "know" in a unique way because the observer becomes a participant in what is observed. At the same time, however, our attempt to remain observers of actions and behaviors maintains a certain distance between the people we want to "know" and us. Unlike autoethnography or native ethnography (Reed-Danahay 1997), the investigator is an outsider, a person who spends "the summer on rope cots at the edges of other peoples' lives, observing them" (Narayan 1995:47).

WHAT DETERMINES THE ROLE
A RESEARCHER WILL ADOPT?

The balance between observation and participation, the specific kind of membership role a particular researcher will adopt (or fall into), and the emotional involvement of the researcher can be influenced by a number of factors. Personal characteristics of the researcher may influence the level of participation that an individual may choose or be forced to adopt. We believe that most researchers who wish to use the method of participant observation can train themselves to do so effectively. However, some people feel so uncomfortable in the role of participant that they will be more effective researchers by primarily relying on other methods.

We have often heard both neophytes and seasoned researchers who have not used participant observation express fear that no one will accept them, no one will talk with them, they will be ignored, etc. In our experience, for most researchers, this is not true. After an initial period of adjustment for both the researcher and the group or community, most researchers using participant observation find that they are integrated at least to some extent into the scene. However, the concern for whether one will be accepted is often a mask for a concern that the researcher does not have the personality to accept the role of participant in a particular setting. And, frankly, some people do not. Briggs (1986) is quite honest about how hard she found it to accept the participant role allowed her by the Inuit group with whom she worked. She was never able to adopt the role of Kapluna daughter and her personality made it difficult to interact intimately with the other members of the community. Many researchers like Briggs, however, with an unsatisfying experience with participant observation in one setting find that in a different cultural setting they can get along quite well. Following Mead's advice cited above, the researcher needs to conduct an honest assessment of his/her skills and temperament. For some, it may be that in some settings other methods and forms of fieldwork will be more effective. For some researchers it may be just a matter of getting beyond culture shock (chapter 4).

Other personal characteristics may make it difficult or even impossible for particular researchers to participate as fully as they would like. Gender, age, class, and ethnicity may pose barriers to participation in some arenas important to research. For example, studies of adolescents conducted by more mature researchers may be limited to observation and interview. Participation of older people in youth culture can be uncomfortable if not impossible. Hecht was able to participate in the lives of street children in Brazil primarily as a volunteer in an organization that served street children and as the "producer" for the taped "radio interviews" carried out by other street children. In Hecht's case, because participation as a street child was not feasible, he recruited participant observers in the sense meant by Lindeman. That is, he was able to work through street children who took tape recorders and interviewed other children.

In research with Chicano youth in Chicago in the early 1970s, sociologist Ruth Horowitz (1996) spent a good deal of time on the streets with members of fighting gangs. She writes:

> Readers may wonder how a woman could possibly have spent time with gang members as they loitered on street corners and around park benches, and developed relationships that allowed her to gather sufficient and reliable data. I never tried to become a member of the community. The research role I developed through interaction with the youth varied from each group to another and was significantly influenced by some of my personal characteristics; I am Jewish, educated, small, fairly dark, a woman, dressed slightly sloppily but not *too* sloppily, and only a few years older than most of those whom I observed. These attributes did make a difference in how people appraised and evaluated me and my actions, and in the activities and thoughts to which I was privy. Careful observations of what kind of information was available to me and how different groups perceived and evaluated me allowed me to see not only what categories were important to each of the local groups and what someone in that role was permitted to see, do, and hear, but also how I should try to negotiate my identity in the field. (43)

One of the key points Horowitz makes in this passage and later in her article is that her role as participant/observer was negotiated with the youth gangs over time. She became a "lady" to some (not available sexually); someone who could go with them to buy guns, but not participate in fights or looking for fights with other gangs.

We will discuss the impact of gender more fully in chapter 6, but the participation of men or women in the activities and lives of members of the opposite sex may be impossible in many (but not necessarily all) cultural settings. Lutz (1988), for example, found that in research on a Micronesian atoll she did not have the access to the activities of men she had hoped to have. More commonly men are unable to participate in the activities generally assigned to women.

Lincoln Kaiser became very close to the members of the Vice Lords gang with which he worked, but he was always a "white guy." William Foote Whyte became well integrated into the lives of people in Cornerville, living in the community, attending meetings and hanging out. However, he several times stepped over the limits of the role that the community was willing to allow him. He was chided by informants and friends for engaging in behavior unbecoming to a "college guy" when he (like others of Cornerville) illegally voted several times in an election, and again, when he used vulgar language commonly used on the street corner. In both cases, despite living in the community and his time spent on the street, his obvious class affiliation limited the extent to which he was allowed to become a full participant (Whyte 1996b; Whyte and Whyte 1984).

For researchers working in settings very different culturally from their own, such as anthropologists working in non-Western tribal settings, the potential limitations should be obvious. The North American or European researcher is immediately identifiable in most South American, African, and Asian settings. While some researchers work quite diligently to achieve fuller participation, they are always limited by being identifiably different. We find it amazing that some researchers are able to participate as fully as they do despite such obvious differences. For many of us, the role adopted as learner or neophyte is the one most readily available to someone so clearly different. However, participation as a cultural baby is participation and may, in fact, provide a good excuse for the incessant and excessive asking of questions.

Participation in illegal activities can pose both legal and physical danger. Adler and Adler (Adler 1985) hung out with drug dealers (wheelers and dealers) and even used drugs during the time they were carrying out research in Southern California. They became close friends with some of the dealers, socialized with them, bailed them out of jail, and reached a point in which they were considered trustworthy. They admit to using drugs (principally marijuana) as part of their participation, arguing that they would not have been accepted in the group if they had not. They declined to become involved in dealing themselves, however, although often urged to do so by their informants. They argue that this reluctance to fully participate placed them in the role of peripheral membership rather than full members. Philippe Bourgois, who studied dealers of crack cocaine, was also on the periphery in the sense that he did not participate in the drug culture as a user or dealer.

Some researchers begin to limit their participation when they feel that they are losing objectivity. A researcher might choose a more peripheral role for several reasons. S/he might be concerned that more involvement would result in difficulty in adopting an analytical stance during analysis and interpretation. Or, further involvement might place the researcher in either physical or legal danger. It is our belief that no research project is important enough to place the researcher in physical danger.

Finally, some researchers choose to take a covert role in fieldwork. That is, they do not make it clear that they are conducting research. Adler and Adler (Adler 1985; Adler and Adler 1987) suggest that they would not have gotten the amount of information about drug dealers if their role as researchers was known by all of their informants. Bourgois (1995), however, was completely open about his role as a researcher, overtly taping conversations both in interview situations and on the street hanging out. We will discuss the ethical issues in participant observation in chapter 11. For us, however, adopting a covert role is not an ethical approach to fieldwork. Moreover, virtually all of our research now has to pass through an Institutional Review Board for the Protection of Human Subjects. Covert research, even of a purely observational nature, when identifiable individuals are observed, is unlikely to be approved. As we will note below, the goal of establishing true rapport requires honesty of the researcher.

LIMITS TO PARTICIPATION?

There are some dramatic cases of the need to establish "limits to participation" because engaging in these behaviors may be illegal, dangerous to the personal health of the ethnographer, or both. Obvious examples include situations in which ethnographers study shamanistic use of hallucinogens or other drugs, drug cultures, prisons, or high-risk sexual practices. Philippe Bourgois (1995, 1996), for example, became quite involved with the drug dealers with whom he was working, although he abhorred the violence and other activities in which they engaged. There are also many accounts of ethnographers being confronted with whether to engage in romantic and/or sexual involvement with members of communities they study (see chapter 6).

On a less dramatic level, there are experiences like those of Bill in Temascalcingo. When we began research there, Bill decided the *cantina* in town would be a good place to find out what was going on in the community. All was going well until one of the inebriated patrons asked Bill what we were doing in the community. Bill's explanation that we were there to study the local culture led his new companion to pull a very large pistol out of his belt and to state: "The Indians around here only understand one thing and that's this. I'll help you find out about the culture of those fucking Indians. Tomorrow we'll go up in the hills to talk to them." The next morning (not very early), the man showed up at our house, pistol at the ready, to assume the role of research assistant to the anthropologist. Bill faced a very difficult situation in getting rid of his newfound friend without insulting him, patiently explaining that we were not there to study only "Indians" and that we would feel much better about using our own methods for getting people to talk with us. Bill ultimately decided that, in the future, there were probably better venues than the cantina in which he could participate to find out what was going on in the community.

Deciding how much to participate or not to participate in the life of the people being studied is not an easy decision for any ethnographer. In addition, there are often occasions during which the ethnographer faces a difficult decision about whether or not to intervene in a situation. Kenneth Good provides a particularly wrenching example of this. During his research with the Yanomama of South America, he came across a situation in which a group of teenage boys and three older women were engaged in a tug of war. A woman whom he had befriended earlier was in the middle. Good ascertained that the teenagers were trying to drag the woman off to rape her while the old women were trying to protect her. He described his dilemma as the young boys succeeded in pulling the young woman off into the bushes:

> I stood there, my heart pounding. I had no doubt I could scare these kids away. They were half-afraid of me anyway, and if I picked up a stick and gave a good loud, threatening yell, they'd scatter like the wind. On the other hand, I was an anthropologist, not a policeman. I wasn't supposed to take sides and make value judgments and direct their behavior. This kind of thing went on. If a woman left her village and showed up somewhere else unattached, chances were she'd be raped. She knew it, they knew it. It was expected behavior. What was I supposed to do, I thought, try to inject my own standards of morality? I hadn't come down here to change these people or because I thought I'd love everything they did; I'd come to study them. (Good 1991:102–3)

Good decided to do nothing but wrote that this was a turning point in his integration into the community. A month later Good did intervene in a similar situation.

Every ethnographer sooner or later faces dilemmas like these that become difficult ethical issues (see Rynkiewich and Spradley 1976 for a useful compilation). We may appeal to "cultural relativism" or to the role of "objective observer" to avoid intervention in situations like those faced by Good. In cases in which we see the people with whom we are working being exploited, subject to violence, or damaged in some other way, however, it is increasingly difficult to justify not intervening. Nash came to the conclusion that the world should not be seen as simply a laboratory in which we carry out our observations but rather a community in which we are "coparticipants with our informants" (1976:164). She used this as an argument for working to try to help the tin miners she was studying in Bolivia fight for their rights. Scheper-Hughes (1996) argues even more strongly that the role of the ethnographer includes activism. She describes how she chose to intervene in the punishment of several young boys caught stealing in a South African village. She intervened to take an accused boy to the hospital to save his life after his punishment at the hands of villagers, even though her research was, in part, on the outcomes of popular justice.

Largely, the establishment of our own limits to participation depends greatly on our own background and the circumstances of the people we study. Our personal characteristics as individuals—our ethnic identity, class, sex, religion, and family status—will determine how we interact with and report on the people we are studying.

BEYOND THE REFLEXIVITY FRONTIER

We noted in chapter 1 that the method of participant observation was developed by Malinowski simultaneously with his development of the theory of functionalism. However, participant observation has been used for data collection by researchers coming from a variety of theoretical perspectives. Agar (1996) observes that contemporary ethnography, especially work carried out at the end of the twentieth century, has drawn more heavily on participant observation as a method than did the work in the previous several decades, which incorporated a more linguistically based reliance on formal elicitation, limited survey research, and analysis of texts. Contemporary ethnography heavily critiques functionalist approaches to analysis in favor of more interpretive approaches but the utility of participant observation as a method of data collection in postmodern approaches suggests that the method is much closer to the core of anthropology around which many different theories are built. While born with functionalism, participant observation is not tied to it. In fact, we believe that holding any theory up to the everyday lives of people has been a major stimulus for theoretical change and development in the social sciences.

Participant observation as a technique of fieldwork has been a hallmark of anthropological research since the beginning of the twentieth century and has been a distinguishing characteristic of anthropology compared with other social sciences. It may be constitutive—that is, it may be essential to anthropology. While tied to functionalist theoretical approaches early in the century, the reliance on participant observation and the recording of chronologically oriented, descriptive field notes, which also include the incorporation of the ethnographer's thoughts and reactions, laid the groundwork for much of the theoretical development autochthonous to anthropology. That the descriptions of the research enterprise provided by Malinowski in 1922 and Bourgois (among many others) in 1995 can appear so similar, suggests that the method, while not atheoretical (no method is), is so closely tied to a relatively unchanging theoretical core in anthropology as to provide the basis for a wide range of theoretical development around that core.

In his award-winning 2008 book, *Living with Bad Surroundings*, anthropologist Sverker Finnström writes thoughtfully about his use of participant observation, his presence in Uganda and the limits to participation as a European researcher, and the way in which he, as a European viewed and was viewed by the the Acholi people in war-torn Northern Uganda in the early twenty-first century:

> In essence, if there is such a thing, I am a European, non-African, or rather a foreigner, even a stranger, to Acholiland. *Muno,* as the Acholi say. Obviously,

my looks resemble those of the expatriate relief and aid workers, development volunteers on short-term or long-term assignments, or the journalists and foreign ambassadors who briefly visit war-torn Acholiland. In practice, I did my best to acknowledge the hospitality offered by my informants. I always ate their food, drank their water, wine, and beers. *Lawak*, Acholi call persons who do the opposite with a proud and bossy attitude. "Like a *muno* [foreigner] who refuses to eat what is offered; who doesn't mingle with locals" as an old man explained. I participated in my informants' reconciliation and cleansing rituals, and I went to their baptisms and funerals. I constantly and eagerly listened to my informants' stories. I especially remember one senior ex-rebel who talked without a single break for more than five hours, as I was seated in an uncomfortable chair doing my best to write down everything he was saying. It was totally fascinating, but my buttocks and my back ached and my writing arm was cramping when we finally decided to call it a day. (Finnström 2008:15)

Finnström goes on to describe his role as a participant observer, rather than as an Acholi insider. Acknowledging that insider or "halfie" ethnographers (native or seminative ethnographers) often claim a methodological superiority, he writes:

I remain, however, an outsider, a visitor, to Acholiland. I cannot claim any essential connection to Uganda. . . . At the end of the day, regardless of our respective backgrounds, it is ethnographic fieldwork that puts anthropologist on firm empirical ground. (Finnström 2008:16)

He also reflects on the role of participant observation (or participant reflection, following (Arhem 1994) as the sharing of experiences that also "works as a tool of intersubjectivity in the endeavor to represent and demystify the other, the unknown" (Finnström 2008:16).

Contemporary anthropology has seen an explosion in literature that is produced by individuals who find it important to examine how their own feelings, prejudices, and personal characteristics influence their interpretations of information. That is, ethnography becomes the interaction of the people being studied (the Other) with the anthropologist (the Self). These approaches have become known by a variety of terms including postmodern, interpretive, critical, or reflexive anthropology. This movement toward more reflexive ethnographic writing has resulted in a quantum increase in the number of accounts of the fieldwork "experience" particularly by individuals who rely mainly on the method of participant observation. The result, we believe, is a continuing demystification of the process of fieldwork and ethnographic writing. Making explicit the process of participant observation allows the reader to better understand the information presented by the ethnographer. Narrative ethnography (Tedlock 1991) and personal accounts of field experience also provide the opportunity for new researchers to begin to anticipate problems, identify alternative strategies, and begin to craft their personal approaches to participant observation early in the fieldwork experience. The approach to training in ethnography common a generation ago, and still extant, in which each new ethnographer is told to go out and reinvent anthropology methodologically and sink or swim on their own ability to do so, constitutes the worst form of intellectual elitism. Fortunately, we have gone beyond that time.

While approaches that emphasize the "observation of participation" are quite useful and important (especially for training budding anthropologists), we see these as complementary to the use of participant observation as a means of collecting verifiable, reliable data concerning human behavior. We accept that none of us can become completely objective measuring devices. We can, however, use participant observation in conjunction with other methods to serve anthropology as a scientific pursuit.

That is, we see reflexivity as a beginning point rather than as an end to ethnography. We need to be aware of whom we are, understand our biases as much as we can, and understand and interpret our interactions with the people we study. Once we have done that, we can strive to determine whether there are regularities in human behavior. From our perspective, Hamilton captured the appropriate balance between reflexivity and social scientific analysis. She wrote:

> the truths and realities on which I must rely take shape in the spaces between observer and observed, between subject and object, between writer and reader. The ethnographic information I collected is a social construct; as an actor, as well as an observer, I participated in the creation of that information. I have placed myself in this book's narrative action and have described relationships with informants and institutional affiliations that limit the field of action I was able to encompass. (Hamilton 1998:33)

However, Hamilton goes on to note that she does "not think it useful to focus" on herself as an actor in the book. Along with including many of the words and actions of the people she studied, she also used considerable quantitative data to elucidate gender relations in highland Ecuador.

There is no question that theory does affect the kind of accounts written by anthropologists and others. From a personal point of view, however, what is heartening to us is that much previous anthropological and other social scientific research can be quite useful in building generalizations irrespective of the theoretical perspective used. Our experience has thus been that, despite differences in theoretical perspectives, gender, ethnicity, and other personal factors, the broad-brush descriptive observations of individual researchers concerning human behavior are relatively consistent. Certainly, if we look at the fine detail or if we look for consonance in theoretical conclusions, we will find many differences. Rather than using the latter as justification for giving up on making participant observation and other anthropological methods more verifiable and reliable, we believe it is more productive to focus on the generalizations that can be derived from such data. The aim should then be to improve our methodological skills, including learning to be better participant observers, to work toward building generalizations that are even stronger.

PARTICIPANT OBSERVATION ON THE FAST TRACK

As qualitative research methods became more incorporated into the planning, implementation, and evaluation of development and health projects, a series of approaches to rapid appraisal using forms of research that were drawn from participant observation have been developed. Rapid Rural Appraisal (Chambers 1980, 1983, 1992) approaches in agricultural research and technology transfer programs became a key component of the "farming systems research" paradigm. In health-related research, Rapid Appraisal Procedures (RAP) advocated by Scrimshaw and Hurtado (1987), Rapid Ethnographic Assessment (REA) (Bentley, et al. 1988), and focused ethnographic studies (FES)(Pelto and Pelto 1997) share the a set of characteristics in which researchers employ several qualitative methods, including aspects of participant observation to collect information on tightly focused topics to be able to incorporate local understandings for the planning and implementation of intervention programs. Coming from the perspective of qualitative research in sociology, Knoblauch (2005) outlines focused ethnography as a form of ethnographic study that is contrasted with conventional in that rather than attempting a comprehensive, holistic view of a cultural setting, it focuses on a single topic, and is typically conducted in a shorter time period than conventional ethnography. Knoblauch notes that focused ethnography, like rapid appraisal procedures and focused ethnographic studies, is more likely to be used in applied research.

It seems incongruous that researchers would talk about participant observation in relatively short-term, focused research approaches. Yet, all of these writers cite examples of the use of unstructured observation and at least limited participation as critical in the collection of information for program planning and implementation. Clearly the role of the participant observer is different than it would be in a more conventional qualitative research project. As Knoblauch (2005) points out, the role of the researcher is closer to the "observer" end of the continuum (Spradley's passive participation or limited participation) than to the "complete participation" end. However, it is also clear that some researchers have managed participation and incorporated it in a novel way into their research (Cernea 1992). The United Nations University 16-country study of health using the RAP incorporated participant observations both in selected households and in community

and clinic settings (N. S. Scrimshaw and Gleason 1992). The use of participant observation in rapid or focused research not only suggests novel ways
of participating, but also different approaches to sampling activities and
people. We will discuss both the forms of participant observation and the
sampling issues related to its use in rapid appraisal or focused ethnography
approaches in health and rural development in later chapters.

This chapter has focused on the important theoretical work that has
been done in recent years on participant observation. We began by indi-
cating that skills for participant observation can be learned and included
a preliminary discussion of some of the important dimensions to doing
participant observation.

We then indicated the importance of understanding that participation
and observation are two different processes that, in some sense, are contradictory. Pure observation seeks to remove the researcher from the scene
of actions and behaviors, while pure participation immerses the researcher
in the scene of actions and behaviors. For this reason, researchers must be
aware of the degree of their participation. We used typologies developed by
Spradley and Adler and Adler to indicate the spectrum of investigators' participation or membership in cultural situations. The investigator has some
degree of control over the degree of their participation and membership,
but we also discussed how the researcher's ethnic, gender, class, and other
characteristics can limit participation and membership.

Contemporary anthropology has led to much more reflexive accounts
based in most cases on participant observation. These accounts emphasize
the interaction between the participant and what he or she is observing.
Although they have led to much useful introspection concerning the fieldwork process and the nature of participant observation, we closed with a
plea for getting beyond the introspection. From our perspective, a social
science is possible and this requires us to engage in comparative research.
This means that we need to improve our skills so that we can better use the
method of participant observation (as well as other methods) in building
social science theory. It is to improving these skills that we turn in the next
two chapters.

NOTES

1. Interestingly, this statement is strategically placed over a photograph whose
caption reads: "Robert Dentan burning the fur off a monkey."

2. Many contemporary anthropologists and researchers using a cultural studies
approach base their analyses on "texts" that can be written or spoken materials. In
the former case, face to face interaction with informants may not be required (see
Murray 1991).

3. We have carried out fieldwork in an essentially commuting situation and as residents of communities. There is no doubt for us either that greater understanding comes from living in the community.

4. Good reports that it was this experience that contributed to his increasing divergence from his then-advisor's portrayal of the Yanomama as "the fierce people" (Chagnon 1983). Although Good saw the violence in their culture, he also saw a substantial amount of harmony and group cohesion.

5. Tedlock discusses a number of cases of anthropologists who are candidates for having "gone native." As she points out, however, in each case the individual continued to publish ethnographic accounts (1991:70).

6. Sanjek (1990d) argues that this is an important part of establishing validity in ethnographic reporting.

✵3✵

Doing Participant Observation

Becoming a Participant

In the previous chapter, we discussed the tension between the roles of observer and participant inherent in the role of participant observer. They appear to (and do) require different sets of skills. In this chapter, we will discuss the strategies and skills necessary to successfully adopt the role of participant. The following chapter will focus on the skills necessary to be a good observer.

Becoming a successful participant in another cultural setting involves a series of practical, logistical, and emotional processes. Some aspects of these processes have been the subject of much anthropological literature, while other dimensions are still part of the "mystery" of doing field research. This chapter will begin with a discussion of how you should approach a new field situation, particularly emphasizing the importance of getting formal and informal clearance to do research. We then discuss the importance of building rapport, establishing close, trusting relationships with people in another cultural setting. Building rapport does not often go smoothly, so we also discuss making mistakes and how a beginning field researcher can successfully recover from errors they will inevitably commit.

ENTERING THE FIELD

Gaining entry to a field site and beginning the process of building rapport can be a daunting experience for new researchers and experienced researchers in new settings. Entrée can be either overt or covert. In covert entrée the researcher does not make explicit that s/he is engaged in a research project. Covert entrée may be a reasonable choice in research that involves nonparticipation or passive participation of the most limited kind, and it is defended by some as necessary under some circumstances (Lugosi 2006). As we express in chapter 11 we believe that taking a covert participatory role is not ethical. In research that includes participant observation, we believe that it is imperative to make the research nature of the relationship clear.

In general, the initial approaches to gaining entrance to a research setting are similar for many different kinds of fieldwork, including fieldwork that will employ participant observation as a method and fieldwork in virtual settings and employing computer mediated communication. First, in research outside the researcher's home country either a special visa for research or a formal research permit may be required. It is important to begin the process of obtaining them well in advance of fieldwork. Even when a special visa or permit is not necessary, it is common courtesy to check in with members of the local community of scholars and researchers. New researchers in a particular setting may want to carry letters of introduction from colleagues with experience in that setting.[1] In recent years the Institutional Review Boards for the Protection of Human Subjects in Research (IRBs) for most U.S. universities and colleges are requiring the research conducted abroad also to be reviewed and approved for the protection of human subjects in the country in which the research will take place. While the method of participant observation is almost always "exempt" in IRB terms, the researcher will need to identify an appropriate institution to review it, and secure a written confirmation that it has been reviewed and approved. In our experience this can take a good deal of time in some countries.

After taking care of issues at the national level, the next step is to identify local leaders and organizations who represent the community in which the research will take place, or who have access to the setting in which the research will take place. That is, the local gatekeepers. While some field situations do not have gatekeepers, this is uncommon (Schensul, Schensul, and LeCompte 1999). Contacting gatekeepers may mean contacting local officials, such as mayors, county executives, presidents of key local community committees, etc. In studies of older adults in communities in Kentucky, Kathleen and her research team made first contacts with the County Judge Executive of each county, and then with the county extension agents, representatives of community development organizations, and leaders of community organizations such as homemakers' clubs, retired teachers' organizations, and the directors of the Senior Citizens' Centers. For a project in a Pittsburgh community that would draw heavily on community participation in the research process (community-based participatory research[2]) anthropologist Kimberly Rak worked to identify leaders in a housing project community and secured their support of the project before approaching other community members. Leaders of the housing project community then became key collaborators on the project. Leith Mullings (Mullings

2000; Mullings and Wali 2001; Mullings et al. 2001) and her colleagues discuss the steps that they followed in order to carry out the Harlem Birth Right Project, a research project examining stress and reproduction that included participant observation with African American women in Central Harlem. In order to gain entrée into a community that was very suspicious of research, Mullings and her colleagues formed alliances with organizations such as the New York Urban League and set up an effective working community advisory board to introduce the research to the community and to guide the specific questions and approaches to the research.

In research in Latin America, we have always identified the organizations that promote the most inclusive meetings of community members. Sometimes this has been regularly organized community political meetings. In Ecuador, for example, the most inclusive meetings were those of the Rural Health Insurance System. In Mexico, we attended meetings of the members of the agrarian reform organization (*ejido*). At community meetings we asked for time on the agenda to present the overall goals of the project, the kinds of methods (in general terms) that we would be using, and to ask permission to work in the community. In each case, we have spoken with leaders before presenting the project at community meetings.

While it has sometimes taken several meetings to secure permission, to date we have never been denied permission to work in a community. However, this does happen. When it does, it may be possible to discover the reasons why the community or community leaders were reluctant to agree and those concerns can be explicitly addressed and the decision changed. In some instances, an alternative research site must be chosen. In still others, it may be that the specific goals of the research need to be examined to understand why a community might be reluctant to allow a particular project to go forward.

Nicole Constable (2003) when using CMC as a critical component to her study of global romance and "mail order" marriages was encouraged by the moderator of an online group to become a member of the group as part of her research. He suggested that she lurk for a few days, and then make her presence as a researcher known to the wider membership. When this was done she received a number of hostile messages—she was "flamed."[3] She finally decided to discontinue her participation in that group. When she withdrew from the group she received a larger number of responses supporting her participation and encouraging her to stay. In Constable's case the "gatekeeper" was supportive, but a number of participants were not, resulting in her withdrawal. However, the supportive moderator initiated an offshoot group of about 40 members who were comfortable with the research and who welcomed her as a participant.

In studies of institutions such as schools, clinic, hospitals, religious groups, or voluntary organizations, gaining entrée begins with the hierarchy of the institutions. For example, this would be principals and superintendents in educational research; hospital officials and chiefs of service in hospital based research. It is our experience that in larger cities some frequently used research sites, such as schools and hospitals, have research review boards that review proposals before permission to carry out research is granted.

No matter the setting, it is important for the researcher to carefully explain the purposes of the research project in terms that are comprehensible to the people who will be included as participants.

> Entrée and rapport are facilitated if the community understands and accepts the purposes of the research. Full disclosure of research purposes is an important ethical principle as well as a key to entrée and rapport. By having a socially recognized purpose, the researcher assumes a less ambiguous role within the group studied. Fieldworkers often find that if they do not actively present themselves in an appropriate role, the community may assign them to an inappropriate one. (van Willigen and DeWalt 1985:20)

Gaining permission is the first step for carrying out research. Gaining access to specific institutions, places, and events may take more time. Often the researcher will find that this is facilitated by particular individuals who essentially take the ethnographer under their wing and help to introduce him or her to their society or group.

FIRST CONTACT

A number of ethnographers have noted that some people in any research setting are much more likely to be open and curious, and to even approach the ethnographer early in fieldwork (Agar 1996; Pelto and Pelto 1978). As a stranger, it is very easy to accept the hospitality and assistance of the first welcoming person or group that appears, but the ethnographer has to be cautious because they may then find it difficult to interact with other groups and individuals. Agar has written that the first people to approach the fieldworker are often either "professional stranger-handlers" or "deviants" (Agar 1996).

Professional stranger-handlers are individuals who are delegated (or delegate themselves) to check out the new person in their midst and limit his/her access to information and situations that might prove uncomfortable to the group. "They can find out what the outsider is after and quickly improvise some information that satisfies him without representing anything potentially harmful to the group" (Agar 1996:135).

Agar described his experience with professional stranger handlers in two research settings. When he began working in Lombardi he was quickly approached by an older man named Sakrya. Sakrya was the first person to approach him, and he materialized any time Agar was doing something "bizarre in the early days of fieldwork, like drawing a map or measuring the size of *tanda* huts" (1996:135). Sakrya also informed Agar that there was no room in the *tanda* for him to live. Several months later, when he had determined that Agar was trustworthy, Sakrya was also the person who introduced him to members of the community and arranged for people from his kin group to act as paid assistants.

The other example Agar gives is from his research in a federal narcotics hospital in Lexington, Kentucky. One of the inmates named Jack first approached Agar and posed the question on everyone's mind: "How do I know that you're not a fed?" When Agar replied, "Try me," Jack took the challenge and began to act as his guide around the unit. He made sure that Agar would not see anything they didn't want him to and fed him with misinformation, until Agar proved that he could be trusted. Later Jack became an important key informant and friend. Agar reported that both Sakrya and Jack were individuals who were respected insiders, "natural public relations experts," and held the trust of the members of the community.

The "deviants" who may approach the fieldworker early in research are different. They are individuals who are, for one reason or another, alienated from or marginal to the community or group. Agar defines them as "members who are on the boundaries of the group in some low-status position" (1996:136). Dentan (1970) described spending some time in the company of a man who approached him early in his fieldwork, who turned out to be the Semai equivalent of the "village idiot."

In our experience, some of the first contacts are often made by people who are "opportunists." They are adept at discovering what resources the researcher might have and how those resources can be diverted to themselves and their families. We have found that these individuals are often from the mid range of the socioeconomic system, neither the most affluent nor the poorest. For example, in our early work in Mexico, after making contact with the president of the *ejido* (the agrarian reform community), we were steered by him to a "research assistant"/guide from his own faction. This individual was younger and a bit more educated than the other farmers, and he was not shy about asking for loans, for help in buying a tractor, and for other resources. After a time, we were able to firmly establish the "economic rules" of our relationship and Pedro became a helpful and savvy collaborator in our research.

Having acknowledged the potential pitfalls and the potential benefits of dealing with those who contact us first, it is important to emphasize that in a number of cases the first contacts can turn out to be outstanding informants and knowledgeable insiders. Finding a sponsor who can introduce and vouch for you can be a key to gaining entrance as a participant. The experience recounted by Whyte (1996a, 1996b; Whyte and Whyte 1984) in his research on a street corner society shows the importance of having a sponsor. Whyte was introduced to his sponsor, Doc, by a social worker. "Somehow in spite of the vagueness of my own explanations the head of girl's work in the Norton Street House understood what I needed. She began describing Doc to me" (Whyte 1996b:75). She made an appointment for them to meet and left them alone. Whyte went into a long explanation of what he wanted to do. "Doc heard me out without a change of expression, so that I had no way of predicting his reaction. When I finished, he asked: "Do you want to see the high life or the low life." Whyte replied: "I want to see all I can." And Doc answered: "Well, any night you want to see anything, I'll take you around. I can take you to the joints—gambling joints—I can take you around to the street corners. Just remember that you're my friend. That's all they need to know" (76). Thus was forged one of the most effective relationships in participant observation research. Doc was not only an intelligent, interested person, but he was personally powerful in the world of Cornerville. Constable (2003) found that recruiting a sponsor from among the online community she was interested in resulted in the creation of a productive online space for her research.

Finding and recruiting a sponsor can be an effective way to enter a community, meet people, and learn the culture. The trick is finding the right kind of sponsor. We suggest that the right kind of sponsor is someone who is in a respected but relatively neutral position in the community, and with whom a relationship of mutual trust can be developed. Agar expressed the response of many of us to William Foote Whyte's relationship with Doc: "We should all be so lucky" (1996:137). Constable's discussion-group-moderator-sponsor was able to identify a subgroup of group members who were comfortable with her research.

Guimaraes (2005), in participant observation in a Brazilian internet multimedia online sociability platform called *Palace,* early on met (through his avatar) a key member of the community who was organizing an online motorbike tour of *Palace.* His sponsor then introduced him to other members as "an anthropologist researching *Palace"* and also assured the other members that Guimaraes was "a nice guy" (149). Guimaraes said:

> while talking about the organization and the pleasures of motorbike riding and traveling (either online or offline), it was possible to introduce myself as and ethnographer and establish rapport with some key members of the group as many of the organizers were Gods or Wizards.[4] (149)

The members of *Palace* came to accept Guimaraes as a participant and researcher.

Agar (1996) noted that in his fieldwork among the Lombardi and in the narcotics hospital, his first contacts eventually became keys to his being accepted into those settings after he had proved his trustworthiness. In our case, Pedro provided a particular perspective on the community and provided us with an entrée into the community. When we recognized that he was allied with one faction, we were soon able to cultivate contacts in the other organized faction and with the nonaligned group. In chapter 5, we return to this theme when we discuss the issue of sampling in participant observation.

Langness (Cohen et al. 1970), however, suggests that in some settings it may never be possible to avoid or overcome being identified with one faction or another. His warning reinforces the need to be clear at the outset about which questions are the most important in the research, and which groups are most important for getting at that information. While relationships with informants present themselves and develop in their own time and in their own pattern, beginning fieldwork with some idea about the types and range of people who will be included among first contacts helps the researcher to move beyond the limitations they might impose. Eventually, it will be important to establish a working relationship, a rapport, with a much larger number of people within the society or group.

ESTABLISHING RAPPORT

The establishment of "rapport " is often talked about as both an essential element in using participant observation as a tool as well as the goal of participant observation. As Villa Rojas (1979) has written about his and his collaborators' field research in the Mayan region of Mexico, "Our close contact with local people has always led to excellent rapport, the only basis on which really reliable information can be obtained" (59). The definition of what constitutes rapport, however, is an elusive one. Merriam Webster's Online Dictionary defines rapport as "relation marked by harmony, conformity, accord or affinity." In our own thinking, we have often used a definition for which we can no longer find the citation. In this formulation, rapport is a state of interaction achieved when the participants come to share the same goals, at least to some extent—that is, when both the "informant" and the researcher come to the point when each is committed to help the other achieve his or her goal, when informants participate in providing information for "the book" or the study, and when the researcher approaches the interaction in a respectful and thoughtful way that allows the informant to tell his or her story.

Nader (1986) suggested a more one-sided view. She wrote, "Rapport, pure and simple, consists of establishing lines of communication between the anthropologist and his (sic) informants in order for the former to collect data that then allows him (sic) to understand the culture under study" (113).

Jorgenson (1989) focuses on the need to develop a situation of "trust and cooperation" between the researcher and the people in a research setting. As Jorgenson notes, the degree to which trust and cooperation (rapport) are established influences to large extent the degree to which information gathered in participant observation is accurate and dependable. Jorgenson suggests that the researcher periodically assess the extent to which s/he feels that a situation of trust and cooperation exists between the researcher and the people with whom s/he is working. Schensul et al. (1999) note that the development of trust, which can be mobilized throughout the fieldwork process, is one of the key benefits of participant observation.

How does one establish rapport? To large extent, rapport is built in much the same way as any other personal relationship. It is built over time. It requires that the researcher put effort into learning appropriate behavior in a setting; showing respect for people in a setting; being a good and careful listener; and being ready to reciprocate in appropriate ways. It means that if the researcher expects informants to tell the truth, at least as they see it, the researcher must also be prepared to tell the truth.

Guimaraes (Guimaraes 2005) argues that the establishment of rapport in online, virtual settings is very similar to offline settings. He notes that the same skills "of knowing how to listen to an informant, learning the proper way to behave and so on are as valuable online as offline" (151). He exercised these strategies in gaining acceptance in *Palace*.

Reciprocity is a critical component of establishing rapport. Clearly, there is a range of level of reciprocity. It certainly includes telling the truth when the researcher is asked about the research, his/her goals in research, or his/her life stories. Telling the truth can pose problems for the researcher but it is our feeling that if the researcher cannot tell the truth about the goals of the research project, it probably should not be carried out. However, deciding how much beyond the general research question and objective to share can be problematical. We should worry about excessively influencing the outcome of the research. In general, it is not necessary to share specific hypotheses, or to attempt a short course on social science research and theory.

Answering personal questions can also be a problem. There are times and situations in which women researchers, for example, may want to leave the impression that they are married or at least in a relationship "back home" to deflect some of the almost inevitable sexual solicitation. We feel that it is acceptable to leave this impression, even when it is not entirely true. (Although, to be frank, if the spouse or boyfriend isn't right on the scene, a fictitious one isn't much help with this aspect of living in the field.) Apart from this, we feel it important to answer questions about religious beliefs and practices, values, opinions, and so forth truthfully. If you feel that you have to lie, how can you expect informants to be frank and open with you? However, the researcher can put their opinions and personal information in the most neutral way possible. For example, when asked about what we think of politicians either of the country in which we are working or our own, we have learned to say: "I agree/disagree with his/her policies" rather than "S/he is a great/horrible leader/crook." When the researcher truly respects the point of view of the informant, it is quite easy to answer religious and other belief questions by saying, "I don't believe that, but I certainly understand why you do."

In many cultural settings, we have found that it is entirely appropriate to ask how much money a person earns. In fact, it makes gathering income information in Mexico a bit easier. The answers may not be truthful, or at least not accurate, but the informants are usually not offended by the question. However, the question often is turned around. In the kinds of research setting in which we have worked, our income, even as graduate students, was incomprehensibly large for a rural, resource-poor farmer to deal with. Over the years, we developed a strategy of not giving a dollar (or peso, or sucre) amount, but to say something like, "I must be frank with you, I am well paid for my work with the university. We are very comfortable." This has seemed to work in most settings.

Another common question is "What's in this for you?" In other words, people want to know what you will gain from this project. Again, honesty is the only viable approach. (And since most of us will not experience large direct economic gain from any project, the researcher can almost always reply that there is no real money involved.[5]) We generally put the answer to this in terms that are understandable in the local setting. For example: "We will write a book that will tell our colleagues what life is like here. This will help us finish our degree," or "get a job," or "keep our job," etc. Sometimes the answer is, truthfully, that we will be able to use the information to help find support for community projects or the development of better policies.

Being truthful with informants does not extend to questions about others in the community. The protection of confidentiality always comes before any other consideration in fieldwork. Researchers must be assiduous in not sharing with other community members' personal information that may have been learned in doing fieldwork. Betraying confidentiality, even inadvertently, is not only unethical, but it ALWAYS comes back to bite you. It can mean, at minimum, the loss of an informant, but can also end a research project, and even affect a career long term.

Engaging in reciprocity may mean sharing personal goods and providing services (e.g., transportation) as they are appropriate in the setting. Responding to numerous requests to share goods or provide services can be very irritating, especially when the requests are beyond the level appropriate in the researcher's home setting. Sometimes an accommodation needs to be made. For example, Rabinow found it easier not to have a car during fieldwork than to respond to constant requests for rides. In Temascalcingo, we also found ourselves serving as the local taxi service but this never became especially problematical.

Reciprocity may mean arranging for material returns to individuals or communities. Malinowski distributed tobacco to informants. In research in 1976 in the Brazilian Amazon, Kathleen and her colleagues brought glass trade beads to distribute to members of the community, and before leaving gave away many personal goods such as soap, flip-flops, and batteries. Guimaraes helped to build and (virtually) decorate *Palace* servers and rooms.

We have always tried to avoid directly paying informants (it seems antithetical to the notion of participant observation) but we have given resources to communities in other ways. In Honduras, people asked whether we could provide the community with a calculator and we were happy to oblige. In the Andean region of Ecuador, our research project sponsored a soccer tournament among the research communities and provided food during the games and a trophy for the winner. We also employed community nutritionists in each region to work with community members, provide community education, and train local health workers. We then supported modest salaries of those health workers. In another project, we provided money to start a rotating credit fund for each community in the project. We routinely employ local assistants and guides. The cost of these kinds of activities is often low for the researcher, but significant for the community and individuals.

Collings (2009) discusses this issue in a report on a recent phase on ongoing research with Canadian Inuit. As part of a staged approach to gaining official, community, and individual agreement to carry out the research he attended a community meeting to present his proposed project:

> I began by explaining the project's aims, methods, and expected results. Not three minutes went by before a hand was in the air. What kinds of benefits will we see from this research? What good will your research be to us?
>
> Ooooh! I was excited on hearing a question I expected, even hoped, to hear. Trying not to sound too smug, I launched into my prepared answer: A database on subsistence production and food networks would be invaluable for community-based decisions on wildlife management and hunter support programs. I had hardly started in on my explanation when I noticed a woman tap the questioner on the shoulder. She whispered but loudly enough that everyone in the room could hear her. "It says on page 3 he is going to give us lots of money." The questioner turned back to me. "OK, it's good then." There were no more questions. The letters of support were ready the next day. (138)

Collings goes on to note:

> In retrospect, I should not have been surprised that money would be the deciding factor in obtaining a permit, although money as an issue did not occur to me until I began filling out ARI's licensing paperwork some time later. The

first section on the application form asks for the investigator's address and affiliations. The first question in the second section? How much money from the research will contribute to economic development? That is, how much money is the investigator going to spend in the community? Only later on the application form were applicants required to explain and justify the research project. To me, the message was quite clear: From ARI's perspective, the most important issue in community-based or collaborative research, at least in the western Canadian Arctic, is financial. (Collings 2009:20)

Even though, as he further notes, collaborative/participatory research is becoming increasing common.

Probably the most common things field researchers provide to informants are photographs. We have made it a practice to provide families with copies of pictures taken of them. When it is possible, we will respond positively to requests to take "family portraits." We have found that sharing photographs makes it less awkward for us when we are taking other photographs to document life in communities.

Finally, reciprocity often includes sharing research results with the community. This is especially important if the community can make good use of the information. In the project in which we employed community nutritionists, we incorporated the results of our study into community education. In other studies, we have been able to assist community members in writing proposals for support, using, in part, information from the studies. Several online researchers have contributed their expertise to building or maintaining the online environments.

This discussion of the process of developing rapport and coming to be accepted in a community begs the question of how long it takes to achieve. In reality, a lot depends on the ability, characteristics, and experience of the ethnographer, the circumstances and characteristics of the group being studied, and the kinds of information that one wants to obtain.

Rapid research methods (RAP, FES) are also based on the establishment of rapport, but under more constrained circumstances. When field work is a matter of weeks rather than months, the definition of rapport is a bit more narrow, but not qualitatively different. We have often, for example, participated in rapid appraisals (Kumar 1993) in which the objective is to obtain a quick impression of farming techniques, agricultural problems, or significant kinds of illnesses in a community. In this situation the degree to which either party understands or shares the goals of the others is, of necessity, quite limited. In these situations, the ethnographer has to achieve an "instant rapport" that is at least sufficient to put informants at ease to answer the questions being asked. Rapport is still based on developing good communication relationships that emphasize listening on the part of researchers (Cernea 1992; Chambers 1992; Slim and Mitchell 1992). At the minimum, it requires that the researcher explain in simple format the goals of the study and treat the responses of respondents and informants with respect and attention to the protection of their rights. The development of rapport by being on the ground, listening, and participating can take place even in emergency settings (Slim and Mitchell 1992). As rapid assessment research has came to include participatory research methods in both rural development and health research, rapport as the sharing of each other's goals has come to include the development of shared goals for programming planning and implementation developed through interaction between the researchers and the participants in research (Chambers 1992; Reason and Bradbury 2008).

For other kinds of topics, much more rapport is required before much information can be gathered. During our fieldwork in Temascalcingo (B. R. DeWalt 1979; K. M. DeWalt 1983) we were unable to get people to talk about topics such as witchcraft or traditional curing practices until we had spent over six months in the field. In other situations in which the people being studied are for some reason very suspicious (e.g., harsh exploitation by outsiders, situations of violence or deprivation, extreme isolation), it may never be possible to achieve a substantial amount of rapport. It has become relatively standard in ethnographic inquiries to think of a minimum of a year of fieldwork as necessary to gain sufficient insight from participant observation, but this is only a general guideline. Certainly, the longer that the investigator is in the field, the higher the level of trust between community and investigator, and the better the quality of the information is likely to be.

To make the point again, rapport exists when both investigator and informants come to share common goals or move to develop joint goals for the research. The participants in the setting or events under study must come to agree to help the investigator, however they understand the project. This means that it is the responsibility of the investigator to describe, at least in general terms, what the project is and what he hopes the product will be (e.g., book, report, or proposal). Clearly, this does not mean explaining the nature of social research or anthropological theory. However, it does mean explaining what one is about at the outset of research and every time anyone asks. Near the end of the research, it may be appropriate to share findings with people in the research through a presentation to the community.

Establishing rapport also means that the researcher must come to accept the goals of the community. At the most basic, this means telling the story to others accurately and fairly, having and showing respect for the participants, and engaging in reciprocity. It can include explicitly discussing goals with informants and finding ways in which the results of research can be useful to the community. It may mean recruiting members of the community to participate in formulating questions and even collecting information. In recent research on the coast of Ecuador, in which we were investigating the impact of income-generating projects on women's social power in rural communities, the questions in which we were interested were, in part, a response to the issues identified by women in the study communities. Members of the study communities were consulted before the beginning of each research phase and community members were recruited into the field teams to serve as guides and assistants.

For most investigators using participant observation, incorporating the concerns and goals of the people with whom we work is not difficult. In fact, the greatest strength of the method is that the researcher attempts to gain the point of view of the participant. Part of the iterative nature of participant observation is that the questions continually evolve as new information is gathered and new insights reached. The big caveat here is that individuals within a research setting have many different goals. Understanding and sharing the goals of the community and individuals within it does not mean laying aside the analytical stance that is also inherent in the method. It does mean that the reporting of research results should not place any individual in harm's way. The Code of Ethics of the American Anthropological Association (American Anthropological Association 2009:4) states:

> Anthropological researchers have primary ethical obligations to the people, species, and materials they study and to the people with whom they work. These obligations can supersede the goal of seeking new knowledge, and can lead to decisions not to undertake or to discontinue a research project when the primary obligation conflicts with other responsibilities, such as those owed to sponsors or clients. These ethical obligations include:
> To avoid harm or wrong, understanding that the development of knowledge can lead to change which may be positive or negative for the people or animals worked with or studied;
> To respect the well-being of humans and nonhuman primates;
> To work for the long-term conservation of the archaeological, fossil, and historical records;
> To consult actively with the affected individuals or group(s), with the goal of establishing a working relationship that can be beneficial to all parties involved.

Sharing goals may also come to mean helping communities to achieve their goals. Many researchers have made the information they obtained available to communities and many have taken on activist roles. Wax writes of her experiences in a Japanese relocation camp during World War II: "I, as a fieldworker, came to participate in this struggle and my behavior and attitudes . . . came to resemble those of a fighter in a resistance movement" (Wax 1971:174). In participatory research programs, researchers and participant develop at least some joint goals.

BREAKING THROUGH

Many fieldworkers find that they can point to a single event or moment
in which the groundwork for the development of true rapport and participation in the setting was established (e.g., Nader 1986; Stack 1996; Sterk
1996; Whyte 1996a; Whyte and Whyte 1984). Clifford Geertz (1973) el-
egantly describes the event that allowed him and his wife to begin to gain
acceptance by the community and to establish true rapport in the Balinese
village in which they worked. The Geertzes had been in the village for about
a month, during which time the villagers treated them as though they were
not there. They were rarely greeted, people seemed to look right through
them; people would move away when they approached. It was truly an
anthropologist's nightmare.

Their breakthrough came as a result of a police raid on an illegal cockfight they were observing. Although the Geertzes could have stood their
ground and presented the police with their credentials and permissions,
they choose to run away with the rest of the villagers when the cockfight
was raided. In Geertz's words:

> On the established anthropological principle, "When in Rome," my wife and
> I decided, only slightly less instantaneously than everyone else, that the thing
> to do was run too. We ran down the main village street, northward, away
> from where we were living. . . . About halfway down another fugitive ducked
> suddenly into a compound—his own it turned out—and we, seeing nothing
> ahead of us but rice fields, open country and a very high volcano, followed
> him. As the three of us came tumbling into the courtyard, his wife, who had
> apparently been through this sort of thing before, whipped out a table, a
> tablecloth, three chairs, and three cups of tea, and we all, without any explicit
> communication whatsoever, sat down, commenced to sip tea and sought to
> compose ourselves. (415)

When, moments later, the police arrived, the Geertzes' adopted host was
able to provide a lengthy and accurate description of who they were, what
they were doing in the village, and what permissions they had. In addition,
he noted, the Geertzes had been in this compound all afternoon sipping
tea and knew nothing about the cockfight. The bewildered police left. The
Geertzes found that after that point they were enthusiastically incorporated
into the community.

An even more dramatic account of a single event that lead to fuller participation is provided by Kornblum (1996) who was called on to stand
with "his" gypsy family when they were attacked by Serbians in their camp
outside Paris. In a moment of crisis, he became one of them.

> As I found my way to the main road through the camp, my worst fears were
> confirmed. It seemed there would be a pitched battle, for the Boyash men

and women were grouped about 50 yards away from a much larger group of Serbian men. Both groups were heavily armed. I saw Cortez flick open his switchblade. Tony was holding a shotgun. The Boyash women kept up a steady barrage of violent oaths and insults. As we slowly advanced toward the Serbians I attempted to find a place in the second ranks, but Persa was there again to shove me to the front. (1–2)

He relates that participating in this (eventually nonviolent) encounter resulted in a subtle change in his relationship with the Gypsies. "Persa and I never discussed that incident . . . but I could tell it had changed her opinion of me from one of disdain to one of guarded respect" (2).

After spending some time studying prostitutes in Amsterdam, Sterk (1996) studied prostitutes in New York in the mid-80s just as the magnitude of the AIDS epidemic had become clearer. Sterk had spent several days "on the stroll" in New York but none of the prostitutes would speak with her. Finally, one challenged her; she explained that she was from Amsterdam and wanted to know something about the prostitution in the United States. Her knowledge of the life was challenged, and apparently she answered appropriately, as she was befriended by the prostitute, Ann. Later Sterk found that her already acquired knowledge of the street from her previous experiences gave her credibility with prostitutes and pimps.

Robert Dentan (1970) describes the day he and Ruth Dentan arrived in the first Semai village in which they would work in Malaysia. They had found an isolated village with relatively little contact with "pale people." While people seemed to view him as "a particularly bizarre museum specimen," they had seen "pale" men before, but never a "pale" woman. However, when Ruth said that she wanted to learn to live like a Semai woman, she was whisked away.

> A swarm of giggling and chattering women immediately gathered around her, swept her up the ladder into our house, stripped her naked, wrapped her in a sarong, stuck flowers into her hair, painted her face, put a machete in her hand, and took her off to collect firewood. (103)

While it appears that it took Robert Dentan a bit longer to be incorporated into the village, Miss Housefly (the translation of "Ruth" as rendered in the Semai language) was quickly incorporated.

Stack (1996) found her acceptance into the community in an African American section of a Southern city happened more slowly but was facilitated by the breaking down of her car. When her car broke down Stack decided not to fix it. Like Rabinow she has been using the car, in part, to transport community members, giving herself a visible role. Without a car, she was more like the people of the community in which she was working, was less visible and more a part of the community. Lack of mobility resulted in her spending more time in people's homes and led, she writes, to her eventual acceptance into the community.

We found in our work in Temascalcingo that the quality of the information we were receiving improved after our return from a three-week trip to the United States to renew our visas and take a break from field work. Until that point, people seemed to be unsure of our interest in them and their lives. We had been able to carry out fieldwork, but did not feel that we had made close contacts or were incorporated into the flow of daily activities. The fact that we had visited our own culture and families, but had returned to renew our stay in Mexico, demonstrated our commitment to the people in this Mexican community. Everywhere we went, people expressed *"Que milagro"* (what a miracle) and greeted us with greater warmth and affection than they had previous to our break. Suddenly, our previous questions about sensitive subjects like witchcraft were answered in detail rather than tossed-off and evaded. The experience of improved acceptance after returning from a trip away from the research setting is so common in the literature that we have come to think of it as one of the most important ways to enhance acceptance.

To summarize, in a number of these cases, the breakthrough in acceptance was achieved when the researchers provided evidence that their relationship with the community was important and serious TO THEM; when they demonstrated a more than passing commitment to a community. We returned to the community of Temascalcingo against the expectations of community members who had assumed we would not. Clifford and Hillary Geertz acted like Balinese villagers when they could have acted like privileged foreigners. Kornblum risked violence to stand with the people with whom he was working. While these dramatic examples are more vivid, rapport generally is established slowly, simply by continuing to live with and interact with a group of people and conducting oneself in a way that shows the researcher's commitment to the community.

TALKING THE TALK

One of the hallmarks of participant observation since Malinowski described it has been the use of local languages in the research setting. Earlier ethnographers, focused on collecting texts, often worked with interpreters. Participation, however, requires being able to communicate effectively in the local setting; being able to follow informal conversations; being able to understand and join in jokes, etc. Discussing how to learn a language, especially an unwritten language, is well beyond the scope of this volume. However, we would like to note that quite a few of the languages that were unwritten and inaccessible before going to the field for researchers in previous generations are now available for study before fieldwork begins. As a result of the work of the Summer Institute of Linguistics (SIL International

2010)[6] and the Wycliffe Bible Translators (Wycliffe Bible Translators 2010), grammars and vocabularies exist for a large number of languages. For example, in 1976 Kathleen spent a few weeks with the Northern Kayapo in Brazil. Only one woman in the community spoke any Portuguese. The only way Kathleen was able to achieve any level of communication in that short period of time was through using the notes of a Bible translator who was working on the Kayapo language.

It is not only worth the time and effort to learn the local language, it is imperative. Debra Picchi (1992) recounts how she relearned this important lesson during fieldwork with the Bakairi Indians in Central Brazil. She went to Brazil as an ecological anthropologist with interests in demography, modes of production, and labor organization. After several weeks in the community, she overheard a conversation held in Portuguese about her.

> "She doesn't speak well," Cici, a young mother of two complained loudly to her friends. "I think she must be as stupid as those giant anteaters that wander around the jungle."
>
> Domingas, a frail old women, answered Cici softly, "You ask too much. She has been with us only a few weeks. You cannot expect her to speak Bakairi as well as we do. Be patient and she too will be a human being."
>
> Maisa, another young mother spoke up, "I don't know. I'm worried. The *Alemao*[7] really is not learning very fast at all. Geraldina told me that she tried to explain to her the story of how the jaguar copulated with a human to produce our people. Geraldina said she didn't think that the girl understood two words of what she told her." (146)

Picchi reflected that she had not been studying the Bakairi language diligently, as the people with whom she had been working also spoke Portuguese, and she was, at that point, more interested in collecting demographic and production data. However, she also realized that the conversation had been staged for her benefit, and carried out in Portuguese to make sure she understood. After further reflection, she realized they were telling her that she would not be considered a true human being in their world until she could communicate in their language; and, finally, "the women were trying to tell her that a grasp of the language was a necessary precondition for an effective study of their tradition" (148).

It is difficult for some people to become fluent enough in a new language to carry out effective participant observation. It takes time and it takes study. But it is sometimes also a problem to work in the researcher's first language. In working within the United States we sometimes know that we will be working in a dialect of English that is sufficiently different from the one we learned as children as to cause some problems. There are times, however, when we think we are communicating but are missing subtle regional and local differences in language.

In the study of nutritional strategies of older adults in rural Kentucky we had been collecting recipes for several weeks before we came to realize that the word "seasoning" meant something different to our informants than it did to us. When we heard seasoning, we thought salt and pepper. It took a bit observation of cooking to realize that "seasoning" referred to some type of fat. Traditionally, it was lard or bacon grease. In the 1990s, it was more often solid vegetable shortening or vegetable oil. Not only did we need to rewrite the recipes, we had to edit the program for calculating nutrient content of dishes. Two tablespoons of lard in the green beans represent a lot more calories than salt and pepper.

All communication in research settings should be approached as cross-cultural communication in which one of the tasks of the researcher is to understand the local language. The formal elicitation of local terms for phenomena of interest is a common activity of fieldwork. In some types of research it is a research end in itself. There are a number of approaches to formal elicitation (e.g., Spradley 1970, 1980; Weller and Romney 1988; Werner and Schoepfle 1987a, 1987b). However, even if the presentation of data from formal elicitation is not a goal of the project, taking time to elicit local terms or to follow-up on statements that are not understood is an important aspect of learning to talk the talk.

How far should talking the talk go? Again, understanding local meanings is critical to understanding what is going on. However, there are times when using the language of the setting can come back to bite the researcher. Depending on the role that the researcher comes to have within a community it may or may not be appropriate to talk like the participants. Whyte found that his informants did not like him using profanities, even though they did all the time. For him to do so was not deemed appropriate.[8]

WALKING THE WALK

The heart of adopting the method of participant observation is to behave appropriately enough to be accepted as a participant at some level and to participate in the daily activities of people with whom the researcher is working. By behaving appropriately, we mean learning what constitutes good manners and practicing them to the best of your ability. It can include proper, polite speech; appropriate reciprocity; table manners; appropriate levels of eye contact: all the many niceties (as defined by each culture) that make up day to day interaction. Fortunately, learning how to behave well enough (never perfectly) is not so very hard. Most of us do learn to do it without dire consequences, even when we make mistakes (see below), and we do so at least partially unconsciously (tacit knowledge?). With enough interaction most researchers begin to adopt some mannerisms and learn to be polite in the local context just by being open to the possibility of doing so. Recall the quotation from Mead (1970b) in chapter 1. She writes that she unconsciously picked up the manners and body language of the various peoples with whom she worked. However, there are some key areas in which problems seem to occur.

North American and European researchers working in another cultural setting routinely have problems with dealing with lack of privacy. Appropriate behavior in many settings includes constantly being with others. Like many others, Robert and Ruth Dentan (Dentan 1970) found they had problems with privacy. As it happened, even defecating was a social event for the Semai. While Robert found he could occasionally slip away to defecate alone, it was an even more gregarious activity for women. Ruth Dentan was not often able to "go it alone."

Ruth almost always had a few companions. As she once remarked, "We squat there in a row in the water, with our sarongs up, like a bunch of ducks." The day Ruth discovered the value of the gregariousness came when she managed to slip off alone and found on her way back a tiger between herself and the settlement. She ran upstream, tried to find another path to the settlement, lost the path, and at last decided that if she had to die she wanted to die in the water. On her return, fortunately, the tiger had gone, leaving only a few paw marks in the sand. After that she preferred having the women accompany her (105).

Intellectually, the Dentans understood that yearning for privacy was partially "pale person's ethnocentrism," which, as good cultural relativists, they were trying to leave behind in their fieldwork. Nonetheless, the Dentans still felt they needed some privacy to remain sane. They instituted a "taboo day" once a month in which they told people that they needed to be alone. The concept of Sabbath was understood by the Semai as a result of contact with missionaries. The taboo day worked pretty well, although even with this in place the Dentans rarely had a completely alone day; but the monthly respite allowed them to manage in the field. Understanding the rules of reciprocity are another arena in which researchers in cultural contexts other than their own find they have problems. Again, as we will note below, Dentan found it difficult to participate in the flow of reciprocity expected in Semai society.

Eating local foods is another aspect of behaving appropriately. Our rule of thumb is to attempt to eat everything we are served, unless we feel that the threat to health is so great that it is worth insulting people. For us, not liking it is not much of an excuse, although it is possible to avoid some items that are particularly distasteful. Bill was able to avoid drinking *pulque*, a mildly alcoholic beverage made from fermenting the sweet sap of the century plant, common in rural Mexico at the time. It was made in homes under somewhat less than fully sanitary conditions (in some homes we observed people shooing away a dog or a goat from the open terra cotta *pul-que* barrel). *Pulque* has a flavor and consistency reminiscent of mild, thick vinegar. While Kathleen came to rather like it, Bill never did. After a bout of amoebas in his liver, he was able to avoid drinking *pulque* as everyone in the countryside understood that one should not drink anything alcoholic while treating liver disease. Bill's liver disease lasted for years, conveniently being used as an excuse whenever he wanted to avoid drinking. Kathleen can't stand the taste of coconut water, a refreshment that is commonly offered in coastal Ecuador. She gets down enough to be polite.

In recent research with Kichwa-speaking people of the Ecuadorian Amazon, Kathleen, two students, and a guide arrived, after a 45-minute climb, in a village in the middle of a local "day of the mother" celebration. The principle food of Napo Kichwa is a "manioc beer"—*aswa*. While a mild *aswa* is consumed every day, it is allowed to ferment to a more alcoholic state for celebrations. As we arrived the *aswa* began to be served. *Aswa* is typically prepared and served by women.[9] In this case it was men serving women as part of the celebration. The two students looked at Kathleen quizzically. Judging that it was not one of those times when a potentially hazardous food could be turned down, she made a mental note to look for the antibiotics when the group returned to their lodgings. The *aswa* was pretty good (as *aswa* goes), the interview with the Kichwa health promoter was interesting; and two hours later the trip down the mountain went a bit more rapidly with all slightly tipsy. Miraculously, no one had even the hint of tummy upset the next day!

It is a good idea to try to check out local table manners early in the field experience. Several of our acquaintances report being overfed in parts of India, before they came to understand that their hostess would continue to fill their plates until they left a bit of food uneaten. Like good North Americans, they were "cleaning their plates," a signal in India that one was still hungry. Saying "no" to another helping is thought to just show polite coyness. In some cultures it is impolite to arrive in a home at a mealtime, as it means that the guest will have to be fed whether or not the resources will allow.

Wax (1971) reports that she realized that she had unknowingly been insulting the Japanese American residents of the relocation camp, because she was unfamiliar with social conventions. When she did become aware, she was able to do well enough to establish many close relationships. We do know people who seem never to be able to give in to local expectations for behavior or who cannot at least in some cultural settings. Frankly, as we noted in chapter 2, they should find another field site or use a different methodological approach.

How do we learn enough to participate appropriately? The most important condition is to want to do so, that is, to be committed enough to using participant observation as a method that the researcher will try to learn. Coupled with a nonjudgmental attitude toward expectations of social life, being open to learning is almost enough for most researchers. A second condition is a genuine respect for the community and the people with whom the researcher will be working. The researcher has to approach participating and observing any particular situation with an open mind and a nonjudgmental attitude. That is, while the activities in which the ethnographer is taking part may be extraordinarily exotic or mundane, a good field researcher must react to the goings-on with sensitivity and discretion.

The researcher cannot be too shy. In order to participate in activities, one must go out and find activities in which to participate. We sometimes get told "no," but unless the researcher asks to go to the event, work in field, hang out on the street corner, gaining access will not happen very quickly. Almost all people love to tell their story and to share their experiences with those who take an interest in them. While we should be sensitive about intruding into situations where we are not wanted or welcome, if an ethnographer shows genuine interest in learning more about behaviors, thoughts, and feelings, he or she will be a welcome guest at most activities. As Picchi's example regarding the language of the Bakairi, the people with whom we are working generally want us to fit in with them, to become part of the community to the extent possible. They are usually ready to teach us how, no matter how painful and humiliating it may be for us.

Which activities and events to choose to participate in is dependent on the focus of the research project, primary research question, and the limits to participation allowed by the community for each particular researcher. The classic ethnographer tries to participate in as many different activities as possible. However, most contemporary researchers have a more focused agenda, and limited time.

MAKING MISTAKES

The book *Nutritional Strategies and Agricultural Change in a Mexican Community* begins with the following paragraphs:

> It was May 3, 1973, the Feast of the Holy Cross—an important feast day for the community of Puerto de las Piedras in the town of Temascalcingo, Mexico. We had been invited to the chapel for services after which an offering was to be made to the Virgin of Guadalupe, followed by a ritual meal. The offering to the Virgin consisted of a handmade basket filled with cigarettes, chocolate, candy, breads, and fruit. The basket was to be thrown off the bridge which straddles the Lerma River, below the chapel.
>
> After the basket had been dropped into the muddy waters of the Lerma, amidst a cloud of burning incense, the office holders in the lower levels of the

religious hierarchy served a ritual meal to the men and women occupying the highest levels of the hierarchy. Large bowls of rice, mountains of tortillas and piece upon piece of turkey in a rich mole . . . were heaped before each of the five couples receiving the meal. Even the gringos were offered a few tacos of turkey and mole. (K. M. DeWalt 1983:1)

Let's stop right there. What the writer does not tell the reader in this passage is that the events that culminated in the description reproduced above also included one of the biggest mistakes in participant observation made by the ethnographers, who were a very young Kathleen and Billie DeWalt. As noted in the written description, food was offered to the two inexperienced ethnographers. However, clear in the field notes, but not included in the published description, was the fact that the ethnographers declined to eat the food offered to them. This event took place early in our fieldwork. Both of us felt very intimidated and anxious about what we were supposed to do on this occasion. It was clear to us that we had witnessed an important event in the ritual life of the community and we did not want to intrude on a ceremonial meal that was to be shared among the community's authorities. Our interpretation was that people were just being polite in inviting us to the feast; based on our norms from the United States, we thought that the polite thing to do was to decline and withdraw from the situation. It subsequently became clear to us that our behavior had offended our hosts.

We heard about this *faux pas* for some time thereafter from a number of people, beginning with one of our key informants who stopped by the very next day to chide us for being so rude as to decline food at a ritual meal. He noted that "the other anthropologist" (a colleague of ours working in a community across the valley) always ate everything she was offered.

Looking back on these events, rereading 40-year-old field notes, we cannot imagine how we could have made such a mistake. Eating all that is presented is probably a cardinal rule of anthropological fieldwork. In our defense, however, we had only been carrying out fieldwork in the community for a few months, our language ability was still rudimentary, and we had not yet begun to pick up on the nuances of "expected behavior." We had been invited by one of our key informants to attend the ceremony and meal, but were unclear as to his role in this event. (As we will note later, he was not only delegated by one of the faction leaders to be our "professional stranger handler," but it was also clear that he expected to gain personally by his association with the North Americans.) The event was clearly for cargo holders in the religious hierarchy. We were afraid he was trying to show off his relationship to the gringos by arriving with us. Our field notes record how much we felt, at that time, like interlopers out of place in these events, gringos. We were afraid that we were taking food out of the mouths of people, who, compared with North Americans, including relatively poor graduate students (as we were at the time), were living on the economic margins.

Our declining to eat a few tacos of turkey and *mole*, however, resulted in the feeling among community members that we were disdainful of their poor food, worried about contamination and illness, aloof. In fact we loved the food, and were not particularly concerned about health. We were uncomfortable and unsure of our participation in the life of the community. We were feeling-out the experience of participant observation and finding our role as ethnographers in the community. As time went on, we became more comfortable with the role of participant observer, feeling less like interlopers, joining, with enthusiasm in any community event or activity to which we were invited.

Even semidisastrous, as it was, the experience of joining in the service, the offering of gifts to the Virgin, and the observation of the meal and the roles of the various cargo holders in the event gave us a much better understanding of the role of the cargo system in the community, the structure of exchange among community members, the role of key foods in both the offering to the Virgin and the maintenance of the highest level of cargo holders. We could never have gained this insight from interviewing alone. To merely talk about the amount of food exchanged in the meal would not have captured the nature of the presentation of truly vast amounts of food, the impact on the families receiving food, the impact on their networks of relatives and *compadres* who would receive leftovers from the feast the next day.

This story also illustrates another point that experience teaches. That is, while this important breach of etiquette probably affected our development of rapport with community members for a time, in the end, our refusal to eat was not a fatal mistake. Over the ensuing months in the community, we had the opportunity to apologize to various individuals involved in the event. We were able to use the time honored (and accurate) excuse that we didn't know what was appropriate; we were inexperienced young gringos with good intentions, but poor manners who needed to be taught appropriate behavior. Our long-term relationship with the community was not appreciably compromised by this event—and our initial *faux pas* resulted in us learning quite a bit about expected behavior in the community.

Bourgois (1995) committed a far more serious breach when he offered a newspaper article in which he was featured, to Ray, a man Bourgois describes as "crucial not only to my continual access to crack scene, but also my physical security" (19–20). Bourgois did not realize that Ray was illiterate, and embarrassed him in front of the people from whom he expected respect. In essence, Bourgois disrespected one of his key links with the world he was studying, a world that revolved around the concept of respect. Bourgois describes how he was still feeling uncomfortable in a situation in which he could be taken as a narcotics agent. He saw the article as reinforcing his identity as a "real professor" and researcher. It was a moment of camaraderie. It took a year to regain the relationship with Ray that he had enjoyed earlier.

Dentan (1970) in talking about fieldwork in two different Semai communities talks about the number of *faux pas* he and his wife made in their early days with the Semai. He likens it to the kinds of mistakes that Semai children make. However, he writes "Since from the Semai point of view we were always rather inept, we could not help feeling very grateful and very affectionate toward them when they came to accept us as people much like other people." (88). Like our experience above, Robert Dentan (1970) writes: "I do not think I would ever have understood the economics of reciprocal food distribution among the Semai if we had not participated so fully in the system that I twice got into hot water for breaking its usually unspoken rules" (92). In one of these instances, after watching one of his Semai friends loading himself down with food from his limited supplies, Dentan asked the friend to wait a week or so before taking any more. The error, as Dentan later realized, was that he had obviously made an overt calculation of the amount of food his friend took. In the rules of reciprocity and food exchange, no such calculation should be made. The friend did not speak to Robert Dentan for several months, although he would come to visit Ruth Dentan.

As Whyte has emphasized: "It is important to recognize that explorations in the field are bound to confront one with confusing situations and conflicting pressures, so that some errors are almost inevitable, but few errors are serious enough to abort a project" (Whyte and Whyte 1984:11). The important thing is to learn from our mistakes.

Whyte describes his role in a local election in Cornerville, where like many of his informants he managed to vote several times for the local candidate in an election. While his Cornerville friends were doing the same, they felt it was inappropriate for Whyte to do so. In another instance, he used rough language, common in Cornerville, but again, his friends let him know that they might talk that way, but it was inappropriate for him.

In some settings, some mistakes can place the ethnographer in physical danger. Philippe Bourgois may have placed himself in danger by disrespecting Ray. Lincoln Kaiser (1970), in carrying out his study of the Vice Lords of Chicago, misread a cue in the behavior of gang members on the streets of Chicago and failed to leave the scene of a possible shooting. As it happened, no shooting took place, but Kaiser makes it clear that he several times felt that not understanding what was going on around him may have placed his life in danger.

Linda Kent (1992) found that a mistake barred her from a fieldwork setting with Irish Travelers (tinkers) in Mississippi. In previous research she had come to know Gypsies well and written a master's thesis on a Gypsy headman. For her doctoral dissertation, she decided to study the Traveling People or Tinkers of Ireland and set out to do a preliminary study of Tinkers in the United States. She settled in Memphis and identified a community of Travelers across the border in Mississippi and began to gain access and build rapport. However, when a local television station in Memphis asked to interview for a human-interest story about Gypsies, she agreed. In the interview she was identified as an expert on Gypsies who had come to Memphis "to devote her life to the study of Gypsies." Two days after the interview was aired, she received a call from the local priest telling her that she was no longer welcome among the Travelers. Didn't she know, he asked, that the Travelers and the Gypsies are sworn enemies? If she was there to study Gypsies, why was she hanging around the Travelers? This event effectively ended her study of the Travelers in the Memphis area.

Mistakes in fieldwork are probably unavoidable. We just don't learn local expectations quickly enough to avoid them. As several of the cases above illustrate, however, making mistakes is often a vehicle to a deeper understanding of behavior and meaning.

In our experience in training fieldworkers, we have noted that the greatest fear of novice researchers is that people will not accept them or speak to them, or that people will be offended by the fieldwork. The experience of the majority of fieldworkers who use participant observation as a technique is exactly the opposite. Personally, it has always amazed us the extent to which people are interested in including us in events, telling us their stories, and how quickly rapport can be established in many settings. We strongly believe that most people underestimate the extent to which people value someone else's interest in their lives and the extent to which people enjoy being "teachers" to eager "students." Our admonition is that if you can overcome your shyness or fear of knocking on that first door, the rest is easy.

As we have seen, however, becoming a participant places the researcher in a unique research role, one where gaining rapport and partaking in a local setting—immersing oneself in a new cultural context—put unusual demands on the social skills and life of the investigator. The payoff is large, a much more nuanced and in-depth understanding of a complex setting than other methods of fieldwork alone can provide. But the cost may also be high. It includes the cost in time of developing the kinds of relationships that grow in trust and cooperation, reciprocity that is ongoing and personal, making mistakes in trying to fit into a new cultural setting, and the psychological costs of having to adjust to a new setting and then readjust on the return to home. Each researcher must find his/her appropriate balance and rhythm in participating in the life of another community, but understanding what to expect and some of the methods that others have used to find their way will help even the novice researcher to eventually find their way.

NOTES

1. The availability of qualified collaborators varies across countries of course, but wherever possible we recommend recruiting local social scientists as research partners. We now rarely engage in fieldwork in another country without the real participation of local researchers as co-investigators. In several settings, we have long-term collaborators with whom we design and carry out research projects on a regular basis. Bill has even begun to insist on having local researchers as partners when doing consulting research (e.g., DeWalt, et al. 2000; DeWalt, Olivera, and Correa 2000).

2. Community-based participatory research (CBPR) is a "collaborative approach to research that equitably involves all partners in the research process and recognizes the unique strengths that each brings. CBPR begins with a research topic of importance to the community, has the aim of combining knowledge with action and achieving social change to improve health outcomes and eliminate health disparities." W. K. Kellogg Foundation Community Health Scholars Program (2010).

3. Wikipedia defines flaming as "hostile and insulting interaction between Internet users."

4. In *Palace*, Gods and Wizards are highly regarded members of the online *Palace* community.

5. In those cases in which substantial income can accrue from the study, the researcher may wish to consider sharing royalties with the community in an appropriate way. We know of writers who have funded scholarships for community students, contributed to community development projects, construction of parks, libraries, etc.

6. The sixteenth edition of *Ethnologue: Languages of the World* published by SIL includes over 6,900 language descriptions.

7. The term *Almao*, literally "German," is used by the Bakairi to refer to all non-Brazilian outsiders.

8. We have found that several different informants in several different settings have found it amusing to teach us words that, unbeknownst to us, have multiple meanings. The entertainment factor comes into play when we are prompted to use them in an ambiguous setting. Researcher in role of clown!

9. To prepare *aswa*, cooked manioc is chewed and mashed. The mash is left to ferment for up to seven days. The fermented mash is then mixed with water (from uncertain sources) and drunk, solids and liquid both. This is another acquired taste, and, furthermore, the water with which it is mixed is most often contaminated. Moreover, since this was a "mothers' day" celebration, the *aswa* had been prepared by men rather than women (YIKES!).

✣4✣

The Costs of Participation

Culture Shock

One of the hallmarks of using participant observation as a key technique in an unfamiliar cultural context is the experience that has come to be known as "culture shock." While classically referring to the culmination of unease felt by the participant observer as a result of not being able to success-fully operate in a new cultural setting, getting all the cues wrong, dealing with not being able to anticipate proper behavior, dealing with behaviors of others that are, to the home culture of the fieldworker, inappropriate, shocking, dirty, immoral, or just plain different, but are perfectly acceptable within the context of the community in which the fieldworker finds her-self, culture shock surely includes what we would call homesickness, and in many cases, the loneliness of leaving all loved ones behind for a while. But culture shock is more than homesickness and loneliness. The demands of trying to operate successfully in a very different cultural context exact an additional toll. For example, Goodenough (1992) describes the complex learning he had to master just to defecate politely on Onotoa.

Anthropologists Cora DuBois (1951) and Kalervo Oberg (1954) are cred-ited with coining and popularizing the term "culture shock" in the 1950s, although, as we will see below, the syndrome they named has been a well-described hallmark of ethnographic fieldwork since the beginning of the enterprise. Although an anthropologist, DuBois introduced the term at a conference dedicated to international education. Interestingly, much of the recent research on culture shock as a syndrome has been conducted in edu-cational and study abroad contexts (Ward, Bochner, and Furnham 2001).

Oberg discussed culture shock as "an occupational disease of people who have been suddenly transplanted abroad. Like most ailments it has its own etiology, symptoms, and cure" (1954:1). Oberg was prompted to discuss the issue of culture shock with expatriate women in Rio de Janeiro after working with a group of international volunteers on a health project, but was also presumably drawing on his own experiences as a migrant and anthropologist outside his native British Columbia. Oberg attributes culture shock to the anxiety that accompanies the loss of familiar signs and symbols (cues) of social intercourse when individuals move into different cultural contexts. Most of the cues of social intercourse are subtle and may be unconscious. The "sojourner"[1] is a "fish out of water" (Oberg 1954:1). He further argues that as a result of frustration and anxiety the sojourner experiences the new culture as culturally "bad" and the home culture is romanticized as "good."

Following such researchers as Hall (1959, 1966), Ward et al. (2001) identify a series of cultural differences in the way that people communicate that appear to be related to the feeling of being a "fish out of water" for the sojourner. These include differences in etiquette, such as the way in which questions are phrased and requests are refused; ways of resolving conflict, such as the differences in the ways in which people in collectivist and individualist cultures negotiate; nonverbal communication, such as mutual gaze, the degree of bodily touching, and the appropriateness of gestures; rules and conventions, such as punctuality and reciprocity; and forms of address. All of which have been shown to vary across cultural settings and to contribute to dis-ease in communications. Oberg suggests that the symptoms of culture shock include:

> excessive washing of the hands; excessive concern over drinking water, food, dishes, and bedding; fear of physical contact with attendants or servants; the absentminded, far-away stare (sometimes called the tropical stare); a feeling of helplessness and a desire for dependence on long-term residents of one's own nationality; fits of anger over delays and other minor frustrations; delay and outright refusal to learn the language of the host country; excessive fear of being cheated, robbed, or injured; great concern over minor pains and eruptions of the skin; and finally, that terrible longing to be back home, to be able to have a good cup of coffee and a piece of apple pie, to walk into that corner drugstore, to visit one's relatives, and, in general, to talk to people who really make sense. (Oberg 1954:2)

Oberg also posited four phases of culture shock that, for many researchers, remain the basis for thinking about the way in which it unfolds. For Oberg, the stages are analogous to an illness:

1. The honeymoon stage in which the sojourner is "fascinated by the new";
2. The "crisis" in which the sojourner becomes hostile and aggressive toward the new context, and critical of the place and the people, often moving to stereotyping;

3. The "recovery" during which the sojourner begins to grasp the new context, to "open a way" into it; gains experience in getting around and communicating and jokes about previous hardships; and, finally,
4. The "adjustment," at which time, the sojourner becomes more competent and moves from accepting foods, drinks, habits and customs and begins to enjoy them.

Drawing on Oberg, a number of researchers studying culture shock among different types of travelers posit a U-shaped curve for the process of adjustment in which at the beginning the traveler is positive and euphoric, followed by a period of much discomfort and distress, and then again returning to a positive state. However, Ward et al. (2001), in a comprehensive review of the literature on culture shock among several different kinds of sojourners such as students studying abroad, missionaries, diplomats, and business people find little support in the literature for a U-shaped curve. For the most part, sojourners appear to be anxious and distressed early in the process and become less so with time. Some longitudinal studies even find that many sojourners experience an inverted U-shaped curve of experience in which they return to a higher level of distress after a period of improvement. However, it does appear that about 10 percent of sojourners do conform to Oberg's U-shaped curve for culture shock.

It appears that culture shock is common among all kinds of travelers, even those traveling for only a short time (tourists), although tourists are increasingly insulated from the conditions that foster culture shock through carefully scripted guided tours. However, sojourners who are participant observers experience several other sources of discomfort that contribute to the experience of culture shock. One of these is the feeling of always "being on," that is, playing the role of being the participant observer and never able to escape, always having to be alert as an observer, when the natural human role is to relax into being a participant. We have often had to repress our irritation when children in communities in which we have worked have stared at us for hours on end, sometimes hanging over house windows or outdoor shower stalls to see what we were doing. Another aspect of always "being on" is the result of being an identifiable outsider in a particular setting, often one perceived to have more resources than members of the local community. This is compounded in cultural settings in which asking those with resources to help out is acceptable. It includes being asked, sometimes continuously, for gifts of food, medicine, tobacco, transportation, and so forth. Paul Rabinow (1977), working in Morocco, describes how much easier his life became after his car blew up and he no longer had to give people rides or, worse, turn them down. Many ethnographers complain about the difficulty of dealing with demands on a daily basis. Finally, "being on" also includes the results of cultural and linguistic incompetence of the neophyte. Some researchers tire of being laughed at or occasionally ostracized for their language and cultural mistakes.

Another element of culture shock for the participant observer is that the fieldworker is not just trying to live in a new setting, but also feels acutely the need to be accomplishing the task of research in this setting—a granting agency is paying for the work and expects a report, an advisor is asking for field notes, an employer is looking for the data, the researcher's degree and career may be on the line, and the researcher is paralyzed with loneliness and anxiety.

For the researcher, as for the conventional sojourner, the characteristics of culture shock include anxiety, depression, anger, and frustration. There comes a day when we just want to be able to defecate in private (Goodenough 1992), throw the toilet paper in the toilet, look another person directly in the eye, communicate effectively without being laughed at by the people with whom we are trying to communicate, etc. Just coping with the logistical difficulties of getting into a new context is a challenge that is often unanticipated by the novice fieldworker. Finally, being alone in the field, at least in the beginning of fieldwork, before rapport is developed, is as lonely as it gets (Mead 1970a).

Paul (1953) calls culture shock one of the costs of the participant observation method. Perhaps understating the extent of the experience for many fieldworkers, he notes:

> The strains of making constant accommodations, of living in the public spotlight, of denying his own preferences, all deplete his patience. He may be able to conceal his exasperation from the people, but he cannot escape the unpleasant effects of suppressed resentment. The first weeks of field work are often trying. The investigator may want to quit and go home, staying only because he is ashamed to give up. (440)

Rosalie Wax describes her entrance into a Japanese resettlement camp in 1943. After an arduous two days of travel, Wax arrived at the Gila camp outside Phoenix in heat that she found "incredible." Alone, in the camp with little preparation for the field experience Wax finally found her room ("cell") by process of elimination from a number of other rooms. She writes:

> It contained four dingy and dilapidated articles of furniture: an iron double bedstead, a dirty mattress (which took up more than half the room), a chest of drawers, and a tiny writing table—and it was hotter than the hinges of Hades. Since there was no one around to ask where I might get a chair, I sat down on the hot mattress, took a deep breath, and cried. I was too far-gone to be consciously aware that I was isolated or to wonder why I had left a beautiful and comfortable university town to stick myself in this oven of a concentration camp. Like some lost two-year-old I only knew that I was miserable. After a

while, I found the room at the end of the barracks that contained two toilets and a couple of wash basins. I washed my face and told myself that I would feel better the next day. I was wrong. (1971:67–68)

Wax goes on to eloquently describe the weeks of ostracism, despair, and perceived failure that followed her arrival at Gila. Few would speak to her, and when she did have conversations, she frequently insulted her potential informants, because she did not understand the conventions of conversation with Japanese Americans. She was clearly not trusted; lonely beyond belief; ready to leave at any moment and sure that the entire project was a failure. All the while the supervisor of the project she was supposed to be carrying out was demanding data. She writes: "Every time I returned to my stifling room after a series of futile 'interviews,' I just sat down and cried. I took long walks in the desert in temperatures of 110°–120°, and cried" (1971:72).

Wax eventually found a way to cope with the situation and to make some progress with her research while she became acculturated to life in the camp, and gained the trust of the residents. She moved from her original room to one even less comfortable in the ruder barracks to which the Japanese were assigned. She avoided the staff. She enlisted the help of another social scientist in the camp and found someone to introduce her to several people from whom she took "Japanese lessons" as a ruse to get to know them better. Finally, she devised a set of "red herring" studies. These were plausible concrete data studies, which, while they had little to do with her real research project, were innocuous enough to be nonthreatening to respondents. She became much more like a formal interviewer than participant observer. She developed structured questionnaires and interviewed women on how evacuation to the camps had affected their lives. She interviewed people on social stratification in Japan. The red herring studies allowed her to meet a number of people in a role they could easily understand. And she says "meanwhile I was gradually pushed into the role of a willing learner . . . friendly respondents now began to instruct me in some of the less confidential aspects and attitudes of center life as well as the rudiments of Japanese etiquette" (77). In the end, Wax found her work in the resettlement camps to be one of the most rewarding of her life. She then describes the difficulty of reverse culture shock upon reentry into her life as an anthropology graduate student.

Mead (1970a) also suggests the new fieldworker begin with more structured data collection to be able to show progress through the difficult first weeks. She writes: "The ability to register progress of some sort is often essential to the field worker's morale, and progress may be noted in counting up the thousands of words of vocabulary mastered, a tantalizing problem solved, a bad cut healed instead of turning into an ulcer . . ." (249). Even while describing the plight of the new and lone field worker she also notes that a person alone in the field may, in fact, be incorporated more quickly into daily life, learning the language more quickly, perforce socializing with "villagers." It is easier for the community to take in a lone field worker, to feed and house him or her. Even Malinowski (1961 [1922], 1967) writes about the

> feelings of hopelessness and despair after many obstinate but futile attempts had entirely failed to bring me into real touch with the natives or supply me with any material. I had periods of despondency when I buried myself in the reading of novels, as a man might take to drink in a fit of tropical depression and boredom. (4)

Indeed, his diary (Malinowski 1967) makes frequent reference to his reading of novels when he was feeling ill or despondent. Deborah Picchi (1992) also relied on novels for the difficult times, especially when she was not feeling well. However, as she had to travel by bush plane to the Bakairi Indian settlement in Mato Grosso, Brazil, she was only able to bring a few novels and had to ration them for the really bad times. We also have to admit to turning to novels at times to escape the community into which we had placed ourselves.

The first few weeks may not hold the only or even the worst patch of culture shock. Paul (1953) agrees with Oberg that, once the logistical problems are long over or at least adequately accommodated,

> a letdown may set in long after the work has gotten well underway. The investigator may school himself to accept physical hardship, he may even gain ascetic satisfaction from enduring deprivation, only to be assailed unexpectedly with a craving for a shower, or a soft bed or a home-cooked meal. More insidious than the material discomforts are the petty and subtle aggravations of social participation. (440)

Sometimes a particular event acts as a trigger for culture shock (or more like a match in dry tinder). Mead talks about how she "burst into tears of helpless resentment when after sitting up all night with a very sick Balinese child, I went home for a moment, and came back in the chilly dawn of the mountain morning and was bitten by the family dog" (Mead, 1949:444–48).

While Wax attributes the depth of her despair on her first day and many subsequent days to a lack of experience, we have found that even after many years of fieldwork in several different settings, we still experience some form of culture shock in a new setting. However, it is less than it was in our earlier experiences and lasts a shorter period of time. Since we expect it, we have become rather adept at identifying the stages as we pass through them: initial elation at finally BEING THERE; loneliness; irritation that nothing works as it should; anxiety that we just can't get our work done, the project will fail for sure; planning to abandon the project; and, finally, the feeling that "we can do this," "it's not so bad," "we are getting the data," "we can cope." . . . While it appears that some field workers never do become comfortable, most do and most, given enough time, find the experience good.

COPING WITH CULTURE SHOCK

Culture shock is a virtually universal experience for investigators pursuing the method of participant observation. As a result, a number of fieldwork narratives discuss the ways in which investigators have dealt with culture shock. Perhaps the most important coping strategy is to realize that the experience of intense anxiety and hopelessness is temporary. As Oberg noted to the expatriate women of Rio de Janeiro so many years ago, "There is a great difference in knowing what is the cause of your disturbance and not knowing" (4). Following Oberg and more contemporary culture shock researchers (Ward et al. 2001), knowing what to expect and understanding that there are cultural differences is one of the key strategies for coping. Today it is called cultural training, but it is in essence the notion of cultural relativity central to anthropology since its beginning.

While some fieldworkers never feel entirely comfortable in the field setting, most of us move through the period of culture shock in a reasonable amount of time. The day comes when the researcher finds that s/he looks forward to talking with neighbors, now friends, and has figured out how to meet the needs of everyday life with the resources available at hand, no longer feels like a fool in attempts to maneuver in the local social setting, and has figured out how to deal with constant demands. While there may well be periods of despair after this point, they can be dealt with. As we have noted earlier, and Ward et al. (2001) also note, some people embrace a new setting to the extent that they adopt it in place of their original one— they "go native."

As Wax and Mead note, it often helps to find research tasks that can be done easily, with little additional stress. As we have noted earlier, we have found that in community studies carrying out a census early in the process helps to introduce us to the community and offers a simple data collection exercise that can allow us to feel that some progress is being made.

While we do not suggest abandoning the field during the adjustment period (we do know the occasional researcher that never returns), it can be very helpful to plan one or more "vacations" from the field when the researcher can leave the community for a short period. Sometimes this is a trip back home to take care of business. Other times it is just a weekend in another town where the researcher does not have to be "on" all the time. In our initial fieldwork experience in rural Mexico we were able to take an occasional weekend trip to Mexico City, about four hours away. There we hung around tourist sites and listened to tourists speaking English, ate hamburgers and french fries (We LOVE Mexican cuisine, but we are talking about *culture shock*, here), and took multiple hot showers. A vacation from the field can also allow for a more objective review of notes, other data, and a bit of analysis. Not all research settings (for example, when you are working on a Micronesian atoll) allow for a weekend trip away. Sometimes it takes more effort to get away from the field, but it can be an effective way of coping. Also as we have noted, the researcher often finds after returning from a trip away, that he or she is greeted as a long lost friend or relation. It often marks the deepening of rapport and the relationships with the community.

Finally, as with the hamburgers in Mexico City or the Pop's ice cream shops in Honduras, cultural comfort food helps. There are some foods we try to take with us and ration out over time. For many anthropologists of our generation, this includes peanut butter. We have found that anthropologists working all over the world have reinvented all of the peanut butter based recipes known. We were able to drive to fieldwork in Mexico and took a case of Campbell's chicken noodle soup (again, it is not about cuisine; it's about comfort). Kathleen still usually packs a couple of bags of M&Ms in a suitcase.

Having a companion or family in the field may help. While it is true, as Mead notes, that the needs of a nonprofessional companion may increase problems, and some of the greatest sources of anxiety for us in the field have been the logistics of trying to meet the needs of children with local resources, couples and families may find that some members of the family have an easier time of integration into the community bringing along the rest of the family. Dentan notes that his wife, also an anthropologist, eased his own entrance into Semai society.

Novels DO help. Kathleen prefers science fiction. Bill likes mysteries and novels of place.

In coping with culture shock, many people have often assumed that having a significant other and/or a family in the field is a great advantage. In our experience, as the following section shows, a family can be both a source of solace and familiarity and a hindrance in doing research.

PARTICIPATING AND PARENTING: CHILDREN AND FIELD RESEARCH

While fieldwork is traditionally portrayed as a solitary endeavor, in reality many researchers bring their families, including their children, to the field with them. The presence of children in the field shapes the research experience in a number of distinct ways. Children can help ease the loneliness and isolation characteristic of fieldwork in foreign cultures. However, children also present a number of challenges to researchers in the field. As part of the trend to demystify anthropological fieldwork, a number of researchers have written about their experiences with children in the field. While each fieldwork experience is unique, a number of themes emerge regarding the effect of children on participant observation.

Many researchers report that their children had a positive impact on participant observation. Bringing children to a field site can lead to increased rapport with the research community. A solitary researcher showing up in a remote area to live alone for a period of a year or more may seem extremely bizarre in many cultures. In most cases, the people who are being studied are able to relate more easily to a researcher living with his or her family. Mimi and Mark Nichter (1987) believed that the presence of their young son made it easier for villagers to relate to them during their research in a rural Indian village. Bourgois (1995) describes how his son's cerebral palsy was diagnosed in a clinic in El Barrio, and that his son's ability to negotiate the neighborhood, rolling his walker over trash and crack vials in the streets of El Barrio, helped to establish Bourgois as a community member.

Also, the presence of children accompanying a researcher can signify his or her adult status. In many cultures a childless adult, especially a married childless adult, may be viewed as strange, dangerous, or the object of pity. During our first field experience in Temascalcingo, it was a concern for many people that we had been married for more than a year without having a child and without signs of Kathleen being pregnant (see also Klass and Klass 1987). During their first field experience in the Sudan, Carolyn Fluehr-Lobban and Richard Lobban (1986, 1987) reported that people had trouble accepting their status as a married couple because they had no children. Many Sudanese doubted that they were truly married but their return to the field ten years later with their daughter Josina reassured their friends and acquaintances.

Bringing children into the field can also open new areas of information to the researcher. Most researchers who bring young children in the field often receive a constant stream of advice about childcare from friends and neighbors. While an overabundance of friendly advice can be exasperating, it can also teach researchers about the culture they are working in. Mimi and Mark Nichter reported that they gained valuable insight into rural Indian ideas about child development from villagers' comments made about their son's "constitution" (Nichter and Nichter 1987). This advice can also challenge the researcher's unexamined cultural biases and assumptions. Renate Fernandez (1987) learned that children sleeping alone in their own room was viewed as a type of social deprivation in rural Spain. Researchers can also learn about a culture from the way people react to their children. When informants are enculturating children, they are also teaching the researcher about their culture. During Diane Michalski Turner's (1987) fieldwork in Fiji, the villagers with whom she lived devoted a lot of time teaching her two-year-old daughter to become Fijian. By watching how villagers interacted with her daughter, Michalski Turner was able to learn not only how one becomes Fijian, but also about Western/Fijian power relationships.

Children can also help gather data that is inaccessible to adults. G. E. Huntington (1987) reports that her nine-year-old daughter was an invaluable source of information about Hutterite children's informal culture. As a result, Huntington learned how Hutterite children engage in very different behaviors in front of adults and when they are among other children participating in their own culture.

Bringing children into the field, however, also has its disadvantages. Some researchers report that the responsibilities of childcare forced them to miss out on certain opportunities. Reflecting on her research in Jamaica, Joan Cassell (1987) relates how she frequently missed nighttime events because she felt compelled to stay home with her two children. Young, unruly children can also disrupt meetings and interviews. In Nancie Gonzalez's (1970) account of her research in Guatemala she talks about how her young son spilled soda pop on the president of the university's rug which did not bode well for the rest of the meeting. Perhaps the biggest disadvantage of bringing children to the field is the amount of time that researchers devote to child care (and hence lose to the field). Many researchers, especially those who are solely responsible for child care, report that the presence of children severely curtailed the amount of time they could devote to field work. Melanie Dreher, who brought three children to rural Jamaica to conduct post-doctoral research with her, states, "I suspect it took me twice the time to accomplish half the work that I would have normally accomplished" (Dreher 1987:165). During fieldwork among an indigenous tribe in the northwest Amazon, Christine and Stephen Hugh-Jones (Hugh-Jones 1987) had to devise alternating fieldwork schedules so that one of them would always be available to supervise their two children.

Our personal experiences with children in the field have been generally quite positive. Our two fair-haired children were an instant magnet everywhere we have traveled in Latin America and led to the opening of many doors for us. We also found that, early in our careers when we were relatively poor graduate students or assistant professors, we could more easily afford childcare and household help in Mexico or Honduras than we could in the United States. We did have some unpleasant brushes with illness, but, in the end, nothing of long-term consequence. We know of others who have had seriously ill children and have even lost children in the field through illness or accident (see Howell 1990). More importantly, as our children moved into their teens and began to have obligations and wishes of their own, it became more difficult for us to take them to the field. More to the point, it was not worth the complaining to which we were subjected. During these years, we began to schedule our time in the field separately so that one of us stayed at home with the children, while the other was engaged in doing field research. A telling incident reminded us of some of the difficulties of children in the field. After our youngest child was a teenager Kathleen returned from several months of fieldwork in coastal Ecuador saying it was the best field trip she had ever had. When Bill asked why, her first reply was that it was the first time in the field that she did not worry about children, whether they were in the field with her or left at home. It must be said, that while we enjoyed having our kids in the field it was a big relief to carry out fieldwork without having to attend to the needs of children.

Whether children help or hinder participant observation depends on a number of factors. It seems that there is a significant effect depending on whether the researcher is returning to a field site or arriving for the first time. Most researchers who are arriving in a field site for the first time with their children seem to experience more problems than veteran field workers (Cassell 1987; Michalski Turner 1987). The age of the children also shapes the field experience. Very young children, while requiring more care, adapt more readily and experience less severe culture shock (Fluehr-Lobban and Lobban 1987; Nichter and Nichter 1987). Older children seem to have a more difficult time adapting to new and foreign cultures (Scheper-Hughes 1987). The field situation itself also shapes the experience with the children. Bringing children to a field site where they already speak the language is easier on both the children and the parent than introducing them to a culture where they are only able to communicate with their family (Cassell 1987; Hugh-Jones 1987). The presence of another parent to share childcare responsibilities certainly facilitates a fieldworker's time in the field with his/her children (Fluehr-Lobban and Lobban 1987; Scheper-Hughes 1987).

REVERSE CULTURE SHOCK (REENTRY SHOCK)

Finally, keep in mind that "return culture shock" is also a problem. Wax writes that when she was beginning work on *Doing Fieldwork* (Wax 1971) she asked a young colleague recently returned from fieldwork in Melanesia what was the most important thing to tell students who had never been to the field. He replied: "Tell them to keep a personal diary in addition to their field notes and tell them that returning to your own society can be as difficult as trying to enter a strange one" (Wax 1971:172–73).

Ward et al. (2001) discuss a growing literature that confirms that reverse culture shock, sometimes called "reentry shock," is extremely common in conventional sojourners. Judith Martin (1984) suggests that one of the reasons for reverse culture shock is that it is unanticipated. New travelers rarely anticipate that they will experience distress upon returning home. Subsequent research has supported this hypothesis (Ward et al. 2001). In addition, there are some demographic differences in the experience of reentry shock. Women are somewhat less likely to experience it. Older people are also less likely to experience reentry shock, and adolescents appear to be the most vulnerable.

In our experience, readjusting to life in North America after extended fieldwork in economically marginal rural communities in Latin America includes a period of time in which the everyday activities of life seem wasteful, too quickly paced, and unresponsive to the "real problems" of the world. (All of which, upon reflection, is true in our everyday North American lives.) Furthermore, many seasoned researchers, and new researchers, once they get over the anxiety of being in the field, find field research to be a very enjoyable break from the kinds of work we do while not in the field. We find fieldwork energizing and intellectually exciting. It helps us gain a perspective on our own lives, to realize that the academic politics that swirl around us are petty and insignificant, and that most of the problems of North Americans are internally generated rather than externally driven. We experience a "let down" upon return to home base.

Wax reports that it took her several years to reengage with her life as a graduate student after her time at the relocation camp during World War II. We find with graduate students returning from the field that the most obvious result of reverse culture shock is an inability to get down to analysis and write-up of research materials. More experienced researchers seem to move through the readjustment period more quickly. Now, it is true that many researchers have a bit of trouble getting to the analysis after the data is collected. These are two very different kinds of tasks. However, the reentry into the home setting after immersion in another cultural setting seems to add significantly to this period. For most, the period of readjustment to home is a few weeks or months. But it does occur, and the wise researcher anticipates this phase of research as well.

NOTE

1. Oberg used the term "sojourner" to describe people, like researchers, who are in a different cultural context for a limited period of time and expect to return home at the end of a defined period. The term has been picked up in the more general literature (e.g., Ward et al. 2001) to refer to such travelers as international students, business people, diplomats and some missionaries, as compared with short-term travelers such as tourists and permanent travelers such as immigrants and refugees.

❦ 5 ❦

Doing Participant Observation

Becoming an Observer

Of course, all crises are grist for the ethnographer's mill—if he himself is not ground in.

Benjamin Paul (1953:440)

While developing an effective participant role is critical to the method of participant observation, it is not a tool of research unless the participant is also an effective observer. In this chapter we will discuss some of the specific skills and details of observation that fieldworkers use to understand people's daily lives, relationships, social organization, values and expectations.

It is a joke among anthropologists that when we have caught an obvious event in everyday life, to point out that we are "trained observers," therefore far more adept than the average individual at capturing nuance. Of course, our peers also cast it up to us when we miss an obvious event, with the implication that we would be truly abysmal observers if we were not trained. Our joke, however, is based on our real assumption that people can be trained, or can train themselves, to be better, more detailed, more objective observers. People do vary with respect to their attentiveness to detail, and their ability to recall detail. Remember that Mead (1953) included innate sensitivity to events as one of the characteristics a would-be researcher should assess before embarking on fieldwork. Anyone, however, can improve the degree to which s/he attends to detail, remembers detail, and, perhaps most importantly, records detail. But, as Wolcott (1994) notes, this is not a very easy thing to convey to others. There is much more discussion about what a participant observer will observe (initially, everything; later, a

79

representative selection of events and situations), but not how one should observe.

In fact, in reviewing a number of discussions of participant observation as a method and fieldwork accounts, we found that descriptions of how researchers developed their abilities to become better observers are rare. Researchers have spent more time describing the nuances of successfully taking the role of participant than they have the concrete details of observing and recording observations. At the same time the literature is full of descriptions of the "aha!" moments when the researcher notes that "suddenly it dawned on me," "then I realized. . . . " That is, the moments in field work in which the researcher came to understand what s/he was observing, but more about that below. In part, this is because, as we noted in an earlier chapter, a good deal of what we learn is the field is tacit. The process of participant observation is, in part, a process of *enculturation* (see Schensul, Schensul, and LeCompte 1999). The researcher gradually absorbs the big picture and some of the details that lead to an understanding of people's daily lives, structure of events, social structure and expectations and values. However, even the gradual development of understanding is based on the accumulation of observations of daily routines, specific events, and conversation, to which the observer has carefully attended and captured in field notes.

At its most basic, observation is just that: the researcher explicitly and self-consciously attending to the events and people in the context they are studying. It is not just a visual phenomenon, but includes all of the senses. "Observation thus consists of gathering impressions of the surrounding world through all relevant human faculties" (Adler and Adler 1994:378). In participant observation, especially, it also includes a kind of self-observation, both of the way in which the investigator experiences the setting as a participant, the particular values and biases s/he brings to the setting (reflexivity); and observation of the impact of the observer on the research setting. In this chapter, we discuss some of the practical steps that should be taken in order for an individual to develop their observational skills.

THE ROLE OF THEORY AND CONCEPTUAL FRAMEWORKS

As we noted in earlier chapters and above and will discuss again in chapter 9, the theoretical framework with which we enter the field is one of the key influences in what we will observe and record. While in an earlier time researchers were often trained (or not trained) to go into the field with no preconceived theories or expectations, most researchers now enter the field with well-defined and specific research questions, well-thought-out theoretical and conceptual frameworks and ideas about social structure, social interaction systems, power relations, networks, etc. Even before entering the field, researchers have thought carefully about what kinds of individuals they will seek out, which venues for observation they will try to attend, what kinds of events they will observe. While the participant observer is learning to become a participant, s/he is also trying to identify the specific actions and products of action that are *indicators* of key concepts and components of a conceptual framework. For this reason, careful observations and the recording of observations in field notes (see chapter 9) are critical elements of the operationalization of the conceptual framework. They are, simultaneously, powerful ways of discovering new elements of a conceptual framework.

TAKING THE OBSERVER ROLE

We find that, after years of experience, we probably observe many situations more closely and more analytically than our noninvestigator friends and colleagues. However, we also observe better when we are consciously carrying out fieldwork; when we define ourselves as being "on"; when we are thinking of what will go into the field notes (more about field notes as critical to the development of the observer below). In a way similar to choosing and taking on a participant role, the participant observer self-consciously takes on the role of observer as well. In fact, the need to be observing, and observing effectively, is one of the strains early in fieldwork that can lead to the experience of culture shock. We find that when we are "on" we have in the back of our minds the fact that, whether or not we are taking cursory notes at the time of the observation, we will be writing field notes later. Keeping consciously in mind that we will have to describe what we did and saw in itself keeps us attuned to the detail of the context.

ATTENDING TO DETAIL: MAPPING THE SCENE

The most important skill the participant observer needs to develop is the ability to attend to details. Effective observation means "seeing" as much as possible in any situation. This can include noting the arrangement of physical space, the arrangement of people within that space, the specific activities and movement of people in a scene, the interaction among people in the scene (and with the researcher), the specific words spoken, and nonverbal interaction, including facial expressions.

It is a good idea to map the scenes in which the researcher is participating. Whyte (Whyte and Whyte 1984) writes about the importance of constructing maps of the interactions in the Cornerville S&A Club. Whyte was interested in studying political and social relations in this community, the structure of action, and the formation and composition of subgroups. He hypothesized that the men who associated most with each other would be allies when it was time to make decisions. He needed to understand the interactions of members of the club in more depth. One of the tools he used to do this was to construct positional maps of Club meetings he observed. Some of this he did surreptitiously. He could see into the room in which the Club met from the front window of his apartment.

> I simply adjusted the venetian blind so I was hidden from view and I could look down and into the store-front club. Unfortunately, however, our flat was two flights up, and the angle of vision was such that I could not see past the middle of the clubroom. To get the full picture, I had to go across the street and be with the men. (Whyte and Whyte 1984:85)

While at the club meetings Whyte observed "who was talking together, play cards together, or otherwise interacting" (86). As he knew the "regulars" well after months of interacting with them, he was able to easily remember who was talking with whom, etc. He made mental pictures of men in relation to the physical objects in the room. He counted the number of people in the scene. He made mental notes of movements around the room. When the scene changed, when people moved around, he went through the same mental processes again. However, Whyte could not keep all of this reliably in mind at first.

> I managed to make a few notes on trips to the men's room, but most of the mapping was done from memory after I got home. At first, I went home once or twice for mapmaking during the evening. But, with practice, I got so that I could retain at least two positional arrangements in memory and could do all of my notes at the end of the evening. (Whyte and Whyte 1984:86)

Whyte's description of his observation of the Club makes several important points.

- Mapping the physical and social scene provides important data for understanding social relationships;
- Mapping is a very good tool for developing the kind of attention to detail and memory that truly effective fieldwork requires; and
- We all get better at this with practice.

Mapping the scene is a fairly common tool of observation.[1] Pelto also describes how he came to a better understanding of social relationships among members of several communities by mapping a reindeer roundup in Finnish Lapland.

We found in our first exposure to a reindeer roundup, that mapping the physical structure of the corral and nearby dwelling units provided a nearly complete outline of the structure of the social interaction talking place . . . the first observation to made about these cubicles is that the Skolt Saame positions tend to be bunched together on one side of the corral, although the segmentation of Skolts from other groups is not complete. Second the cubicle of any one reindeer association tend to be together and the relative positions of the associations are visible in the organization of the cubicles. . . . The positions of the cubicles in this case correspond to both the social and territorial placement of these people. (Pelto and Pelto 1978:201–2)

Creating the map and attending to the details of position and interaction allowed Pelto to draw important conclusions regarding social relations, ethnic interaction, and political and economic power.

In addition to mapping the physical and social scene, Pelto observed and recorded a running record of the activities of the roundup as they occurred. He does not tell us if he took running jot notes, periodically left the scene to take notes, or was able to commit all of this to memory and write up the notes later. But the information gained through participating in the roundup became a key part of the description of economic and social relationships among various Saame groups and Finns.

In a study of women's social power in Ecuador (K. M. DeWalt 1999; Poats and DeWalt 1999) we were interested in the ways in which women and men interacted in community meetings. We attended a sample of community meetings in four communities, observing who spoke, whose opinions appeared to influence discussion, the ways in which decisions were reached. We also made sketch maps of who was sitting and standing, where men and women were seated, where specific individuals we believed were community leaders were seated and where speakers were sitting or standing. Figure 9.1 (p. 162) shows a rough sketch map captured in jot notes during one particular meeting in one of the study communities. Our notes regarding who spoke showed equal participation by men and women. However, the sketch map shows an all male cluster seated apart from other members of the community. While they were not officers of the organization (the officers were seated in a cluster at the head table and were both men and women), by attending to where decisions were being made, it became clear that all decisions were being made within the cluster of men. Vogl, Vogl-Lukasser, and Puri (2004) mapped the home gardens in which they and the gardeners they were studying were working in order to better understand the ethnobotany of home gardens in Mexico, Austria, and Indonesia.

Mapping the social scene and the spatial layout of living and working spaces, whether it is a corral, a meeting, or a garden, becomes not only a way to examine spatial arrangements in various venues and events, but also a tool to focus observation and a way to train the observer to note detail carefully and record it faithfully.

(PARTICIPATORY) COMMUNITY MAPPING

In addition to the mapping of social spaces and venues, more detailed and accurate mapping of communities is also an important activity in field work and can be a component of participant observation. The mapping of communities can be a means of defining the study area, understanding and analyzing the geographical distribution of community members, describing the activity spaces (as compared with living spaces) in a community, and identifying locational problems inherent in the research area (Cromley 1999). In community-based research we have always begun the process by making maps of the community, position of houses, public spaces, and services.

There are several good reviews of concepts and techniques for community mapping available (Chapin, Lamb, and Threlkeld 2005; Cromley 1999; Kuznar and Werner 2001; Spier 1970; van Willigen and DeWalt 1985; Werner and Kuznar 2001). Increasingly, community-based maps are available from census bureaus, geographic services, and land management agencies. It is also easy to secure aerial photos and remote sensing images of regions and communities. Satellite images are readily available for free from sites such as GoogleEarth (earth.google.com). All of these can be used as bases for community maps. In some, individual structures such as houses and community spaces can be identified. Others provide a backdrop on which structures and spaces can be mapped in more detail. Werner and Kuznar (Kuznar and Werner 2001; Werner and Kuznar 2001) note that detailed community mapping has been part of ethnographic practice since the early twentieth century. They outline the basics of sound ethnographic mapmaking emphasizing attention to accuracy, scale, and measurement. Kuznar (Kuznar and Werner 2001) found it helpful to grazing areas in research with both the Navajo and the Aymara.

Chapin et al.'s (2005) review of mapping land in indigenous communities reviews the history of participatory approaches to mapping in indigenous communities in both rapid and long-term research, and reviews the key methods of participatory mapping. Participatory and rapid assessment approaches frequently use participatory mapping to integrate community interests and views with those of the researchers. Participatory community mapping is also a useful method for the development of rapport (Bastidas and Gonzalez 2009; Cromley 1999; Maman et al. 2009). Bastidas and Gonzalez (2009) describe a set of methods for participatory mapping and social cartography they used to identify community conflict and approaches to resolve conflict in Robles, Colombia. Maman et al. (2009) drew on participatory mapping not only to assist in their understanding of the limits and meanings of spaces to the people in the communities in Thailand, Zimbabwe, South Africa, and Tanzania in which they were conducting randomized community trials of HIV testing and counseling, but also to build opportunities for the development of trust and rapport for the experimental more quantitative phase of the research.

We should note here that mapping raises some ethical concerns regarding the maintenance of confidentially, especially if dwellings are noted on maps. Also, as Kuznar found out in his research with the Aymara, some information on important resources such as grazing areas is contentious and a breach of confidentiality, a potential source of conflict, even violence.

Finally, mapping can be a means of doing something useful while learning a language or while building rapport. One of the first things we encourage new researchers to do when entering the field is to do a sketch map of the community (see van Willigen and DeWalt 1985:42–45). This serves a number of purposes. It gets them acquainted with the physical surroundings and settlement pattern of the community. Walking around the community also makes you visible so people become accustomed to seeing strangers in their midst. In addition, there are lots of opportunities for informal conversations while mapping that encourage new researchers to get over their shyness and to begin interacting on a regular basis with people in the community.

COUNTING

Participant observation is often described as the quintessential qualitative research method, and, in fact, it is. However, that does not mean that no quantitative data can or should be collected. All researchers make some quantitative statements such as "very few people attended the meeting," "many children miss school because they are taking care of the animals," "most of the vendors are women," etc. In fact counting, both during events and activities, and later in analysis, can be a key component of improving the level of description and objectivity of observation. Counting can take place in every situation. How many of what kind of people are in a particular setting? How many are doing what? How many men as compared with women as compared with children are acting, moving, speaking? How many chairs, chickens, cows, cars, corporate executives are present? In other words, the researcher should train him/herself to count people, things, and actions in all sorts of routine and everyday events and activities. Seemingly trivial "countings" can form the basis of latter conclusions regarding change over time, or differences in distributions of things and actions across subgroups.

More importantly for this discussion, counting is an exercise that can aid in developing stronger observational skills.

One of the first training assignments given us as beginning researchers was to observe the weekly market in the Mexican community in which we were living. Although we had only rudimentary Spanish during our first field trip, careful observation was a useful thing for us to do that did not require verbal skills. However, we were not just to observe, but to count the number of sellers of each kind of good, count the people, count the number of people without shoes, etc. There is a big difference between being able to report that the majority of sellers are women, and to report that 60 percent of the stalls were attended by adult women, 30 percent by adult men, and 10 percent by children; or that 15 percent of the people in the food section of the market were without shoes and only 5 percent in the clothing section were without shoes.

Some people are natural counters. We realized this one day when an acquaintance stopped by our home in the United States to pick something up. As she walked in the door she noted that the door (which was original to our 100-year-old bungalow) had 30 small panes of glass. We had lived in the house several years and could not have told anyone how many panes there were if asked. Since then, we have met a number of natural counters. Such people immediately note how many chairs are set up in a room, how many groups of people there are, how many pounding strokes it takes a woman to reduce a pile of corn into meal. Unfortunately, neither of us is a natural counter. We have to consciously think about the importance of counting people and things. The effective observer can cultivate the habit of counting, and either record the count immediately or commit it to memory for later inclusion in field notes.

At this point, the new researcher might well ask: How much recorded detail is enough? The very best answer is: there is never enough. One could observe the same event for hours or days, or a hundred times, with all of the very best powers of observation and still find something new each moment or time. However, this is not a reasonable approach. There are diminishing returns, even to the time spent in observing and recording observations in field notes of a single event. Also, the researcher carrying out extended fieldwork will likely have more opportunities to observe and participate in similar events and activities. As in most aspects of fieldwork, the researcher does the best s/he can at a particular time and in a particular setting.

With mapping, counting, actively listening, and keeping a running mental stream of observation, observing complex events as a researcher can seem to be an overwhelming experience, especially for a new researcher. To be truthful, it is. But with time, practice, and experience it is not only possible but likely that most researchers will do it well, certainly well enough.

ATTENDING TO CONVERSATION

The participant observer is also attending carefully to what is being said. We will discuss informal interviewing in more detail in chapter 8. However, much of the time a researcher is participating in an event or activity, s/he is also engaged in active listening. Active listening is listening attentively, using casual facilitation techniques, making mental (sometime written) notes about the conversation(s), and sometimes being prepared to offer a prompt when an aspect of the conversation touches on material important to the researcher, but when the information being offered is not entirely clear to the researcher. With respect to the last point, it is sometimes a good idea to let a point pass, with a mental or jot note to follow up on it in a more directed interview later rather than break the normal flow of conversation when hanging out.

Even in participant observation, as compared with informal interviewing, the written record should contain as much verbatim conversation as possible. Realistically, however, unless the researcher is making rather detailed jot notes, or audio or video taping while interacting, reproducing much of any verbatim conversation will be difficult.[2] Finally, nonverbal expression and gestures are also important to understanding what is going on. Attention to detail in observation should also include noting nonverbal cues and communication. These are the kinds of data that are (obviously) not picked up in audio recording, so even an researcher who audio records informal conversation should be observing and noting the nonverbal aspects of conversation.

FIELD NOTES AS A TRAINING TOOL FOR OBSERVATION

We have found that doing detailed field notes (see chapter 9) is an important means of training one's mind. As one replays (in the mind) and recounts (in field notes) conversations and events, many different details emerge than when one just simply participates. Although neither one of us seems to be able to remember even the main topics of conversations as we go through our daily academic lives (and this is definitely getting worse as we age), when we are "on" in the field, we can write pages of detailed field notes, often capturing people's verbal and nonverbal expressions. Writing field notes becomes an additional training tool for improving a researcher's observational skills. When a new researcher sits down to write an accurate detailed account of the day's observations, the areas in which more comprehensive and detailed observation would have been critical become immediately clear. The meta-notes (chapter 9) for the next day of work should include comments on the elements of activities, events, and conversations that will need more detailed attention in subsequent encounters.

SEEING OLD EVENTS WITH NEW EYES

The participant observer in a new scene may often feel overwhelmed by the complexity of events, the amount of new detail to be observer and recorded, and the difficulty of understanding exactly what is going on. As difficult as it seems at the outset, this situation is far easier to deal with than entering a scene after having participated in it as a native. While autoethnography (Reed-Danahay 1997) has a number of advantages, the researcher knows at least parts of the context intimately; its major disadvantage is that it is difficult to attend to level of detail necessary to gain new insight, when the context is so familiar. Furthermore, the naïve observer not only sees detail the native does not, but also does not take many things, including social relations, for granted.

Through many years of teaching field methods to students, we have come to believe that the students who write the poorest field notes at the outset are those who are carrying out their project in a familiar context. They have to see their world with new eyes. Our approach to working with students with this problem is to force them to take detailed jot notes and later write extensive field notes about things that seem obvious to them. We require them to make spatial maps, map out interactions, and take notes as though they were carrying out running observations.[3] Invariably we find that when they review their notes they find aspects of the scene they had not "seen" before.

While this is quite true of native researchers, it can also be a problem with fieldworkers who have been in a context for some time and are observing and participating in the hundredth occurrence of an event or activity. As we note in chapter 10, a researcher who has been in the field for some time runs the risk of not looking carefully enough for new insights; not seeing contradictory material; not seeking out new explanations for phenomena. It is a good idea to go back to basic observational techniques later in fieldwork, just as a self-check on the potential effects of ennui.

PRACTICING AND IMPROVING
OBSERVATION AND MEMORY

Over the years, we have seen and used a number of exercises to help new researchers improve the level of detail they observe and record. One such technique is not worrying about memory but keeping a running observational record. This is a technique used in some types of structured observation, but can be used to improve observation of detail. The researcher observes an event or activity keeping a running record, writing a stream of observation record. Every observed action, conversation, expression is recorded while in the scene. This can be done in written form or even audiotaped, if it is possible in the particular context chosen. The goal is to see how much the researcher can observe in a certain period.

Several researchers can observe the same event or activity, keep a record, and then compare records. It is a humbling experience to realize that each observer attends to different aspects of the context, but the comparison can help each to be more attentive to aspects of events they have a tendency to miss. We do enough team research ourselves to continue to use this technique to keep up our skills and check the accuracy of our observation and recording. When more than one team member is in a particular event or activity, each writes his/her own set of field notes and then circulates them to the other researchers. Discrepancies can be discussed, and if possible resolved. Otherwise differences in observation are noted in analysis.

New researchers should have the opportunity to carry out observations in a context in which someone reviews field notes and critiques them for content and detail.[4] This is much of what happens in the field methods courses we teach. Again, as in team research, experienced researchers can continue to circulate field notes to their colleagues for critiquing, using this as a check on detail and accuracy. Even the most experienced anthropologists can improve observational and recording skills when colleagues help by pointing out gaps in the record.

The only key to improving memory is to practice observing, making mental notes, and then writing detailed notes. Being conscious that we will be writing notes seems to make remembering a bit easier. Each one of us has a natural limit on the capacity and accuracy of our memory, and, unfortunately, the capacity appears to change with time. We are strong believers in taking jot notes or even more detailed notes when the nature of the activity and the people involved will allow it.

WHAT TO OBSERVE

The tempting answer to the question: "What should I observe?" is, "everything." Not only is this not feasible, it is probably completely impossible. In chapter 6 we discuss the importance of choosing a representative set of activities and events in which to participate and observe. What kinds of activities and events in which to participate and observe are also influenced by the specific research questions addressed and theoretical approach adopted for any particular piece of fieldwork. Participant observation is an iterative process, so a list of the events and situations that one will observe will change over time. What is observed in a particular setting will also be shaped by the interests of the observer (see below). All observation is partial (Agar 1996; Wolcott 1999).

Most of the activities that researchers record in their notebooks consist of mundane, frequently repeated events. That is one of the underlying assumptions in almost all social science studies: there are patterned behaviors, embodying and exemplifying culturally significant knowledge and attitudes. Many behavior patterns are daily events—eating, washing, caring for the animals (and the children), going to school, going to regular jobs and so on. Others are weekly (weekly market; weekend activities, reading the Sunday newspaper), still others are repeated several times, or hundreds of times, daily such as store transactions or physician-client interactions. On the other hand, every field worker also experiences very unusual events—some of them periodic, others unpredicted and aperiodic (such as police raids, floods, and gang fights). The participant observer should do the following:

- Observe the activity and study the "story line"
- Identify the component segments of action
- Try to sort out the regular, nonvarying components from the more variable items
- Look for variations in the "story line" that reflect differences in SES, education, ethnicity, seasonality, etc.
- Look for "exceptions" (e.g., "mistakes," "poor manners," "insults")

If the observed behavior is important for one's theoretical purposes, then the researcher should develop a plan for systematic observation, including an estimate of how many observations will be "enough" (depending on the degrees of regularity and "structuredness" of the behavior).

One of the inherent biases in observation, especially participant observation, is the likelihood that unusual and rare events will be more closely observed and recorded than commonplace events and activities. The compelling nature of unusual events and situations can lead to a bias in which they are more likely to influence analysis and dominate description. Events, activities, and situations experienced early in fieldwork are also likely to take a more central place in analysis and write-up.

It is also common that the researcher, after having participated in an event or activity one or two times, tends not seek out opportunities to participate again but "moves on" to other events. In this case, there is less opportunity to compare the way similar events unfold on different days, under different circumstances, and at different times of the year. To take one simple example of the problems this might cause, there is the everyday consumption of food. Because we and the people we study do it several times a day, it may not be noteworthy to include what foods are consumed at every meal. Yet, nutritional anthropologists know that the "seasonality" of food (i.e., what foods are available and when they are consumed) may be critically important. Not having certain foods available can lead to nutritional deficiencies and/or health effects in a population. The point is that the researcher should continue observing commonplace events over time throughout the course of the project.

One of the other key uses of observation is to allow for the juxtaposition of what people say they do, and what they are observed to do, as part of analysis (Agar 1996). For example, Bill and his students have had experience in studying agricultural credit programs in Latin America in which development banks provided fertilizer to farmers to use in producing cash crops. While farmers reported using the fertilizer for its intended purpose, observation showed that farmers were either using the fertilizer on subsistence crops or selling it. Knowing this, further investigation was able to show that farmers did not see it as being in their economic best interests to produce the cash crop. For them, the cash benefits of selling the fertilizer or using it to produce food for their families was a better use of the resource.

It is also important for the researcher to observe and experience those activities and events that are core to the processes the researcher hopes to describe and interpret. Eileen van Schaik (1992), who carried out a study of workplace issues among community health aides in rural Jamaica, collected a number of accounts in which the aides discussed the problems of fulfilling their obligation to visit the homes of their clients regularly using only public transportation. However, she never fully understood the concerns until she began traveling with the aides on local buses and could observe the constraints on mobility this imposed. Descriptions of events and activities that appear to be important to the research question should provide prompts for seeking opportunities to observe and participate. Going the other way around, observing events and activities carefully generally produces a number of questions that can be addressed through interviewing.

The researcher also needs to keep in mind that what s/he is observing changes with time in the field. What seems overwhelming at the beginning becomes much more manageable as the researcher has more information and observations. The nature of the enterprise changes from trying to observe and record everything, to one in which more attention is paid to new activities, or events that have an unusual twist, or an aspect that the observer has not previously observed. One of the benefits of longer-term participant observation research is that we may get a chance to observe rare events. But more importantly, we are allowed to observe more as individuals and communities become more comfortable with us in their midst and come to trust us. Wolcott (1994) notes that he portrayed one of his informants as a teetotaler in an early publication, only to find out after knowing the informant six years that, in fact, he did occasionally take a drink socially.

Some rare events may never be directly observed. Brymer (1998) notes that he spent years working with Mexican American "gangs" in a Southwestern city before he saw a real gang meeting. Most of the time, the young men with whom he was working hung out in smaller groups (8–10 guys) called *palomillas*. The large gangs that most people agreed existed actually came together only under unusual circumstances when it was thought that a fight with a rival gang would take place. In the case Brymer was able to observe, gang X was represented by a large number of heavily armed young men and a number of women. No fight took place because gang Y never showed up, but the situation provided Brymer's only opportunity to observe a meeting of the larger gang.

JUST EXPERIENCING

Finally, while we have just spent a good deal of time arguing that the participant observer should be consciously aware of observing most of the time in which s/he is engaged in research, one of the inherent contradictions in the methods is sometimes, it is a good idea to "just experience" events. It is the tacit understandings and insights that being a participant bring to research that make participant observation an important method. To the extent to which "being on" interferes with that experience, the researcher may sometimes need to lay aside the explicit observer role and attend not to remembering but to feeling and experiencing. The irony is that, after some experience as an observer who is "just participating," the experienced participant observer finds that s/he can come away from an afternoon off with the ability to write hours of field notes. In other words the observer role becomes second nature, almost automatic.

LIMITS TO OBSERVATION

Observer bias in what is observed, how it is observed, and how it is recorded is not limited to the method of participant observation. Niels Bohr, the theoretical physicist who was a major figure in the development of the theory of quantum mechanics, understood the critical importance of the idea that every observer observes a phenomenon from the place from which the observer observes. Furthermore, he noted that one only observes a phenomenon when it intersects with the observer. An observer has no idea what is happening when not connecting with the phenomena in some way (Bohr 1963; Frisch 1967). Following Bohr, biologist René Dubois (1968) argues

What scientists really try to do . . . is to develop ways of stating, without am-
biguity the *experience* they gain of the world, either directly by observation, or
indirectly by instrumentation and computation. The word "reality" thus has
large subjective components because it involves the nature of personal experience. (108)

Finally, Bohr also noted that the act of observation (because it includes
the need to intersect) always has an impact on the object observed (and,
of course, the observation).[5] Bohr's discussion of the nature of observation
in particle physics anticipated a similar reexamination of the nature of observation in social science that became a dominant theme in the critique
of ethnography and ethnographic representation in the last quarter of the
twentieth century. While social science has mostly backed away from an
extreme relativist position and the paralyzing debate about the nature of
observation and an outright rejection of the notion of objectivity, the result
has been the now routine inclusion of reflexivity in the planning, conduct,
and reporting of research. Being reflexive involves a careful examination by
investigators of the "place from which they observe" in order to better understand the relationships among the observer, the observed, and the report
of the observation. We do not care to contribute to this debate, but to say
that we are with Bohr (and many others) on this question. We don't ask
the question "is the research/researcher biased?" *All researchers and research
are biased*. We need to ask the question "How is the researcher biased?" We
believe that there is an object reality "out there" and that the researchers
can report more or less well on reality, depending on the degree to which
they carry out careful and reflexive research. The "place from which the
observer observes" and the impact of the observer on the observed then
become part of the methodology of research and the reporting of research.
Perhaps more interestingly, there is enough experience with a number of
the more common sources of observer bias that we can anticipate some of
the sources of bias.

The "place from which the observer observes" is influenced by a mix of
a large number of characteristics, experiences, and situations that exist in a
particular time and place for a particular observer. As we will note below,
after the theoretical crisis in social science, especially ethnography, in the
last quarter of the twentieth century, the need for the researcher to clearly
examine his/her biases in a reflexive way before, during, and after research
became commonplace in research design and the creation of ethnography.

Clearly, the research question and the theoretical position taken by the
researcher are obvious sources of bias in the collection of data and analysis. In addition to limitations to what will be observed as a result of the
research questions and theoretical approach, personal attributes can substantially affect participant observation in field research. In chapter 7 we
will discuss some of the constraints placed on observation by the gender

of the researcher. Other personal characteristics include age, ethnic back-ground, or class physical characteristics. Postmodernist writers particularly emphasize that the observer and his or her circumstances and biases cannot be separated from the accounts that s/he writes. As a result, as Agar (1996) notes, all observations are partial. A different observer with different per-sonal characteristics and interests is likely to report quite different aspects and dimensions of the same event.

In addition, ethnographers surely differ in terms of their abilities and qualifications. Until recently, however, it has been rare for the accuracy of field reports to be questioned. This is so despite an increasing number of con-troversies coming to light in which the data collected by different researchers who have worked in the same area differ substantially (e.g., Redfield (1930) and Lewis (1951) concerning Tepoztlán in Mexico, Mead (1928) and Freeman (1983) on Samoa, Benedict (1934) and Barnouw (1963) on the Zuni). This acceptance of the reliability of data contrasts markedly with the controversies embroiling anthropology and other social science disciplines concerning the interpretation or theory built with the data.

Building theory depends upon having reliable data so it is lamentable that so little attention has been placed on the issues of reliability and va-lidity of the information collected. The relatively small amount of formal examination of ethnographer bias in anthropology provides evidence that these issues merit much more attention than they have previously received.

ETHNOGRAPHER BIAS

The notion that characteristics of the researchers and of the research situ-ation have a predictable impact on reporting—ethnographer bias—was examined by Raoul Naroll (1962, 1970) who became concerned that his cross-cultural research results may have been affected by systematic biases in ethnographic reporting. In the most striking finding, Naroll (1962:88–89) found that the incidence of witchcraft reported in particular societies was related to the amount of time the ethnographer spent in the field. He showed that ethnographers who spent more than a year in the field were significantly more likely to report the presence of witchcraft beliefs among the societies they studied than ethnographers who spent shorter amounts of time in the field.

Our own research in Temascalcingo provided a striking personal confir-mation of Naroll's finding. We have referred earlier to leaving the field for a three-week period of time after our first six months in the field. Before our brief hiatus, we had asked people many times about magical and witch-craft beliefs, particularly because these topics were so relevant to Kathleen's medical anthropological research. Everyone had denied that there were any such beliefs in the community. Almost the very day of our return, however, one of our key informants began regaling us with a recounting of a conflict that had occurred during our absence. The conflict included accusations by one of the parties that witchcraft was being used against them. During the remaining months in the field, witchcraft became a common theme of our conversations with people who had denied its existence before. We are convinced that the willingness of people to talk with us about such themes reflected a break-through in their level of confidence and comfort with us. Thus, as Naroll (1962) and we can attest, the length of time that a person spends engaged in participant observation does make a very large difference in the kind of findings that may be reported.

Another example of predictable ethnographer bias comes from the work of Rohner, DeWalt, and Ness (1973). Their work focused on the effects of bias in reporting about parental acceptance/rejection and its importance in personality development in children and adults. One striking finding of these analyses was that those ethnographers who use multiple verification efforts report more parental rejection and other "negative" personality traits among the people they study. They reported that this seems to be linked to a "bias of romanticism" among anthropologists. Unless ethnographers use methods other than just participant observation, they are unlikely to report the negative aspects of their subjects' personalities and lives. They quoted Levi-Strauss (1961:381) who observed that

> at home the anthropologist may be a natural subversive, a convinced opponent of traditional usage; but no sooner has he (sic) in focus a society different from his own than he becomes respectful of even the most conservative practices.

This argues for a mix of methods in which participant observation is just one of the tools that anthropologists use in order to find out the behavior of the people they study.

The "quality" of participant observation will vary depending on the personal characteristics of ethnographers (e.g., gender, age, sexual orientation, ethnic affiliation), their training and experience (e.g., language ability, quality of training), and their theoretical orientation. As interpretive anthropology makes clear, all of us bring biases, predisposition, and hang-ups to the field with us and we cannot completely escape these as we view other cultures. Our reporting, however, should attempt to make these biases as explicit as possible so that others may use these in judging our work. What is also apparent, however, is that by utilizing more formal methods of data collection in conjunction with participant observation, we may improve the quality and consistency of our reporting.

Much of the recent trend in postmodernist writing in anthropology explicitly aims toward presenting both "the Self and Other . . . within a single narrative ethnography" (Tedlock 1991:69). The point is often made that "objectivity" is not possible in the study of human behavior. While we can agree with this position, we do not accept the corollary that is often drawn that therefore we should not strive to improve our observational skills or search for explanatory theories concerning human behavior.[6] Understanding ourselves and our reactions to field research and the individuals we study should be a beginning point, not the final product of ethnography. Indeed, psychoanalysis was commonly used by anthropologists like Cora DuBois, Abram Kardiner, Ruth Benedict, and others both as a method of studying other cultures as well as a personal means for coming to terms with their own reactions to their research. They then went about the business of trying to construct social scientific explanations of people's behavior through ethnography. Our perspective is that we should go beyond the individual postmodern musings that are too common in contemporary anthropology to more systematically examine how the anthropologist's race, gender, sexual preferences, and other factors affect their observations.

This chapter has explored different dimensions of becoming an observer. As we have shown, observational skills can be enhanced by attending to detail, mapping, counting, seeing old events with new eyes, and comparing observations with others. Although we acknowledge that there are limitations and biases in the observations made by any individual, we continue to believe that we can improve the quality of participant observation and that these observations can be used in comparative and theoretical social science. Explicit attention to sources of bias, and controlling for these, is a better approach than giving up on the scientific enterprise.

NOTES

1. Doing this kind of mapping in everyday life is often illuminating as well. In that aspect of our lives that has occasionally involved academic administration, we have found that charts of who sits next to whom at faculty meetings provides us with clues about potential or real coalitions and alliances.

2. Some researchers do routinely leave a tape recording going during meetings and even hanging out. As long as the participants in research know they are being taped, a taped record can be a great aid to memory when writing field notes, or even be transcribed verbatim. Bourgois (1995) had a tape recorder running much of the time.

3. Running observation is a technique for structured observation in which the observer takes running notes on all events as they unfold.

4. As we will discuss in chapter 11, we believe that it is unethical NOT to experience a period of supervised research before undertaking a completely independent project.

5. Kathleen has come to use the film version of the Michael Frayn play *Copenhagen* which examines the nature of observation through the interaction of Bohr and his former colleague, Werner Heisenberg, during World War II.

6. Marvin Harris went even further in criticizing those anthropologists with a post-modernist or reflexive bent. He said that the solution to the criticisms they raise "is not to abandon one's attempt to be scientific but to attempt to overcome subjective limitations by being more scientific. The phenomenological obscurantists would have us believe that no objectivity is better than a little objectivity. They blow out the candle and praise the dark" (1979:327).

❧ 6 ❧

Gender and Sex Issues in Participant Observation

As we have shown in the previous chapters, one of the important contributions of theoretical discussions in social science over the past two decades has been the axiomatic acceptance of the ethnographer as an individual with a specific gender, race, class affiliation, and any number of other characteristics that will have had an effect on specific ways in which a person will approach a research project, experience the research setting, be experienced by informants, and the expectations and perceptions he or she will bring. No one argues that the researcher enters the research setting as a neutral research tool. Being a man or woman may be the most significant social fact concerning an individual and obviously will have an impact on participant observation.

This chapter includes a discussion of gender and sex issues in participant observation. Our discussion of gender examines how being male and female can affect access to, and the recording of, information from field research. The discussion of sex focuses on how one intense kind of participation with some individuals in a society can affect the observations of the ethnographer.

THE GENDERED ETHNOGRAPHER

The gender of the ethnographer has an impact on several areas of the ethnographic enterprise. A quite important influence relates to the experiences of the ethnographer during the field research. Women in the field have often been harassed and have become victims of violence in ways different from men (Warren 1988). Just as men are often barred from situations in which they can know the intimate worlds of women, women ethnographers are sometimes barred from important parts of the worlds of men. The reports of ethnographers, however, suggest that women may find it easier to gain access to some aspects of men's lives than male ethnographers find it to gain access to the worlds of women (Nader 1986; Warren 1988). Other researchers have argued that, in general, women make naturally better field workers because they are more sensitive and open than are men (Nader 1986; Warren 1988). Some feminist and ethnic writers argue that true rapport and accurate portrayal of the voice of the participant can only be achieved by researchers who come close to matching the informants in gender, race, and class (hooks 1990; 1989). Although, in contrast, Lunsing (1999) argues that as a gay European man in Japan, Japanese women were much more open to him about their sexuality and sexual harassment than to other Europeans including women. Lunsing also recounts personal experience of a level of sexual harassment from men in Japan that rivals that reported by many women researchers.

Differential access to the lives of women has resulted in generations of predominantly male-biased ethnography, which has often paid little heed to the lives and concerns of women. Several classic ethnographic debates are, at least in part, the result of the different vantage point of the ethnographer. The gender of the ethnographer, for example, may be partially behind the discrepancies in the reports of Mead (1928) and Freeman (1983) concerning the sexual lives of Samoan girls. The view of economic exchange in the Trobriand Islands that Malinowski (1961 [1922]) presented is enlarged and enhanced by the work of Weiner (1988) who focused more of her work on exchanges involving women.

Katherine Lutz (1988) has written about the experience of being a woman in Ifaluk, a Micronesian atoll. She noted that the lives of men and women on Ifaluk are sharply divided. Men and women, husbands and wives, may spend very little time together. This is not to say that women do not have high social status in many domains of life on Ifaluk. It is a matrilineal society, in which women contribute strongly to the economy through control of agricultural production, but Ifaluk world is highly gendered. Lutz, however, had anticipated that she would be able to achieve the "genderless" or "generalized gender" status that a number of women ethnographers reported in other settings (see Fluehr-Lobban and Lobban 1986; Jackson 1986; Lederman 1986; Warren 1988). In fact, she found that she could not achieve this, but was required to conform to the gender expectations of the community around her. Lutz recorded the event that finally convinced her to abandon the hope that she could create a role outside of the Ifaluk system of expectations. She wrote:

> On the first evening, Tamelakar [her fictive "father"] and my "mother," Ilefago-mar, gave me a first elementary primer on what I should and should not do; I should say *siro* (respect or excuse me) when passing a group of seated people; I should use the tag *mawesh* (sweetheart) when addressing someone; I should

crouch down rather than remain standing if others were sitting; and, Tamela-kar emphasized, I should not go into the island store if there were more than two men inside. I was to consider myself their daughter, they said, and Tamela-kar would from then on refer to me before others as his daughter. A week later, a *toi*, or "mass meeting," of the island's men was called; on hearing this, I said that I would like to see it and was brought over to the meeting site by a middle-aged man from the village. Tamelakar was already there. Seeing me, he anxiously asked, "Where are you going?" and looked both uncomfortable and displeased when he heard I was interested in observing the meeting. As direct requests are rarely refused, he did not respond, but waved me to sit off to the side by his relatives. With this and subsequent encounters, such all-male occasions soon lost their interest for me, and I spent the great majority of my time with women in cook huts, gardens and birth houses. (Lutz 1988:36–37)

Lutz expected to be able to choose the role that she would adopt in Ifaluk and anticipated that she would "allow" (1988:33) herself to be socialized in arenas in which she was interested. If one is to be successful as a participant observer, however, that is not always possible.

Jean Briggs (1986) also reports that she was never able to adopt the role of *kapluna* (white) daughter to the satisfaction of her fictive Utkuhiksaling-miut "family." As a result, she reports many months of stymied research, in which community members essentially shunned her due to her inability to keep her temper and act like an Utkuhiksalingmiut woman.

A number of women, however, have successfully stepped outside the pre-scribed roles for women within a particular cultural setting. Women have been involved with research on agricultural production or other economic activities in which both men and women might work, but the spheres of men and women are different. Allen (1988), for example, was able to study the tasks of both men and women in her Peruvian research, although she notes that her original entrance into the community was eased because she was accompanied by a male colleague.

Some of the most successful and fascinating fieldwork is conducted by teams of men and women. Murphy and Murphy (1974) provided a view of Mundurucu society that was almost unique for its time in the way that it placed in counterpoint the perspectives of men and women. The Murphys were able to do this because they had simultaneous access to different events and to different informants during the same events.

Having the perspective and/or assistance of a member of the opposite sex can often be quite important. In research on food security of older adults in rural Kentucky (Quandt, Vitolins, DeWalt, and Roos 1997) in which Kath-leen participated, we had tried to discover information about the use of alcohol. After a number of months of in-depth interviewing with samples of key informants in each of two counties, we had heard virtually nothing about alcohol use or production of moonshine. Direct questions, care-fully worded oblique interviewing, and "knowing" questions had all been answered with flat denials. One day the research team traveled to Central County with Jorge Uquillas, an Ecuadorian sociologist and collaborator on another project, who had expressed an interest in visiting the Kentucky field sites. On this trip they visited Mr. B, a natural storyteller who had spoken at length about life of the poor during the past 60 years. Although he had been a great source of information about use of wild foods and recipes for cooking game, he had never spoken of drinking or moonshine production. Within a few minutes of entering his home on this day, he looked at Jorge, and said "Are you a drinkin' man?" (Beverly whipped out the tape recorder and switched it on!) Over the next hour or so, Mr. B talked about community values concerning alcohol use, the problems of drunks and how they were dealt with in the community, and provided a number of stories about moonshine in Central County. The presence of another man gave Mr. B the opportunity to talk about issues he found interesting, but felt would have been inappropriate to discuss with women alone.

Men and women have access to different settings, different people, and different bodies of knowledge. Our own experience has been that having a man and woman involved in field work at the same time has provided a more balanced view of community life, of key relationships and of the interaction of households and families, than we would have had if we had worked alone. We base this not only on our experience in working with one another in a number of projects, but also on other projects in which we have worked with larger teams involving men and women. Fortunately, for many decades, men and women have been about equally represented among students entering cultural anthropology programs. For this reason, it is much more likely that collaboration by males and females in field research can occur.

At the same time, we would not claim that working as a couple has given us any "special" insight into the communities and people we have studied. Any ethnographer brings their own special perspective to the field. Single ethnographers with characteristics that differ from our own would not have discovered some things that we noted, but at the same time, there are other behaviors that our own perspective did not allow us to see. Kathleen's interests in medical and nutritional topics, and Bill's interests in economic and agricultural issues, resulted in rich data on those aspects of life in Temascalcingo (B. R. DeWalt 1979; K. M. DeWalt 1983) and other locations in which we have worked together. On the other hand, we have much less data on issues like kinship, sexuality, religion, symbolism, or ethnohistory.

UP CLOSE AND PERSONAL: SEX IN THE FIELD

As several writers have noted (Caplan 1993; Kulick 1995; Lewin and Leap 1996a, 1996b), even in the climate of reflexivity, until the late twentieth century the sexuality of the fieldworker has not been much discussed by ethnographers, in either their monographs or methodological notes. Discussion of sex in the field was not a part of the methodological or theoretical training of many anthropologists. Esther Newton has written that she learned in graduate school "because it was never mentioned—that erotic interest between fieldworker and informant didn't exist; would be inappropriate; or couldn't be mentioned" (Newton 1993:4).

Ashkenazi and Markowitz (1999) in the introduction to their edited volume on sex and sexuality in anthropological research (Markowitz and Ashkenazi 1999) cite their experience with a young woman researcher who was very distressed by an unwelcome, unanticipated sexual advance experienced at the end of the collection of a life history interview with a male narrator.

> After describing the interview setting, she recounted how, as she rose to leave, the interviewee turned her hand shake into a passionate embrace. Then she looked up from her coffee visibly shaken, and tearfully asked, "What did I do wrong?"
>
> "Nothing!" we declared. We explained that the closeness temporarily created during the course of a life history interview is open to interpretation and that a narrator may regard it as an invitation to more intimate contact. "Surely you know this," we added. "No," she replied, "how could I?" (Ashkenazi and Markowitz 1999: 1)

They go on to note that these issues are little discussed, either in fieldwork accounts or in discussions of methods.

Kulick and Willson (1995) found the reluctance of many researchers to discuss sex and the sexuality of the ethnographers somewhat curious, as ethnographers have not hesitated much to discuss the sexuality of the people they have studied. Some early well-known exceptions include references in Malinowski's diaries (1967), Rabinow's (1977) discussion of an affair in Morocco, Turnbull's (1986) mention of his Mbuti lover, and from one of the very few women to speak of this, Cesara's (1982) reflections on her fieldwork experience among the Lenda.

Good's account (1991) is less about sex and sexuality, but describes the evolution of his relationship with a Yamomama woman. He first agreed to become betrothed to Yarima when she was less than twelve years old. Although his initial agreement to this arrangement was made almost casually in a conversation with a village headman, Good became more attached to Yarima during several years of returning to South America. He describes his increasing emotional involvement, the eventual consummation of their relationship after she began menstruating, how he dealt with his rage and jealousy after Yarima was raped by another Yanomama, and their eventual marriage and moving to the United States. The book also includes observations from Yarima's perspective (Good 1991). An engaging and personal account, Good makes no claims that this relationship enhanced or hindered his understanding of the Yanomama.

Jean Gearing (1995), however, describes how she became attracted to her "best informant" on the island of St. Vincent, became his "girlfriend" and eventually married him. She argues persuasively that her romantic relationship with a Vincentian, which was viewed as completely appropriate by the community, not only increased her acceptance in the community, but opened up the opportunity to gain significant insight into Vincentian life, both through a shifting in her relationships with others and with her husband as an informant.

In the introduction to one of several recent volumes on sex and sexuality in the field, Kulick (1995) reviews some of the factors implicated in the reluctance to discuss sex and sexuality in field work. He includes among these the supposed objectivity of the observer (Dwyer 1982); that sexuality should not make a difference in the objective recording and analysis of the customs and habits of other people; the general disdain (until recently) in the discipline for personal narratives (Pratt 1986); and more general cultural taboos about discussing sex, or at least our own sexuality (Kulick 1995:3). Kulick suggests as well, following Newton (1993), that silence about sexuality has served the purpose of "fortifying male heterosexuality by keeping above the bounds of critical inquiry and of silencing women and gays" (1995:4).

Cupples (2002) discusses in detail the ways in which her work in Nicaragua was highly sexualized, with a number of instances of what would be considered sexual harassment in the United States (but perhaps not in Nicaragua) and the ways in which she both handled the sexuality of men with whom she was working and even used it to gain access to data. She writes about the impact of being an obvious object of sexual desire in the field on her own experience of sexuality. She also notes the sexualized nature of the "arousal" of just being "in the field" and being "in love with the field."

> Over the course of my fieldwork, my sexual and gendered subjectivities shifted and I found myself renegotiating my femininity and performing it more self-consciously. Gender is performative . . . and these shifts and renegotiations are particularly valuable in highlighting the performative nature of gender, which can have a destabilizing impact on normative heterosexuality (Cupples 2002:386).

In recent years, several volumes of essays have been published that deal more directly with the issues of sex and sexuality in the field (Whitehead and Conaway 1986; Bell, Caplan, and Karim 1993; Kulick and Willson 1995; Lewin and Leap 1996b; Markowitz and Ashkenazi 1999). Several factors have contributed to this increased attention. The first is the contemporary emphasis on reflexivity which suggests that the ethnographer is situated sexually as well as with respect to gender, class, race, and so on (Kulick 1995; Caplan 1993; Lewin and Leap 1996b; Altork 1995; Ashkenazi and Markowitz 1999; Cupples 2002; Lunsing 1999). Discussions of sexuality, then, became part of the process of reflexivity. A second trend is the increase in research on gay and lesbian communities by gay and lesbian ethnographers; this has resulted in a number of accounts of the experience of being a "native ethnographer" in a sexualized context. Finally, there is increasing acceptance of the discussions concerning sexual relationships in the field for all researchers.

Several ethnographers have written about the impact on their research of a fuller participatory involvement in the community itself, both the effect of being accepted as a "native" and the information they gain as a result of sexual activity (Bolton 1995, 1996; Leap 1996; Murray 1996; Gearing 1995; Cesara 1982; Lewin and Leap 1996b; Newton 1993; Lunsing 1999). Bolton (1995, 1996), for example, discusses not only the ways in which his homosexuality influenced his examination of gay communities in the "years of the plague" [AIDS] but also how his sexual activity became "data."

Murray (1991, 1996) has written several thoughtful essays on the use of information gained during sexual activity as data in research. For Murray, having sexual relationships with other gay men in Guatemala became fieldwork on eliciting terms relating to homosexuality in Central America only in retrospect. His primary motivation for having sex with Guatemalans was not to recruit informants, although he does admit to having thought about the "representativeness" of his "sample" at one point. In the one instance in which he reports that he went with a man out of curiosity, rather than attraction, they ended up not having sex. However, Murray argues that "Having sex with the natives is not a royal road to insight about alien sexualities" (1996:250). Further, he is concerned that "conclusions based on sexual participation are distorted by confusing the intimacies possible with strangers with natives' everyday intimate lives" (1996:242). Coming from a more textually oriented theoretical and methodological approach, he suspects that even behavior under these circumstances is adjusted to fit what the participants believe the researchers want to know. He prefers "native documents not elicited by foreigners" as data (1996:250). Even this conclusion, however, is, in part, the result of his juxtaposing "experience near" data from participant observation with interviews and other research materials.

To summarize sexual relationships in the field raises two issues that are quite important to review here. One has to do with observation. Increased attention to reflexivity suggests that sexuality is a key characteristic of the observer, apart from gender (although obviously these two cannot be separated). As Kulick puts it, it is time to ask the question, "What are the implications of the anthropologist as a sexually cognizant knower?" (1995:6). The answer to this question, provided by a number of contributors to his and several other volumes, is that there are a number of implications, and recognizing the observer as a sexually situated observer is important in both the writing of ethnography and the reading of the ethnography.

The second issue has to do with participation. As several writers have noted, participation in sexual relationships may be important to acceptance in a community and the development of rapport (Turnbull 1986). More commonly, ethnographers who discuss these issues argue that intimate relationships not only allowed them to participate more fully in with the community, but provided access to information that might not have been available otherwise (Gearing 1995; Murray 1996).

Intimate relationships, however, raise several ethical questions. What is the potential for sexual exploitation of research participants? Despite the feeling of many ethnographers (especially new researchers) that they are dazed, confused, and relatively powerless, differences in race, class, gender, and status put most ethnographers in a more powerful position than the citizens of the communities in which they work. Gender differences may not be an issue for gay and lesbian researchers, but class and ethnic differences are still likely to be important. What are the implications for the use of information gained during sexual encounters as "data"? As we note in chapter 11, participant observation raises a number of ethical questions, principally because it is not always clear when the ethnographer is conducting research. This potential would be magnified in the context of intimate relationships.

In this vein, the matter of informed consent, which is becoming more important in research involving human subjects, becomes extremely relevant. Should we be developing informed consent scripts that can be whispered at an appropriate moment? This is not an idle question. Professional societies and universities have developed elaborate guidelines for insuring that the people we study are given a full explanation of the purposes of the research and that no harm should come to our research subjects. Physical intimacy and/or emotional attachments between the researcher and members of his or her research population clearly raise significant ethical issues.

Another disturbing question that arises for us is: What will be the impact of sexual relationships on the experiences of subsequent researchers in doing ethnography? Several women researchers, Kathleen included, have experienced reluctance and even hostility from potential women informants as a result of their expectation that "U.S. women" were out after their husbands. Several of our female graduate students have found themselves in awkward situations because of the perception among some Latin American men that all U.S. women are "loose." In several instances, these problems were the results of previous female researchers from the United States who did have intimate relationships with men (including married individuals) in the community.

Finally, to what extent does sexual activity place researchers, especially women, at risk for sexual assault? The very work of participant observation puts researchers, both men and women, at risk for sexual harassment (at least in U.S. terms), and assault, but the risk for women is higher (Lee 1995; Warren 1988). Harassment of all types, from the mild, such as the propensity to *piropo*[1] of Latin American men, to outright rape is not only possible, it may be very common. Rape of the researcher in the field is not often talked about, but we know of several women who have been raped but are, understandably, reluctant to write about it. In the literature, Eva Moreno (1995) discusses how a combination of ambivalence and inattention to sexual cues resulted in her rape by a male research assistant. Howell (1990) reports that 7 percent of a sample of women anthropologists reported rape or attempted rape in the field, noting at the same time that this probably represents a significant underreporting of rape. Some women attempt to assume a "sexless" identity when in the field to help protect them against assault. Others have, or invent, burly husbands and boyfriends, who, even in their absence, can serve as male protectors. An interesting byproduct of the discussion of sex in the field provided by Murray (1996) is his mention that his beginning sexual activity with other men in Guatemala may have compromised the position of his woman companion. She had been using him as a foil against other men, a strategy that became much less effective when he became sexually active in the field.

Like a number of other anthropologists, we have always strongly advised students that sexual relationships with informants or other individuals in communities in which we were working should be avoided. Bernard (2006) notes this advice as common for beginning anthropologists. The risks—ethical, personal, and to the research enterprise—have always seemed too high to us. The narratives of researchers who have developed intimate relationships in the field, however, suggest that the risks are not always great and a "blanket prohibition" is not only impossible (ethnographers are, after all, human) but perhaps not even desirable. Our own advice to graduate students has often been ignored, although the results of these encounters (and sometimes marriages) have further reinforced our contention that sexual relationships and fieldwork are not a good combination.

This chapter has shown how the gender of an ethnographer can affect access to some aspects of different societies, as well as affecting the kinds of observations that may be made. One advantage that cultural anthropology has as a discipline is that there are relatively equal numbers of male and female researchers. Although no one has done a systematic analysis of this, it may be that anthropological theory and research are consequently less gender-biased than other social science disciplines. Team research may also be a means for reducing the potential biases introduced by the gender of the ethnographer.

Our discussion of sexuality in the field showed how this formerly taboo topic is now increasingly written about by anthropologists. Sex in the field clearly affects the observations and insights of the ethnographer, but it also raises a variety of practical and ethical considerations. While we applaud the fact that many more researchers are sharing their thoughts concerning intimate relationships while in the field, we continue to believe that placing sexual limits on participation is warranted.

NOTE

1. The website www/piroposkc.com/whatis.html (2009) has a good definition of *piropo*:

Pi-ro-po \pi-'ro-po\n. pl-pos [Sp. Piropear]
1. An amorous compliment 2: A flirtatious remark.

There are some words that simply cannot be exactly defined, except within the Spanish language, *"piropo"* is one of those. A *"piropo"* is "a flirtatious or poetic compliment to a woman." In Argentina these expressions of admiration, when well constructed are not only traditional but even an art form. The more clever the *piropo* the more it is appreciated by its intended recipient.

Known throughout Latin America, *piropos* are especially prevalent and practiced in Argentina's capital city of Buenos Aires. Considered one of the most elegant cities in the world, its women are acknowledged as some of the most charming and beautiful in Latin America. A *piropo* is an expression of gratitude for that beauty.

Piropo combines the Greek words for fire (pur) with eyes (oops) and while poorly constructed *piropos* can be obvious and callow ("don't get too close to me, I don't have fire insurance") creative *piropos* are subtle with refined machismo that arrive quietly like an anonymous gift.

Some examples of a *Piropo*:

"If beauty were a sin, you'd never be forgiven."
"I'm now sure there is a heaven because I've seen an angel."
"You move like the Bolshoi Ballet."
"Oh! If you could cook like you walk, I want to eat scraps!"
"I must be asleep to dream of such beauty."
"Where you go, flowers must spring up."
"So many curves, and me without brakes."

Piropos are good fun, and only thought and practice make them perfect and more appreciated.

❧ 7 ❧

Designing Research with Participant Observation

The first part of this book has focused on some of the theoretical and practical aspects of doing participant observation. Part two emphasizes topics concerning the incorporation of participant observation into field research, how to record and analyze these observations, and ethical issues related to participant observation.

In this chapter, we focus on how we can better incorporate participant observation into research design. Unfortunately, participant observation has too often been treated as a method that does not require the researcher to think much about research design. Like a lot of early field research in anthropology, the presumption seems to be that by going to a unique location and participating and observing, the researcher will come back with insights into human behavior. Our position is that participant observation requires even more attention to the design of research so that the results of this relatively flexible method can be ultimately analyzed and interpreted. Moreover, more attention to the detail of design issues enhances the potential for securing funding for research using participant observation.

PARTICIPANT OBSERVATION AND RESEARCH DESIGN

Research involving participant observation as a method is not different from any other empirical research endeavor in that it is a way to take ideas (theories and hypothesis) and hold them up against the real world to see if they can survive. We agree with Kirk and Miller (1986) and many others that "There is world of empirical reality out there. The way we perceive and understand that world is largely up to us, but the world does not tolerate all understandings of it equally" (11). The trick in participant observation, as in any other method, is to allow for as fair a test as possible. The goal for the design of research using participant observation as a method is to develop a holistic understanding of the phenomena under study that is as objective and accurate as possible given the limitations of the method. In the terms of science, the researcher will try to maximize the validity of the data that are collected and present a fair and objective analysis and interpretation of them.

Paying explicit attention to the design of research enhances the likelihood that the test is as fair as we can make it, and also allows for others to be able to evaluate the degree to which our particular understanding of the world has been influenced by our theoretical position, the particular methods we used to approach the question, and the particular vantage point from which we observe. In considering the design of research that includes participant observation as a method, we would like to make several points at the outset. The first is that one of the goals of designing research that includes participant observation is to improve the degree to which the products of the research (written accounts/ethnography) provide as valid a view of the context and phenomena under investigation as possible.

The second is that participant observation is rarely the only research method used in a project, nor do we believe it should be. While projects based virtually completely on participant observation are carried out, we believe that the most effective research includes a number of methods that can be used to investigate different aspects of the phenomenon and to improve the likelihood of accuracy and objectivity in a project.[1] A particular project might include the use of other qualitative methods such as more structured forms of interviewing and observation, as well as more quantitative methods such as interviewing with interview guides, or interview schedules, and questionnaires, structured observation, and formal elicitation. For some, in fact, participant observation is an approach to getting deeper more solid contacts with people and situations rather than a method in itself. In this case it is a backdrop to other research methods. The use of participant observation allows for the building of greater rapport, better access to informants and activities, and enhanced understanding of the phenomena investigated using other methods. Again, we are approaching participant observation as a technique in and of itself, capable of providing valid data on a number of aspects of social life.

The third is that, while researchers generally use participant observation to address descriptive research questions as the data base for interpretive studies or to provide information from which to build new theory and generate hypotheses, participant observation can be used as part of design that tests certain kinds of hypotheses.

Fourth, whether participant observation is the primary method being used or one of several methods, the degree to which participant observation can provide a valid view of context in which research is being carried out is based in part on taking several aspects of research into consideration before and during the research. These include an assessment of the types of questions that can be addressed with participant observation; selection of the research site; attention to the representativeness of venues and activities for participating and observing; attention to the representativeness of informants; development of a strategy for recording observations as completely as possible; and planning for the ways in which the materials collected during participant observation (data) are analyzed. For projects that will include other methods of data collection in addition to participant observation, the researcher should also address the specific place of participant observation in the overall project design.

Finally, in the method of participant observation the observer is the research tool. The limits to objectivity flow from this fact. Understanding from where any observer is observing, is fundamental to understanding the products of research. It also means that successful use of participant observation supposes that the researcher is able to assess the impact of his/her own viewpoint on the collection of data, analysis, and the written product. Self-reflexivity has become central to understanding the impact of gender, sexuality, ethic group class, theoretical approach, etc. on observation and analysis. In chapter 2 we quoted Finnström regarding his up-front assessment of where he, as an observer, stood and his assessment of the probable impact on the kinds of data he could collect and his approach to analysis.

FUNDAMENTALS OF DESIGN OF PARTICIPANT OBSERVATION

Objectivity

The main goal of explicit design is to enhance the objectivity of the research. But can any research be objective? If objectivity is conceived of as an absolute state, the answer is clearly no. Objectivity is not a concept that has to do with the discovery of *truth*. Rather, it represents a continuum of closeness to an accurate description and understanding of observable phenomena. It does imply that there is a real world "out there"; and while one can construct any number of views of the world, not all will stand up to a fair test equally; and that any one observer can know aspects of that world to greater and lesser degrees of accuracy based on his/her carefulness in observation, recording, and analysis. However, the understanding that any researcher (using any method) develops is partial.

All observation includes an observer. Every observer observes from where s/he stands. Tools of research—gages, telescopes, survey questionnaires, formal elicitation frameworks—allow for more precise observation and standardization of measurement tools, but it is still observation from a particular theoretical position and, as increasingly acknowledged, from particular gender, class, ethnic, etc. perspectives. In the case of participant observation, the observer is the primary tool of research. In some sense, then, there is greater burden on the participant observer to understand the tool.

In social science research, objectivity is often broken down into two concepts: validity and reliability. Reliability refers to the extent to which results can be reproduced using the same approach over time and under different circumstances. For example, would two different observers observe the same thing in similar ways? Would the same observer observe the same thing in the same way at two different times? Would two different analysts reviewing the same set of transcripts or field notes identify the same themes, characteristics, and interpret them in similar ways? As we noted above, reliability is difficult to assess in research using participant observation, as it is rarely replicated. That is, it is not common for two different observers to approach the same question in the same setting using similar techniques.

Reliability

There are two issues regarding reliability that we would like to discuss. The first is that careful documentation and reporting of the methodological choices including how observations were made, under what circumstances, and how they were recorded and analyzed allows the reader not only to assess the validity of the work (see below and the discussion of audit trails in chapter 10) but for interested individuals to attempt to reproduce the results.

The second issue has to do with the several kinds of reliability. First, classically, reliability is assessed in laboratory or experimental research by conducting multiple observations, over time, of phenomena that are thought to be unchanging (test, retest situations). When dealing with social phenomena, the assumption that change has not taken place over time is a very shaky one. It is almost axiomatic that social conditions are always changing. Several classic debates in anthropological research, between Oscar Lewis (1951) and Robert Redfield (1930) on the nature of social life in Tepoztlán, Mexico and Derek Freeman's (1983) critique of Margaret Mead's (1928) analysis of adolescent sexuality in Samoa, are based on research carried out several decades or more apart. Therefore, even when two researchers make observations in the same physical setting, it may not be a fair test of the reliability of the observations. However, current analyses of both of those debates suggests that differences in methods and conceptual frameworks[2] also contributed to the differing conclusions arrived at by each researcher (Shankman 1996, 2000; Wilk 2001).

Another way to test the reliability of observations is to carry out several at much the same time. This is commonly done by researchers who attempt to observe or participate repeatedly in similar events over the course of field-work; or to discuss the same issues with a number of different informants. In some cases, a research project has several researchers working at the same time. In much of our recent work, this has been the case, and it is possible to compare observations of the same event generated by different observers. Table 7.1 presents two sets of field notes written by two researchers observing the same event, in this case a meeting of members of the Rural Health Insurance Program in a community in Ecuador. Comparison of the two sets of notes shows that while both observers noted the same series of events, each attended to somewhat different details. Researcher #1 identified groups and individuals, and focused on the details of the meeting. Researcher #2 attended more to the layout of the room and its occupants, and on the ways in which consensus and decision making were attained.

Table 7.1 Two Sets of Notes: Meeting at *Seguro Campesino:* Cruz Alta de Miguelillo

Notes by Researcher #1

Setting: Ramada next to the dispensario at Cruz Alta de Miguelillo, about 80 women, 30 males.

Meeting set for 1pm and actually began about 1:20pm. KD and I entered the ramada when more than half of the women were already seated greeting them and taking our place on the front left side. I recognized so many groups women, who were all seated in organized places to me. There were the San Antonio INNFA moms, the Chirimoya Seguro, the PLAN crowd from Cruz Alta. It was comforting to feel that I really have interacted with a wide range of the women from the entire community when I had been doubting this a bit. I talked to a woman next to me about what there were so many women and no men. She said that they are affiliated under the male head of household but that the men work and the meetings are always during their work day so they send the women to represent. But she also explained that even if the meetings were at 3pm the men would be too tired and not interested in participating. Up at the front the almost all female directive was collecting past fines from some member. When the meeting was about to begin in filed all the men to tallying about 30. Unlike the spatial arrangement of San Vicente there was no way that the men could have stayed outside and just looked in through the windows. There was about 2 meter cane wall all around mandating that they enter if they are going to be part of the meeting. The men found places dispersed among the women and a group of about 8 filed up to the front left corner and took their places (very reminiscent of the San Vicente meeting). MI stood up and read the agenda, we were point II and then Ramon opened with a few words from the President of the Committee Central. He was the only male seated with

(Continued)

Table 7.1 Two Sets of Notes: Meeting at *Seguro Campesino*: Cruz Alta de Miguelillo (*Continued*)

the directive. [But the actual President of the three-group Seguro is Angela Parraga. So what is his role?]

President of the Comite Central – Ramon

Presentation by research team KD. BB, Hernán

Acto Anterior: last meeting's minutes

Words from the President

Asunto Varios

KD stood up and gave a speech thanking the community for the hospitality and welcoming us into the community and that we all had a good experience. She asked for permission to come back once more in October and do the health portion of the study. They received her well, and the only thing that may have been left out was a recap of what the study was about specifically, women's participation. Health, decision making, etc. . . . She also promised to give a report on the analysis of the data and what we have learned from the study to the community in October. (Note: This will coincide with the 3-Seguro meeting). Next, I stood up and thanked them and said I would be in the community for a little while longer. Hernán said a few words that his work in the community was not over, thanked the 3 women who helped us out and hinted that he'd be back. AP stood up and on behalf of all said we were welcome there and that as well any benefit that we might bring would be welcome as well. She ended with the words that the door of the community would always be open to us.

Minutes of the last meeting: Secretary began with the wrong date then got on track.

Words of the President: That we are 3 different patronos but under one dispensario and this is the meeting that we all need to be at to be informed of the expenses and purchases of the funds collected from the members in the Seguro. You should come to understand to learn about where the money goes, and then not just talk and assume where it goes. There are monthly purchases, paper transmissions (when have to go to other clinic), medicines etc. She said that people don't know (is she avoiding some deeper issue), and that other people are new affiliates and don't know what rights they are entitled to. All need to pay the dues on time, to get their service outside of the dispensario. She talked about having been in PV and went to the Seguro, said that they will only attend parto de cesaria, no normal. That they will only attend the cesarean births and that normalize births will have to go back to their homes for the births!!! [This hit me as atrocious! And more and more makes me question the high reported cases of Cesarean births here in Manabi—could make an interesting study, on the social and medical levels, what is going on socioeconomically in the system that may influence the birthing options or more important the diagnosis by the doctors???]

[The doctor entered at this point and came to the front; Pres. gave her the floor to talk.]

Doctor: She delivered her words in a vague and uninterested manner, not making eye contact with anyone, although looking towards KD and I a few times. She began with the fact that there are always problems, the bridge being out, the river, the roads and that they need to be fixed and the new government will hopefully do that. That she has only been there for 6 months but mucha queja de la columna. She is worried that because of all the walking that they have to do since vehicles are out. She talked about rheumatic fever [ASK KD] and that to get the lab results analyses you have to go to several different lab to believe the results. (she was jumping all around during the talk with out a focus about what she was saying). She mentioned that many of the señoras complain of arthritis because they wash clothes in the rivers, in the cold water and they should avoid this. "That this is a very sick community." (what she had told me in the interview the week before) that everyone has problems con el hueso, that they need to get the bridge fixed and the roads better and coop transports that enter (are all of these things realistic—what does the community make of these statements). She told the assembly that they need to not smoke, boil water which many of them are not doing and she tells them this all the time. Don MT silenced all to listen better. She mentioned that a child recently died from having too many antibiotics, and that they should prevent the illness and not just use antibiotics for everything including acne. That the nurse would be going on vacation for 3 weeks and that there is no $ for the replacement, so the dispensario will be closed. That with the Nueva Reforma—that is happening with the government doesn't seem to be of any good for them, the government has no $ and what will that mean. She'll visit the houses, and do the transference.' That if there is an emergency they should go to the Seguro hospital in PV, but only if they are emergencies. Then from the men emerged jokes that death will not wait 3 weeks and neither will emergencies. (What will the community do? Would be interesting to observe the health during these three weeks) She continued that the Seguro at the national level is cutting back in all in the meds that they give by ½. That she will attend 20 patients and 4 emergencies and that is it because she gets tired and then the service will not be that good, and you know how that is.

Don MT raised a point that he had asked her a few months back to put together a chat about AIDS for the community and had she done that. She agreed and said she looked for laminas and that it was a lot of work, (totally avoiding but then went into an impromptu talk—not what I understood to be his desire). She began a dialogue about the AIDS that was very interesting. "First the symptoms: weight loss! Loss of appetite, hot skin and this all depends on what it attacks, your lungs, bronchitis, weak organs. Anny B jumped in and said that she saw a movie in the high school the night before about AIDS. Diarrheas also. The doctor then flowed into a cancer talk and isn't that what AIDS is, yes, a Cancer." She said that some are malignant. "That the people who have AIDS are mainly homosexuals, and that if you did an exam of them, the majority would have AIDS. Be careful of these people!!" Mentioned the one AIDS case in La Floresta/La Chirimoya. Then that you need to do prevention. No tiene estar dispuesta con ellos. That men should have just one woman and then went into a talk about marriage and the Bible that says men should have just one woman. The men jumped in and said that women should be with just one man. She continued with men giving the disease to women like venereal disease when they visit prostitutes. That men get AIDS and then bring it home to their wives in the house. AB jumped in again about and that condoms don't prevent the transmission of AIDS, right, the doctor agreed. At this point the nurse walked in and corrected some of the information and took over the talk.

(Continued)

Table 7.1 Two Sets of Notes: Meeting at *Seguro Campesino:* Cruz Alta de Miguelillo (*Continued*)

[I have to admit that I was having a hard time holding professional composure during the talk, a bit disappointed in myself.]

Nurse: "only way that you can get it is blood to blood, and saliva and that condoms don't protect. But she said that we should not isolate people with AIDS but yes take certain precautions like not have sexual relations with them. AB jumped in again that with conversation you can't translate, don't isolate them, but tratar de animarse, but treat them well.

The doctor continued with una sola mujer para un hombre (bringing religion in as a reason for the people to have one partner). But then she jumped to "es la persona que busca el problema, -- the person her/him self is the cause of the problem—just like girls who get pregnant. It's their fault destroying their life. Then their babies have no father." Said that they found a kind of cure but now AIDS is stronger than ever 1,800 cases in Ecuador (AB). The doctor said that you need to avoid blood transfusions. And that everything is like a " cancer!"

Ramon asked her for her address if they needed it while the nurse is gone. Portoviejo – Sucre/Espejo. Nurse said I am tired and taking vacation. That the doctor will attend to patients but outside the building. [Why can't she have keys and get into the building?] And she told the community to pay attention to the situation in the Seguro in the coming weeks with the installation of the government. [This has the potential to be a highly politicized problem for the communities and will have interesting impacts on the unity of the community.] Her idea is that there are a few meds but she wold like them to be there when the people need them.

Nurse addressed a big issue that I had sensed a before. She straight forward said, ask me any questions that you have about her or for her please bring them up now. Don't wait until the meeting is over and she leaves because it then gets back to her later. From the directive asked about what about new affiliate, nurse answered they'll have to wait until she returns at the end of August, this was not the answer they were waiting for. Brought up the issue of the Licenciada that comes once a month but is fat and will not come past the bridge, a big companion for the community. And then she encouraged the community to enter into a dialog with her and not with harsh words but to ask her to come up, they have the right for her to come all the way up to Cruz Alta and not just to Cascabel, [incentivizing them to act on their own behalf— interesting in light of the first conversations I had with her.]

Nurse: that she knows that some people in the community are uncomfortable with the way that the doctor attends the patients but then they need to tell her, that when you talk to people, they will understand "que hable con ella."

Order of attention of patients: MD from the Chirimoya said she is not against anyone but would like to know why the policy changed from attending children and elderly ended and now is not in use. That mothers with small children have to wait. Nurse said changed it because of complaints from the community, she has always preferred children then elderly but what do they think. The Pres intervened to moderate the situation. The assembly got involved with opinions about how the system should be. Let's vote raise hands for priority attention to children under 12 years. Most did. Don

MT who made the compliant, and nurse directly pointed this out to him. Lost to the argument. Woman in yellow, margarita's mother, who is over 60 and said well, I am not elderly. Why not under 6 years. Then AB said that not fair should under 12 (she has daughter under 10). Nurse, let's compromise how about less than 8 years. That was decide. At one point looked to KD and I what we thought, I said no me meto en esto. MS was quite vocal about how people have to get up early to coger turno and then AB said not right that the mothers from La Chirimoya wait until the nurse passes on her way up to the health center and that is not right, and then they complain that they are not attended to. They should be conscious and not do this, Nurse reminded that they are 3 groups but one dispensario and need to unite.

AB stood up and made quite a speech "Angelita, Yo hablo en una voz alta y clara no para ofender pero para que todos me escuchan, y entienden" Shaking her finger in the air at the directive. (people we laughing at her a bit) I was not the one who collected the fines from the woman for s/5,000. The woman who was refused her slip for the fine stood up behind Anny to counter her, spoke much less fluidly than A.B. and said you charged me the fine when it was the meeting during the paro. A.B. definalty has a sharp tongue and it had come out in the Chirimoya meeting the Sunday before.

Nurse said that there is a risk to close the dispensario because there are few socios and they need more people to join to keep them alive. At this point the nurse excused herself and I followed her out to catch her for the interview I was waiting on. (SEE KD"S NOTES FOR REST OF MEETING.)

Manual had a big presence form the past, one of only two men who really voice in the meeting. Forgot who he was at first, then recognized.

Notes by Researcher #2

In the road we greeted people in the house of the familia "Br," where BB stays sometimes, and the house of A B (called by BB: "Ann from Plan").

In the truck we arrived in Cruz Alta at about 11:45. We stopped at the dipensario and got down from the truck. The driver was kind enough to lower the tail gate so I didn't have to climb over the side.

BB asked about the meeting which was now scheduled for 1pm. BB took me into the dispensario and I met the Auxiliadora, briefly. We then went over to the house of M P, who was a young woman who had helped in the encuesta. Hernan wanted to pay her and get her informe. We stayed a few minutes and then went on to the house of the woman with whom BB was going to stay, in order to tell her than BB would not stay with that night but would in the coming week.   The woman's name is D.

Impressions of Cruz Alta. This town appears somehow more prosperous and well maintained than most I have seen. Many of the houses have front yards with decorative plants and actual lawns. Houses seem to be in good repair, clean, open and airy. Several I saw seemed to have ramadas which were also neat and clean. I had the sense of more agricultural equipment around. [Ask BB to count or confirm this, BB says that she has not seem farm implements, I may have been reacting to the having seen

(Continued)

Table 7.1 Two Sets of Notes: Meeting at *Seguro Campesino:* Cruz Alta de Miguelillo (*Continued*)

the open bus (chiva).] The town seems to be sort of set up on a grid, at least close to center.

At about 12:45 we moved on to the ramada by the dispensario where the meeting was to be held. As we waked into the courtyard, Hernan called us over to meet a couple of men. He said we should meet them, one was "interesting." He was talking in such a low voice I could not really understand what he was saying. As people seemed to be moving into the Ramada, BB and I went in, Hernan stayed outside with the men he was talking to. I thought this was curious at the time.   As we entered there were a number of people sitting on benches along the wall and relatively few on the benches in the middle. At this point I counted over 60 women and 4 men. People continued to trickle in, and filled in the center benches. At a bout 1:10 a large group of men (who had been standing outside talking) all filed in. Hernan was one of this groups. He sat next to me on the far left side almost to the back wall. And several of the men who walking in at this time sat next to him, filling the benches on the far left and back left wall. [I now feel that he was waiting to come in with the rest of the men. I wonder if this is common pattern.] In the end, just as the meeting started we counted 84 women and thirty men. Over twenty came in at the last moment after virtually all of the women were in the ramada. Many of the men sat along the wall in the left hand corner of the room. Others, however, were dispersed among the rest of the participants. There was no group of men who sat with authority in any special place, as there was in San Vicente.]   [Hernan said that one of the men who came in with him was a former assasin.

The president of the "comité central" is a woman named AT

The meeting was the three monthly meeting of all of the patronos. The Seguro Campesino of Miguelillo has three distinct groups with their own organizations, presidents treasurers, etc. They are: La Chirimoya, the smallest, San Antonio and Cruz Alta, the largest with 137 families. In all however, the number of families affiliated with the seguro is only about 200. Several times in the meeting this was mentioned by the president that it was a small number and if they didn't get more members, they were in danger of losing the Seguro. Each group meets separately two months out of three and in the third month, they meet together and the meeting is run by the comité central.

[Themes of the meeting brought up several times: we are under attack, the government wants to reform the seguro campesino system; we have too few members, they might close us down and we would not have anything; complaints about the way in which people were attended at the clinic. Apparently in the past children and older people were given preference.]

The first punto was a call to order. The second punto was our "thanks" I spoke, BB spoke and Hernan said he would not say "thanks" since that meant that he would not come back and he intended to continue to come to the community. I thanked them for their collaboration and hospitality.

At about this point the doctor came in. She is woman who I would guess at 55 years of age, short, partially gray hair.

The third point was a presentation by the doctor. Side comments suggested that she rarely gives "charlas" for the community. She talked about all of the complaints that she got about "dolor de los huesos y de la columna." She attributed it to the need to walk from the road now that the bridge is out. She said that the community needed to organize to get the authorities to repair the road so that buses could come in. She said that she would complain about this as well. She feels that this in one of the most important health problems in the community. She went on about this for some time.

She then made a point of how she could only attend 20 regular patients and 4 emergencies in her visits. She said that in reality she gets very tired and could not attend more than this number well.

[Later it became apparent that people often come to the dispensaria at 4 or 5 am to get a number or ficha which determines the order in which they will be seen. If they come too late and all of the fichas are gone, and it is not a true emergency, they cannot be seen that day.]

Some one (president) reminded her to talk about what will happen during the time that the auxiliadora is on vacation beginning on Friday July 31, and for three weeks). The dispensary will be closed for the three weeks that the auxiliary health worker is out. The doctor will come on the Tuesdays and Thursdays, as usual but will not be able to get into the dispensary. She will go to houses or dar consulta outside of the dispensary. In between times any with an emergency will have to go to the seguro hospital in PV, but they must have their cedula, carnet and a referral order. The auxiliadora will leave a number of signed slips available for people who need it. This was reinforced several times. By the auxiliadora, doctor and the presidenta.

The man sitting next to Hernan asked the doctor if she would tell him what the first symptoms of AIDS were (apparently there was a case of AIDS in La Chirimoya recently]. She actually sort of hesitated and then went into an explanation of AIDS that was essentially incorrect. At one point she said that AIDS was a cancer. Later she reversed and said it was a virus that destroyed blood cells and lowered immunity. She said that it was infectious and no one should go near anyone with AIDS. That almost all homosexuals had AIDS, that the bible said that a man should have only one women and if he did he wouldn't get AIDS. The first symptom was weight loss, but she did say that it would attack whatever organ was weakest, so it could manifest as diarrhea, bronchitis or cancer. AB said she had been at a seminar about AIDS in which it was said that condoms didn't prevent aids, that one could get it from saliva, or if one hugged another and both had open wounds. No one corrected her about the condom part.

The doctor then left. The auxiliadora said that she gets a lot of complaints about the doctors and that people should talk to the doctor directly, not be groseros—rude—but tell her directly their complaints. She made a snide remark about the coordination of the vacations saying that her (the auxiliadora's) vacation had been requested a long time ago, and if the doctor had coordinated it would have been fine. But it was the doctor's problem not hers.

There was discussion of the need to get new members and the member list is low. There are several people who want to affiliate, but they need to get the licenciada (Lawyer) here to do the paper work. She doesn't want to walk in and wants the people to come

(Continued)

Table 7.1 Two Sets of Notes: Meeting at *Seguro Campesino:* Cruz Alta de Miguelillo (*Continued*)

out to Cascabel to see her. The auxiliadora said, "just tell here to come out one day. I come out every day. It takes me an hour and a half but I do it. She can do it too."

Margarita from Chirimoya raised the issue of who should be attended first. She noted that mothers with children have to sit for a long time, the children get hungry and restive, they pee, etc. And it is hard. She feels bad for the mothers and children. She wanted to know when the policy of seeing children and ancianos—old people—had changed. The auxiliadora had a frustrated expression and she finally said, that she had gotten "1001 complaints" about the policy. Sr. Assassin (one of the "familia" R's) said that it wasn't fair that someone would come to stand in line at 4 am and a mother with a child would come and take a place in front of him. There was a more general discussion and a finally the auxiliadora suggested that within the 20 places that children and older people would be seen first. That is that 20 people would get fichas, and then among those, children and older people would be seen first.

There seemed to be general agreement, consensus was apparently acknowledged. The discussion then followed as to what age would constitute children. The first proposal (I think from MD) was that 12 years and below. A man in the back said that was too old, twelve year olds were capable of waiting, so 6 and below would be more appropriate. There was some discussion and the auxiliadora suggested the compromise of 8 years and below. MS spoke saying he didn't much care, 8 years seemed Ok with him, but that everyone could come and take their ficha. That if he had to come at 4 am they could too. He said he got there the other day at 5:30 to get an appointment for his child, and he was 11th, most of the fichas had already been given out at 5:30. He also took the opportunity to say that he didn't understand why people were complaining so much about the cost of the seguro, even the fines. That it was cheap, even if they got fined. That a single operation in Guayaquil costs millions of sucres. He said that he couldn't understand why anyone would threaten to resign because of a fine, as the cost is still so low.

[MS appears to be someone of influence in the community. Hernan use the work "caudillo" to refer to him. He is from Cruz Alta, but now lives in Cascabel.]

There was a brief discussion of how old "old" was someone suggested fifty, but there was a general clamor against it and people settled quickly on 60 years of age and older.

The auxiliadora asked if there were any more complaints or comments, if not she would go home. Which she did. BB left to interview her on the way out.

The president (a man) of the San Antonio groups stood up and said no one from his community had complained, but if there were any now to speak up. No one did.

MD then raised the question of the funeraria, that there were no curtains. She asked if there was any money to buy curtains. Someone suggested that money from the central comité be used to buy curtains. Someone said that someone had rented the funeraria for 200,000 sucres and this money could be used. Then someone mentioned that Dr. Humberto (the "prefecto") had sent for and paid for curtains two times and both times they had gotten lost in Quito. There was some sniggering. Clearly some people felt that the money was lost but not the curtains (i.e., that he had taken it). A decision was made to put some money into the funeraria. But first to find out how much it would cost. Again, MD brought it up, but both men and women contributed to the discussion.

The final points had to do with two meetings to which they had to send representatives. The first is the national meeting in Quito that we heard about last month in San Vicente. It is to discuss policy changes . It in now supposed to take place on Aug 6. It was not clear who was going to attend. Then someone raised the issue of a meeting of seguros in PV in the sala de choferes on Aug. 8. They sent an "encuesta" to be filled out by each SC group before the meeting. They will organize and present their vision a nivel campesiono on Aug 10.

Important things about the meeting:

Consensus was reached in much different way than in San Vicente. People spoke aloud and proposals were made, counter proposals were made and compromises suggested. The president would then say OK we will do this. . . . If there was no more discussion, she apparently assumed that there was consensus. There was no period of open simultaneous discussion, as there was in San Vicente.

The whole meeting seemed to me to be much more well organized. The presidenta seemed to be tentative at the outset, but actually stayed pretty much in control of the meeting without seeming to put n a lot of effort. When more general talking, among neighbors would break out, a number of people would shout that they should respect order and the talking would stop and individuals would be allowed to talk.

There was a general feeling of being under attack, both because of the changing national policy, and the low number of affliados.

Both women and men spoke and it appeared that the points of both women and men were taken seriously. Both women and men suggested solutions and compromises. The number of women speaking was similar to the number of men. Three men (outside of the men who were there representing the patronatos of the sub groups). One was the assassin, one was Manuel Sornosa (guy who rents the "planta" Miguelillo to make almidon) and another I didn't know. At the point in which AB got into an argument, there was a man outside the back wall of the ramada who spoke through the window.

There is apparently some factionalism between Chirimoya and the other communities. One of the main points of discussion was the decision that had been made by the general (full 3 group meeting) about the forgiving fines for late payments during the strike in Feb(?). But Chirimoya had decided to collect their 5,000 sucre fine from a woman who did not pay. This provoked an argument between AB, who seemed to be the treasurer of the Chirimoya. MS, who is from Cruz Alta said that every patrono should be able to make their decisions independently in fact, they have different policies for fines; Cruz Alta charges 2,000 s and Chirimoya charges 5,000). The presidenta de la comité central disagreed and said that the whole group, including representatives of Chirimoya had come to this decision. They also read the minutes from that meeting to reinforce this.

AB got very angry, she felt that several people were misrepresenting her comments at the meeting they were discussing (the one in February). She kept asking if they had heard HER say, what they were attributing to her. Finally the man who was saying" but

(Continued)

Table 7.1 Two Sets of Notes: Meeting at *Seguro Campesino:* Cruz Alta de Miguelillo (*Continued*)

you said . . ." backed down and said that he had not heard HER specifically say these things, but that they were said.

There is apparently a good deal of tension between the Dr. And the auxiliadora. The auxiliadora seemed to be talking behind the doctor's back at several points after the doctor left. Even thought the aux. Had made of point of people speaking and complaining directly to the Dr. and complaining directly to her (the aux.) when they had problems with her (the aux) work. BB said that people really liked the last doctor, but do not like this one. She came as a replacement 6 or 7 months ago. BB also believes that the Dr. does not like it in Miguelillo.

When similarity of results is achieved either by researchers observing at different times or by several observers at the same time, there are times when the reproducibility of results is not meaningful. Kirk and Miller (1986) use the term quixotic reliability to refer to a phenomenon we have all observed. This occurs when we ask the same question of a number of informants and get the same answer. In research in Ecuador, we asked a number of informants at what age they weaned their children. We received the answer—at 24 months—from almost all of our informants. There was virtually no variation. We immediately discounted these results. We realized that we were getting the culturally appropriate response to the question. In actuality, there was a relatively large range of variation in the length of time of breastfeeding in the community, but our question, which produced reliable answers, was not a valid measure of the age at weaning of children. Only through a longitudinal observation of a cohort of children did we get a more valid picture of the range of variation in weaning practices. We are always suspicious of responses to either formal or informal interviewing that are always the same. While quixotic reliability can be a problem in participant observation, participation in and observation of behavior often provides an important check on the responses of people to questions about behavior.

We noted above that a series of measurements (recorded observations) can be reliable without being valid. What then is validity? Validity is a quality of any type of observation that has to do with the extent to which the results of the observations correspond to the presumed underlying reality. In other words, the description accurately represents the phenomenon studied. For practical, applied research we can also speak of the degree to which the results provide sufficiently accurate descriptions so that that they prove useful and productive for programs of planned change (Pelto 2001).

Again, while we would like to have absolute validity of observations and conclusions produced through research, in practice, it is not attainable in any research setting. Much of research design is aimed at enhancing the validity of observations to the extent possible, given the limits of any method. In some sense, because participant observation is an experiential approach in which the characteristics of the observer are part of the mix, any observation that is carefully recorded is valid (that is, it truthfully represents the response of the observer, but is not reliable in that there is no assumption that a similar description could be produced by another observer). However, this does not mean that it is a valid view of the phenomenon under review if an objective view of that phenomenon is the goal. While some theorists say this "personal" level of validity is all we can achieve, we disagree. Experience and comparison of the writing of others convinces us that observations of trained, self-reflexive observers, using several different approaches to a phenomenon can achieve an acceptable level of reliability and validity and are, to the extent of the method, objective. Attention to the elements of design can enhance the reliability and validity of observation and, hence, the objectivity of research.

ELEMENTS OF DESIGN

The elements of research design in field studies are:

- The positing of a question, or questions, for research drawn from the literature and theoretically grounded, whether or not specific hypotheses are articulated
- Selection of a research site in which the question(s) can be addressed
- Selection of methods and techniques of research that can address the question
- Development of a strategy for the selection of places, activities, individuals, etc. from which data will be collected in a way that maximizes the likelihood that the materials collected represent the range of variability in the setting
- Development of a strategy for management of data for effective analysis
- Development of a preliminary strategy for analysis that suggests a set of analytic categories and techniques that responds directly to the research question(s) and hypotheses

These elements of design also correspond to the kinds of questions that must be satisfactorily answered in the various components of a research proposal.

Choosing a Question

All discussions of research design, whether from the laboratory sciences, natural sciences, or social sciences, have to deal with the types of questions that can be addressed with a specific method; issues of objectivity, validity, and reliability associated with the method; and the generalizability of conclusions drawn using the method. In the last two decades, epistemological discussions of social science have focused on the limits to objectivity of experiential methods such as participant observation. However, the same debates also have a history in other disciplines. It should be clear that we approach social research, a position that places this type of research within the context of scientific approaches. The ongoing discussions of the limits to objectivity when the primary research tool is the researcher him/herself has been not only part of healthy scholarly debate, but has also reinforced and sharpened the discussion of the concern (that we believe has always been part of social research) that both the researcher and the reader must continually evaluate the impact of the particular vantage point of the observer on what is observed and how it is interpreted. This is no less true of research and scholarship in the natural sciences and humanities (Bohr 1963; R. J. Dubois 1968; Harding 1998).

Again, following many other researchers, we would argue that any account of any phenomenon, approached scientifically or not, is partial. It is a fundamental characteristic of scholarship. Arguing points from one's disciplinary, theoretical, and methodological perspectives is central to the fun of scholarship. We live for this stuff! It is not only part of the fun, it is also central to the development of knowledge of the world around us. As Agar (1996) notes, drawing on the well-used analogy of the six blind men and the elephant, the point is not that any particular view is ever complete or true, but that the integration of information from different observers or different methods provides a better understanding. As we will note below, however, one of the limitations of fieldwork, in general, and fieldwork that uses participant observation as a method, is that the cost in time and money often means that any one setting or set of phenomena are unlikely to be investigated by a large number of researchers. There are often only one or two views available. This limits the degree to which we can assess the reliability (reproducibility) of any particular analysis. It also means we often have only one or, perhaps, two views from which to build a more complete picture. In the laboratory and clinical sciences, it is common to see dozens of studies of the same question, from different disciplinary and theoretical positions and using differing sets of methods in different types of research settings that are trying to achieve reproducible results.

Appropriate Questions

There are three different kinds of questions that can be addressed in any empirical research project including qualitative research: description (descriptive/exploratory/theory generating), interpretation, and explanation (Bernard 2006; Johnson 1998). While different research methods and techniques are more appropriately applied for different goals, participant observation can be used to address all three. Historically, participant observation has been used most commonly to provide data for descriptions of societies and phenomena. The classic ethnographic study seeks to provide a theoretically relevant description of aspects of social life. The description, then, can be an end in itself or the basis for interpretation of some kinds of hypothesis testing.

Like all research methods and techniques, participant observation is more appropriate for some kinds of questions. First, it is essentially a synchronic method. That is, it is a method that is used to understand what is happening NOW. The researcher's experience is tied to a specific time and place. Participant observation cannot be use to understand change or changing conditions, unless the change is taking place during the research period or the researcher engages in serial research projects. While informants often comment on their perception of changing conditions, technically, the researcher only knows that they say they perceive that there has been change. While change can become a theme of analysis, it is the perception of participants that is under research with participant observation. Other methods such as review of documents and other texts, oral history, and life history approaches also have limitations, but are more appropriate to understanding change.

Participant observation is also an experiential approach. Data come from observation gained while experiencing and participating in events. This implies several important limitations to the method. First, participant observation is used effectively to understand phenomena that are observable, which implies that they are available for observation. Some kinds of events and activities are rare enough that a researcher may not observe/participate in them during a period of fieldwork. Again, other methods of data collection may be more appropriate for the study of rare events.

Second, without careful thought, the experiential nature of the method can also allow researchers to ignore the importance of processes taking place outside the rather circumscribed world of the local community. The participant observer can report on the perceptions of these events and processes from the point of view of members of the local community. But participant observation provides an inherently emic view of phenomena. Other data and methods are critical to understanding the wider context within which communities and groups exist. One of the greatest limitations of ethnographic research that was criticized by Eric Wolf (1982) in his book *Europe and the People without History* was the tendency of anthropologists to depict non-European societies as isolated and frozen in time. Wolf's point was that all peoples have a history and that, in particular, the history of non-Western societies was profoundly altered by European colonialism. While many researchers approached ethnography and qualitative studies using theoretical approaches that were based on critical theory or political economy approaches before 1982, it is now uncommon for any researcher to ignore the impact of global processes on local communities. Originally, a tool for understanding the local using an isolationist mindset, participant observation is now often a tool for understanding the local response to those processes.

Participant observation has most frequently been used in descriptive and interpretive research approaches. However, it can be used to test hypotheses when the hypotheses can be phrased in terms of presence or absence of traits and characteristics; or rather the presence of traits and characteristics. [The absence of a trait may be meaningless using this method (see chapter 9)]. In experimental designs, in which the researcher consciously manipulates some aspect of the context, the absence of a response to that manipulation is meaningful. In observational designs (e.g., participant observation) absence of observation may be suggestive, but may only mean that the observer failed to observe or to have the opportunity to observe any particular response. However, every phenomena, characteristic, or trait that is observed can be said to present. The distribution or importance of particular ideas, traits, characteristics, etc. may not be known, but if observed, we may suppose that they exist.

Participant observation is also part of a strategy that can allow us to discover the existence of patterns of thought and behavior. Again, it will not help in completely understanding the distributions of characteristics, but it can assist in identifying patterns of thought and behavior.

Finally, as we have noted, the method of participant observation, and recording of observations in chronologically organized field notes was developed, or at least originally described, within the context of a functionalist theoretical approach. The holistic, interrelated, and isolationist view of social processes of the functionalist approach fit well with the method. Some of the most well known products of participant observation research are synchronic descriptions of "cultures" and the interconnectedness of social institutions. However, as we noted above and as others have discussed (Agar 1996; Picchi 1992; Sanjek 1990c), the method is such that it challenges many assumption about a setting made before beginning fieldwork. It is more commonly used now as the primary method, for researchers taking a more interpretive approach to the study of ethnography. It is our belief that the method of participant observation is so close to the central core concepts of disciplines such as anthropology that it is compatible with a number of theoretical approaches and, moreover, has been instrumental in theoretical change in anthropology.

Choosing a Site

In a perfect research world, the site of a research project involving fieldwork and participant observation is chosen because it is the best site in the world to address the research question chosen. In the real world of research, sites for research are chosen for a number of other reasons, which include the practical considerations of the life of the researcher, that is, can the researcher conduct research outside his/her own local area; will family concerns, funding, or health considerations limit the range of places in which the research can be conducted; what are the language skills of the researcher and what languages is it feasible to learn; how will the personality and other personal characteristics of the researcher limit the extent to which the researcher can become an effective participant. In addition to conditions related to the personal situation of the researcher, disciplines such as anthropology usually require a specialization in a small number of geographical and cultural regions, with an in-depth knowledge of existing research in the prehistory, history, current economic, political, and social conditions, in addition to the existing ethnographic literature. This "culture area" concept is still central to training in anthropology. Researchers develop interests in culture areas and particular regional and country settings for all sorts of reasons. While these are sometimes theoretically driven, more commonly for whatever reason a particular region or country has an intrinsic appeal to the researcher. In other words, in an ideal research design the question drives the site. In the real world, the site selection often drives the question. There is nothing inherently problematic about this, as long as the particular question chosen for study can be effectively and usefully addressed within the geographical context in which the researcher is comfortable. One cannot, for example, study questions involved in understanding legal polygyny in North American settings (although the study of covert polygyny might be quite interesting). The site does not have to be the ideal place to address a question, it just has to be good enough in theoretical terms.

The advantages to specialization in a particular culture area are many. The researcher has a strong incentive to learn the languages important in the region before embarking on a research project. The researcher often has a broad understanding of the extra local economic and political setting. The researcher begins fieldwork with a fairly good idea of what to expect culturally, socially, and logistically.

Appropriate Methods and the Benefits of Triangulation

In well-designed research, the choice of methods of investigation flow directly from the specific research question to be addressed and the goals (e.g., description, interpretation, explanation) of interest to the researcher. In this book, we are dealing exclusively with the method of participant observation, and presume that the question being asked is one that can be answered, at least in part, with this method. However, we would like to stress that in any fieldwork project, participant observation is usually only one of several methods being used. Other methods commonly used in fieldwork include more formal in-depth interviewing; life history interviewing; oral history interviewing; formal elicitation approaches (e.g., pile sort, free listing, elicitation frameworks); survey research using interview schedules or questionnaires; review of documents and texts; and structured observation. Each has its strengths and limitations, and there is an extensive literature surrounding their appropriate use in research. It is our belief that the use of different techniques with different strengths and limitations allows for the cross validation of conclusions by comparing them using data collected in different ways. This is sometimes spoken of as triangulation, but is also part of the classic approach to assessing validity. Insights gained through participant observation can be cross-checked through the appropriate use of other methods.

Some researchers argue that the most effective use of participant observation is as a means to generate hypotheses that can be tested using other methods of data collection. We think that this is a limited view of the strengths of participant observation, but in research proposals written to agencies that generally do not fund much participant observation, we have successfully argued that a phase of research based on participant observation was necessary before we could formulate the appropriate questions for a precoded interview schedule.

In general, however, our own research projects generally include some more formal, often audiotaped, interviewing, using interview guides and schedules, in order to generate some data that are comparable across individuals (see chapter 8 for a discussion of the limitations of comparison in informal interviewing approaches). We use structured observation to gather comparable data on food use, childcare, health practices, agricultural practices, sources of income, etc. At the same time, the insight gained through participant observation allows us to assess the relative saliency of concerns and enables us to interpret the results of more structured approaches in ways that are closer to the understandings of participants. We believe that each method, with its own special strengths and limitations, gives us a slightly different viewpoint from which to observe the elephant.

ENHANCING REPRESENTATIVENESS: SAMPLING IN PARTICIPANT OBSERVATION

Sampling is a process more generally associated with quantitative research subjected to statistical analysis. The validity, and, more importantly, the generalizability of statistical analysis depend on the extent to which the probabilities in the sample reflect the true probabilities in the population being sampled. In qualitative research in general, and in participant

observation in particular, we are more concerned with understanding a setting or question in depth and from the perspective of a participant than we
are in knowing the distribution of variable across a population. However,
we know that no community or group is homogeneous. Communities are
collections of individuals and groups that share some understandings of
the world, but individuals have their own perspectives and interpretations
depending on their individual experiences and places in the social system.
If we wish to go beyond the most general and superficial generalizations
about a setting or community, it is necessary to understand the range of
variation of experiences and perspectives. Therefore, assuring the representativeness of information gained through participant observation is no less
important to the enterprise of ethnography (Honigmann 1970; Johnson
1990; Mead 1953; Paul 1953) than it is in quantitative research.

Mead (1953) was very interested in the issue of sampling in qualitative
research and in assuring the representativeness and hence the validity of
descriptions. In discussing the criticisms of anthropological work leveled by
sociologists and psychologists regarding the limitations of anthropological
sampling she argued:

> Anthropological sampling is not a poor and inadequate version of sociologi-
> cal or sociopsychological sampling, a version where n equals too few cases.
> It is simply a different kind of sampling, in which the validity of the sample
> depends not so much on the number of cases as upon the proper specifica-
> tion of the informant, so that he or she can be accurately placed, in terms of
> a very large number of variables—age, sex, order of birth, family background,
> life experience, temperamental tendencies (such as optimism, habit of exag-
> geration, etc.), political and religious position, exact situational relationships
> to the investigator, configurational relationship to every other informant, and
> so forth. (654–55)

She went on to note that while the sociologist might be concerned with
questions such as *how many* middle-aged men will express dissatisfaction
with their jobs, the anthropologist is asking a different question: *how* are
job dissatisfaction and satisfaction integrated within "cultural character."
While quantitative researchers are interested in the quantity and distribution of phenomena (variables), the qualitative researcher is interested in
the nature of the phenomena within a particular setting and in identifying
broad patterns. The nature of sampling in participant observation is of critical importance, but different from sampling in quantitative studies.

As Honigmann (1970) pointed out, sampling begins when the research
question and site are chosen. The choice of a particular question for research limits the kinds of information and types of people and events that
must be observed to answer it. A specific site, out of all the possible sites in
the world, is selected and this also places important limits on the research.

While the process of participating and observing may appear to respond primarily to external cues, in fact, we are continually choosing individuals, places, and events. How do we make decisions regarding places and events in which to participate, and with whom to have informal conversations?

The issue of sampling, even in participant observation, is intimately related to the research question and theoretical approach of the investigator. As we have noted above in chapter 1, while one of the strengths of participant observation is to discover new insights into a question, good research starts with a clear question and theoretical framework. The question and theory influence the kinds of places, activities, events, and people that are likely to be important to the research. One of the first steps in sampling for participant observation is to make a preliminary identification of places, activities, events, and people. Others will be added as the investigator gets a better sense of the context and new questions that arise in the fieldwork. The preliminary list then provides a sampling frame. In fact some of these can be anticipated from preliminary information about settings and should be included in research proposals.

Johnson (1990) has discussed the importance of choosing informants to achieve representativeness. While Johnson was concerned with more formal ethnographic interviewing, his arguments about the importance of attention to representativeness are critical. In the more formal language of sampling, when we talk about representativeness in the individuals with whom we interact and the activities and events in which we participate, we are referring to types of judgement and opportunistic sampling. In judgement sampling (Bernard 2006) the investigator chooses individuals and events on the basis of a set of criteria for inclusion. The criteria are drawn from theory, existing literature, and fieldwork (What do you want to know, and from what kinds of people: experts, participant, neophytes, etc.?); and include a determination of the degree of expertise of an informant (Does this person know about what the researcher wants to know about?) and the articulateness of the informant (Will she tell you, and in detail?).

Opportunistic or convenience sampling is even less structured and relies on talking with people as they are encountered by the investigators. The researcher participates in and observes events as they arise. While in the real world of fieldwork using participant observation a proportion of people with whom the investigator interacts and an even greater proportion of the events and activities in which s/he will participate will be of this sort, researchers should make an great effort to get beyond opportunistic sampling to achieve greater representativeness.

One of the early goals of fieldwork should be to understand the kinds and sources of diversity within a setting or group. Some of the obvious sources are age, gender, economic strategy, income, ethnic identity, religious affiliation, and household type. But there may be other unique or more subtle sources of diversity. In our research in an agrarian reform community (*ejido*) in Temascalcingo, Mexico we discovered very quickly that there were two identifiable factions, and a group that saw themselves as non-aligned. There was also a small but active group of Evangelical Protestants in a predominantly Catholic community. The size and type of household had an impact on how agricultural work was organized. While most *ejido* members were men, the few women members were quite different depending on whether they had adult children to help them in agriculture or were single mothers of young children. We were able to identify informants and events related to the different factions and churches and then attempted to develop relationships with a variety of people and to visit occasions during which different members of the community would be present.

In rural Kentucky, the counties in which we were working were large enough that it was more difficult to get a handle on diversity. However, we knew we needed to include men and women, living alone and in unions, and of different ages. We also knew that there were marked economic differences within the communities. In this case, we identified a series of organizations and agencies we felt were likely to have contact with different kinds of people. We identified homemakers clubs, retired teachers clubs, senior citizens centers, several different service organizations, including home care organizations, food banks, religious charity groups, and farmers' organizations. We used club meetings and senior citizens centers as venues for observation, and club lists as sources of names for individuals to contact as potential informants. With careful attention to age, gender, and household differences, we made it our business to find people with whom we should interact, and different places in which to hang out to meet diverse parts of the population. While not everyone we identified in this way turned out to be a good informant, we did establish a number of relationships that led to opportunities for participant observation, as we were invited to parties and picnic, meetings, and food procurement and preservation activities such as harvesting, gathering, canning, and hog butchering.

It is not only important to identify a diverse pool of informants, but also to identify a representative pool of events and venues. Again, in the work in rural Kentucky we were interested in the food resources for older adults. Part of our strategy was to observe people in eating establishments. To do this we identified a range of eating establishments used by older adults. These included a range of restaurants of varying prices, including fast food restaurants, corner stores that served some hot food and sandwiches, and the senior citizen centers. We also accompanied the drivers for the meals on wheels programs. We then included "hanging out" in these different places as part of our research strategy.

Another way to gain an acquaintance with a wide range of people in a particular setting, especially in a community study, is to carry out a census or other short formal interview with a sample of people or households chosen in some structured or random way. In our experience in community studies, this has been a way to identify people from a wide range of social and economic circumstances with whom one might want to establish more of a relationship later in the fieldwork. Surveys and censuses are common enough in the contemporary world that it is not so odd for an interviewer to knock on your door, especially if the researcher has been introduced in community meetings and has obtained some official community recognition and approval for the work. In research in Latin America we have often conducted a census early in the fieldwork experience and then used both the contacts and the data from the census to guide more informal research. In Mexico, it allowed us to quickly move beyond the contacts provided by Pedro, our assigned guide. This kind of an approach, of course, will not work in settings where a survey or census phase is inappropriate or difficult. Philippe Bourgois could probably not have surveyed crack dealers early in his fieldwork in the Barrio. Likewise, if Agar had tried to do a survey among the inmates of the narcotics hospital, he would probably not have met with much success.

Participatory research approaches most frequently include the incorporation of the insights of community participants in the selection of places, events, and venues. This adds to the strength of the participatory designs. Mullings and her associates (Mullings 2000; Mullings and Wali 2001; Mullings et al. 2001) drew on the recommendation of the member of the Community Advisory Board in identifying the specific neighborhoods and work places that would be most important for the participant observation phase of their research in Central Harlem. Since the time devoted to participant observation was comparatively short (several months rather than a year or more), the identification of meaningful sites was even more critical and attending to the experience of community members was an important component of the design.

Rapid appraisal procedures that include some form of participant observation require even more careful attention to the choice of places, activities, venues, and events for observation as the time frame is often weeks rather than months. The shorter time available for the development of a closer understanding of the experiences of participants means that sampling must be focused even more carefully on those places and activities that are most likely to yield insight. Since most research projects using RAP are quite tightly organized around a particular issue or program, the particular questions being asked focus the sampling procedures. RAP approaches are much less likely to result in information that radically refocuses research, as participant observation over longer periods of time frequently does.

On the other hand, a period of participant observation at the outset of a RAP project can help identify precisely the people, places, and activities for which more quantitative techniques, such as semistructured interviews, structured interviews, and surveys would be appropriate. In this sense participant observation can assist in the development of more appropriate sampling strategies for other types of data collection. Schensul, Schensul, and LeCompte (1999) refer to this as "exploratory observation" and suggest that a period of observation can enhance the design of subsequent research.

An even more abbreviated form of rapid observation (with very little participation) is the "windshield survey" approach developed for rapid rural appraisal techniques (Chambers 1980, 1983, 1992; Mukherjee 2004) used in rural development programs and now frequently incorporated into community health research. A windshield survey is a technique in which the observer walks, bikes, or drives through a region, neighborhood, district, observing the spatial placement of structures, people, fields, and so forth. However, it also includes talking with people along the way, observing what is done, and getting into fields and markets and homes and other venues to get a "feel" for what is important. Schensul et al. (1999) further suggest mapping the route during a walking "survey" of a community.

PROPOSING PARTICIPANT OBSERVATION

There are a number of reasons for writing a formal research proposal before beginning a new project. Some are merely pragmatic. Submitting a formal proposal is usually required to obtain funding for research, your master's thesis or dissertation committee requires it, or you need to submit a request to do research with human subjects. While funding research and meeting the demands of committees for completing your degree are very important reasons for writing proposals, and often critical, they are perhaps not the best reasons. The very best reason for writing a formal research proposal is that it allows the researcher to develop clear research questions and a strategy for data collection and analysis before beginning the actual fieldwork. All of this work, even when it is modified and refined in the field, enhances the efficiency and effectiveness of the fieldwork.

Some people believe that it is difficult to obtain funding for research that is based mainly on participant observation. We have often heard our colleagues complain that review committees do not understand the value of qualitative research in general, and of participant observation in particular. Between the two of us, we have sat on over a dozen different review panels for the National Science Foundation, National Institutes for Health, Centers for Disease Control, Agency for Health Care Policy and Research, U.S. Agency for International Development, Inter-American Development Foundation, and the Fulbright Program and we have reviewed, literally, hundreds of proposals. On review panels, we are often chosen to represent anthropology or "qualitative researchers." While on a handful of occasions we have felt that our colleagues on the panels truly did not understand qualitative research and/or devalued it, it has been far more commonly the case that researchers who want to do qualitative research have written poor proposals. It is not enough for a researcher to say that he or she will do a descriptive study of "Group X" because they have never been studied before, or to describe the design of the research, including sampling, recording of observations and analysis of field notes and other materials in terms so vague that a reviewer is asked to take a leap of faith that the researcher knows what s/he is doing.

In a proposal submitted for funding the proposer has to convince a panel of other researchers, most of whom will not be experts in the specific field of study, that:

- the question is important to answer
- answering it will add to existing knowledge (i.e., you contextualize it within an existing literature)
- the research site is appropriate to answer the question
- the theoretical approach/conceptual framework to be used is valid and flows from existing research
- the methods used will allow the question to be answered
- the proposer is competent to carry out the proposed project

When an economist, epidemiologist, sociologist, or another anthropologist is reviewing a proposal, to say merely that participant observation will be used is not enough. We have to justify why this is the best method for answering the question, or how it relates to other methods we will use to answer the question. Moreover, the description of what will be done has to include the elements of design that both seasoned qualitative researchers and researchers from other more quantitatively oriented disciplines expect to see in a research design. That means being clear about sampling (representativeness), being clear about the ways in which data from observation and informal interviews will be captured (field notes, recordings), and the provision of a detailed description of how the data will be analyzed.

The research proposal represents a specific genre of writing and most proposals conform more or less to a standard format. While there are variations, and some funding agencies emphasize some aspects of the proposal over others, most proposals must include:

1. A succinct statement of the objectives of the research project. Objectives may be descriptive, interpretive, explanatory, or any combination of these. The statement generally includes one or more specific research questions and may include specific hypotheses (but need not).

2. A "background" statement (drawn from the literature and previous research) that summarizes existing knowledge on the subject; identifies debates or lacunae in the record; and demonstrates how achieving the goals of this project can add to existing knowledge.
3. A summary of research design that presents an overall design that can directly address the goals and questions of research. It should describe why the particular setting chosen is the appropriate, indeed, the best setting to study this phenomenon; how the project will be set up to meet descriptive, interpretive, or explanatory goals; how any comparisons proposed will be carried out; how hypotheses, if proposed, will be tested; what kinds of data collection methods will be used. It is here that the researcher must clearly state the utility of including participant observation in the mix of methods and the specific kinds of data and knowledge it will generate.
4. A detailed discussion of specific methods of data collection. For participant observation this should include a discussion of how representativeness will be assured ("sampling" of people, places, activities, and events); how data will be captured (jot notes, field notes, tape recordings, video recordings); how field notes and other data will be managed in the field.
5. A preliminary discussion of the strategy for analysis, including a preliminary indexing system; a specific strategy for identifying themes; any software that might be employed to assist in analysis; what kinds of data will be used to address the specific goals and questions of research.

RESEARCH OBJECTIVES

At least some of the objectives of the project must be addressable with participant observation. For example, one of the most common problems we see in proposals is a stated objective to study change or changes in a phenomenon using participant observation. As we noted above, participant observation is essentially a synchronic method. It tells the researcher about what is happening now (ethnographic present) but little about what has happened in the past. While including oral history or a review of documents can allow for a reconstruction of some of the past, participant observation per se cannot.

While most research objectives to be addressed by participant observation will be stated in terms of description, they may also include the testing of hypotheses. If the research objectives include explanation and the testing of hypotheses with participant observation, the hypotheses need to be stated in terms of the presence or absence of phenomena, or the existence of patterns of ideas or behavior.

This chapter has emphasized that a project based upon participant observation requires as much, indeed more, attention to research design than any other kind of research. Careful attention to research design at the beginning of a project will enable relatively unstructured method to be more easily justified to funding agencies, as well as for the results to be ultimately analyzed and interpreted. Just as with other methods of research, in participant observation we need to pay attention to issues like research objectives and sampling.

NOTES

1. The strategy of using several different methods or techniques to examine the same phenomenon is often referred to as triangulation of methods.

2. Mead interviewed adolescent girls; Freeman talked with adults and focused on the ideal behavior of young girls. Redfield used participant observation and interviewing as his principal methods and focused theoretically on community cohesion; Lewis used more structured interviewing and focused on intra-community heterogeneity.

❧8❧

Informal Interviewing in Participant Observation

Most researchers who use participant observation as part of their approach to research also use a number of more structured data collection methods. The other techniques used will include mapping and counting, informal interviewing, semistructured interviewing, formal interviewing, formal elicitation frameworks, and very structured interview schedules and questionnaires. In this chapter we will explore the more informal end of the interview continuum, particularly the collection of data from conversations and very informal interviewing.

The type of "interviewing" that is part of participant observation is usually informal and is usually more like a casual conversation among acquaintances. After all, the goal of the technique is for the researcher to participate in naturally unfolding events, and to observe them as carefully and as objectively as possible. The researcher is looking for new insights into the point of view of the participants. The basic rule in carrying out interviewing or conversing during participant observation is that the researcher is intent on following the lead of the informant, exerting only minimal impact on the topic and flow of the interaction. The goal is to get out of the way of the participants or informants and let them talk (Bernard 2006).

This is not, however, the same as participating in a conversation in a nonresearch setting for at least two reasons. The first is that, ultimately, the researcher is interested in some phenomena more than others (answering the research question or questions). The second is that the researcher will soon be writing notes about the conversation, and knowing this he or she is likely to conduct the interaction in a different way than if this were not the case. In other word the researcher is likely to be directing conversation and asking many more questions that would usually take place in a casual conversation among acquaintances. Because verbal interaction between the researcher and those with whom he or she interacts in the project has some of the characteristics of an interview, ethnographers should know about different kinds of interviews and be able to use some of the techniques commonly used in interviewing.

TYPES OF INTERVIEWS

There are a number of types of interview and they can be classified along two continua. The first continuum is the degree of control by the researcher and informants (Bernard 2006; Dohrenwend and Richardson 1965; Spradley 1979). At one extreme, the end in which there is the least control by the researcher and the most by the informants, lies the pure observer, who observes but does not participate in the conversation (on the Internet, this is a "lurker"). At the other end of the continuum is the precoded written questionnaire filled in without the presence of the researcher. In this case, the form and content are completely controlled by the researcher, with no accommodation for the concerns or understandings of an individual respondent. A respondent can only choose one of several precoded responses or can choose not to answer a question at all.

The second continuum is the degree to which the stimuli (questions) presented to each informant are uniform. At the conversation end, each conversation is unique; there is no intent or attempt to raise the same topics or ask questions in the same way with each participant in the conversation. At the other end of the continuum, it is presumed that the self-administered questionnaire presents each respondent with an identical stimulus (the questionnaire).

Between the extremes on both continua lie most of the forms of interviewing carried out by qualitative researchers (see figure 8.1). Bernard's (2006) category of informal interviewing includes much of the verbal interaction in which the participant observer engages with informants and other participants. Bernard (1995) has defined informal interviewing as being characterized by:

> a total lack of structure or control. The researcher just tries to remember conversations heard during the course of a day "in the field." This requires constant jotting and daily sessions in which you sit at a typewriter, unburden your memory and develop your field notes. (209)

We would call the situation he describes in the quote as conversation, and in another, closely related category we would put informal interviewing. In "remembered" conversation the researcher is observing informants as they go about their daily activities and are interacting and conversing in culturally

Conversation	Unstructured Interviews	Semi-structured Interviews	Structured Interviews	Self-administered Questionnaires

←

Control by Informant/Participant/Respondent

LOW   HIGH

Uniformity of Stimulus Presented to Informant/Respondent

→

Figure 8.1: Continuum of control and uniformity of stimulus for different types of interviews.

patterned ways. As Bernard notes, the researcher makes notes, tries to remember verbatim passages of conversation, and records those in field notes.

In informal interviewing the researcher follows the lead of the participants, but asks occasional questions to focus the topic or to clarify points that s/he does not understand (Spradley 1979). In this case, the informant may be more aware that s/he is explaining something to the researcher, training them in his/her culture. In both conversation and informal interviewing, the researcher is not necessarily directing the topics for discussion, but is following, or following up on points raised by another person during the natural flow of conversation.

Other forms of interviewing are more directive and are clearly understood as interviews by both the researcher and the informant. In unstructured interviewing, the researcher typically has a plan for the interview and may have a brief interview guide that includes the topics to be addressed as an aid to memory, but he or she presents topics in an open-ended way and exerts as little control over the interaction as possible. In semistructured interviewing, the interview guide includes a list of questions and prompts in order to increase the likelihood that all topics will be covered in each interview in more or less the same way. A somewhat more structured approach would include a guide with opening questions and suggestions for prompts to be used as needed.

When a formal set of questions is used in an open-ended way, we can refer to the result as structured interviewing. In this, the questions asked by the interviewer are scripted although the responses of the person can be relatively open-ended. Finally, the step before questionnaire use is the use of an interview schedule (often precoded) and administered face to face by the interviewer. With the administration of an interview schedule there is still an interaction between the researcher and respondent, and the respondent can have a small amount of impact on the interchange, but the researcher is clearly in charge and usually attempts to administer the interview in the same way to each respondent.

Both of the dimensions in figure 8.1 have an impact on the nature of the data collected. The extent to which the researcher, as compared with the informant, controls the flow of the interaction has an impact on the degree to which the content of the interaction reflects issues and information that are salient to the informant. Even the best of open-ended interviewers, that is, those who intervene minimally in the interaction, direct the content to some extent. If the goal is to understand the way that participants view a phenomenon, then it is important to allow the flow of conversation to reflect those aspects that are salient to the informants. On the other hand, the degree to which information gathered from different individuals is comparable across individuals is dependent on, among other things, the degree to which they were responding to similar stimuli (questions and probes). While individuals may interpret and respond to even precoded questionnaires differently, the likelihood that the responses of different individuals can be considered comparable is higher than in a more unstructured interview. When different individuals are engaged in free-ranging conversations, even when the topics discussed are similar, there is no way to assess the extent to which the individuals are responding to the same ideas or questions.

Noncomparability of responses is most important when there is a wide range of disagreement about information or interpretations. For example, in one project, Bill had conversations with a wide variety of people from industry, government, nongovernmental organizations, communities, and universities about the social and environmental effects of shrimp farming (aquaculture). Responses from these different stakeholders reflect considerable disagreement about the effects, and sorting out claims and counterclaims has been important for policy purposes (see DeWalt et al. 2000). At the same time, if several informants in different contexts voice similar ideas or concerns, it is in fact powerful evidence that the issues are salient and that understandings are widely shared. In research in Mexico in the early 1970s, Kathleen found that the phrase "The illnesses no longer understand the herbs" (*Las enfermidades ya no entienden las hierbas*) kept coming up in open-ended conversations about health with different people, in different contexts over the course of several months (K. M. DeWalt 1977). It appeared that this was a widespread interpretation of medical change in the community and the consequences (the need to seek biomedical treatment rather than use traditional medical remedies) were becoming consciously appreciated by people.

On the other hand, when conversations or unstructured interviews do not turn up information about a particular topic, the lack of information is not interpretable. That is, if a description or comment by one informant is not voiced by another, it does not mean that that issue is not salient to the second person. It only means that it did not come up in conversation with that person. If asked directly, the second informant may or may not have articulated something similar. The absence of information in the conversation and in the record is not interpretable in any way.

More structured approaches to interviewing are more likely to yield data that are comparable. Clearly there is a trade-off. Most research projects will include several different types of interviews. A common strategy is to begin with less directive approaches. Later, the researcher can follow up themes of particular interest in a more structured way, with a sample of informants.

While any one researcher may employ all of the types of interviewing mentioned in course of fieldwork, when in participant observation mode the investigator will be engaging in conversation and the most informal interviewing. Even conversation, however, will probably not be as completely "nondirective" (Whyte and Whyte 1984) as Bernard's definition suggests. Because researchers always have their research questions in the back of their minds, they are likely to consciously or unconsciously direct interactions toward their interests. Even showing a bit more interest in some topics rather than others will direct conversations toward those topics. The interests of the researcher will always have an impact. The trick is to use this impact to encourage informants to discuss more fully the topics that relate to the research question, but to direct the content of the conversation as little as possible beyond that.

One of Bill's first experiences in doing research exemplifies some of the important points about interviewing. During one summer, he was hired as a research assistant by the Labor Education Center at the University of Connecticut to examine discrimination in the construction industry. He was sent out with a semistructured interview and showed up at a job site, pen at the ready, to begin interviews. It did not take long before he realized that the direct questions he was asking about numbers of, and attitudes about, minorities on the job site and in the union were being met with silence and/or hostility. After discussing the problems and potential solutions with the researchers directing the project, Bill changed strategies to use informal interviewing. Keeping the main objectives of the research in mind, he abandoned the use of an interview schedule and through informal conversations was able to gather much more information about perceptions and attitudes. He did explain the general purposes of the work to the people he interviewed and was able to make jot notes to help him recall information. After the interview, he entered as much of the information as he could on the original interview guide.

It is important, then, to understand that different kinds of interviews are more appropriate depending on the populations being studied as well as the research questions of interest. Self-administered questionnaires are obviously useless in nonliterate populations but we have both seen examples of researchers committing errors that are nearly as silly. Most typically, this involves researchers who put together complicated and impressive (at least on paper) structured or semistructured survey interviews that, when they are actually used, generate results that are nearly meaningless. We agree with Chambers (1983) who wrote about surveys in rural development:

they are more limited, less reliable, and less able to generate insight than is commonly believed. By capturing and enslaving so many researchers, especially social scientists, they also raise questions of cost-effectiveness and opportunity cost, of alternative uses of those same resources of staff and funds. (51–52)

In many cases, more participant observation and informal interviewing can generate more meaningful and interpretable results, more insight for the researcher, and be much less intrusive for the population being studied.

INTERVIEW TECHNIQUES

Even at the least intrusive, researchers should be aware of the techniques of interviewing and be able to use those that are the least directive. The following discussion of techniques can be used in conversation and informal interviewing and also in more structured interviewing, such as unstructured, semistructured and formal interviews. However, we have included for discussion only those that are least intrusive here. For discussions of how to effectively conduct more structured interviews, the reader is directed to Babbie (1973) and Dillman (1978).

Active Listening

The most fundamental technique for being a good interviewer is active listening. Active listening is first and foremost, listening. As Doc said to William Foote Whyte early in research in Cornerville:

> Go easy on that "who," "what," "why," "when," "where" stuff, Bill. You ask those questions, and people will clam up on you. If people accept you, you can just hang around, and you'll learn the answer in the long run without ever having to ask the questions. (Whyte and Whyte 1984:69)

Doc's advice underscores the most important aspect of conversation and informal interviewing in participant observation: the researcher is quiet, primarily a listener and, more importantly, is gaining information in the terms used by participants, and in a progression of thought that is natural to them. However, active listening is also "active." By this, we mean that the researcher is more actively aware of the conversation than in conversations in a nonresearch setting. The researcher is making mental notes about what is said, who said it, and what it might mean in the context of the project. In other words, the participant observer is "on," with heightened awareness of the context and increased attentiveness to detail. S/he may be making mental notes of specific words and information, or may be talking jot notes during the conversation. The researcher is not only attending to verbal communication, but is also noting nonverbal cues as well. The researcher is also trying to communicate that s/he is interested in what the informant is saying and respects the ideas and opinions of the informant (whether or not the researcher agrees with them).

Being an active listener also means using the least directive types of probes and prompts in order to facilitate the conversation. Probing is used when the researcher feels that something is left out, that the informant might say something more about an issue if encouraged in some way (Yow 1994). There are several ways of using probes to facilitate a conversation or informal interview that stop well short of asking even the simplest of questions (Enelow and Swisher 1979; Mishler 1986; Wiese 1974; Yow 1994). Some of the least directive probes are meant merely to communicate that the researcher is listening and interested.

Sensitive Silence

We think of sensitive silence as silence with an edge. The researcher is engaged in a conversation in which s/he is not saying anything but shows attentiveness to the interaction through body language and eye contact (Yow 1994). The researcher/interviewer may be leaning in toward the participants. S/he assumes a position in the most intimate level of closeness that is appropriate to the expectations of personal space in the culture, the particular setting of the interaction, the degree to which the researcher knows the participants, and the gender of the participants.

Appropriate personal space differs in different culture settings (Hall 1959, 1974). One of the aspects of learning the rules that a participant observer has to deal with early in research in a new setting is how to judge personal space. It generally takes a few weeks of pulling away from people who the researcher feels are "too close" or backing people into corners as they try to get farther away from the researcher to develop a tacit feel for personal space. Also, appropriate space is likely to be different for men and women, in mixed or same sex groupings, and for people who know each other as compared with relative strangers. Again, the researcher attempts to adopt the most intimate space appropriate for gender and degree of acquaintance.

The degree to which eye contact is facilitating or offensive is also influenced by cultural differences. For most North Americans and Europeans, attentive eye contact is facilitating. It denotes interest in what is being said and suggests that the researcher would like to hear more. In our experience, this is also true in the Latin American contexts in which we have worked. However, it is also true that in mixed gender settings, strong eye contact can sometimes be mistakenly interpreted as an invitation to more intimacy.

Again, it is important to figure out relatively early in fieldwork what degree of eye contact is appropriate and facilitative.

Researchers should not underestimate the difficulty of remaining silent ether in conversations or informal interviews. It is probably the most difficult technique to use. For North Americans, especially, silence that continues several seconds is threatening and very difficult to maintain. Our colleagues who have worked with Native American communities in the United States assure us that the tolerance for silence is much greater in those cultural settings. Our experience in Latin American settings suggests that remaining quiet even a second or two encourages our informants to continue with their discussion, without active intervention by the researcher. In years of teaching interviewing techniques to first year medical students, Kathleen found that remaining silent is the most difficult thing they have to learn. Not many are successful at the start.

Researchers speak when they should be quiet for a number of other reasons as well. The most common is that a comment by an informant reminds the researcher of another issue, also interesting, and the researcher breaks in with a question or comment about the second issue before the informant has finished his/her comment on the first issue. Sometimes the new idea seems so compelling that, without thinking the researcher jumps to the new idea. The new idea may seem to be closer to the core interests of the project. The researcher may feel that s/he will forget to follow up on the second idea later. (As we age, we realize that this particular problem increases in salience for us.) In all of the cases, the researcher can and should focus on not interrupting and waiting for the informant to come to the natural end of the first idea before moving on. Make a jot note of the idea so that you do not forget it and will come back to it later. Usually a single word in the margin is often sufficient to act as an aid to memory.

In the following excerpt from a taped conversation with Mrs. L, she and the researcher are talking about what Mrs. L plants in her garden. The reader can see that this section of conversation has a very choppy, jumpy feel to it. The reason is that the researcher keeps interrupting Mrs. L and does not allow her to finish her sentences. We join this conversation speaking of tomatoes:[1]

Mrs. L: . . . yes, pulp in them, and they're just great, I think. Then I too, raise the big yellow ones, and I also raise the big purple ones. I like some of that old kind . . .

Q: You save that [seeds]?

Mrs. L: Oh, yes . . .

Q: What else do you raise besides the lettuce, radish, and tomatoes?

Mrs. L: Well, I . . .

Q: What else did you put out?

Mrs. L: I hadn't put out anything, but I will put out peas . . . I have onions out now. But I will put out the sweet onions later . . . maybe 200 of them.

Q: You don't use the sets?

Mrs. L: Yes, I do . . .

Q: You use onion sets?

Mrs. L: I put out . . . oh . . . !

Q: Is that for your own use?

Mrs. L: Oh, I like to divide with my neighbors . . .

Q: And your son?

Mrs. L: Yes, he has a garden, too. He lives right over there. They have a garden . . .

Some researchers, especially inexperienced interviewers, are nervous enough in a new setting to—frankly speaking—blather. Blathering often takes the form of sharing far too much (unasked for) personal information, often in response to a comment by the informant. (Please note that in conversations in nonresearch contexts, we often offer such information as part of the conversation. However, let us say again, even in a conversation-like situation in a research setting the researcher is not engaging in a common conversation). New researchers often feel that offering unrequested personal information and opinions is part of keeping up their end of the conversation. However, it is very poor interviewing style.[2]

After years of training and supervising social science graduate students, medical students learning communication and interviewing skills, critiquing our own and colleagues' audiotaped interviews and field notes, we have come to the conclusion that the most common mistake made by interviewers using any type of interview strategy is not keeping quiet and letting the informant speak. Even after years of experience, we are humbled by listening to our own taped interviews in which we cut off informants, or say something that changes the subject before the informant is ready to end. We are far better than we were, but our assessment is that every researcher can improve on their use of silence as a research tool.

The Uh-huh Prompt

The uh-huh prompt is no more sophisticated than using nonintrusive verbal cues to let the informants and participants know that the researcher is listening. Many of us do say something that sounds like "uh-huh" or "hmmm-hmmm" or a grunt (Bernard 2006). Or, we use a real word such as "yes" or "OK" or "really" (when speaking in English, of course). The intent of the "uh-huh" prompt is to add a verbal component to active listening that says: "I'm listening," "I'm following you," "I'm with you," "Please go on." Many of us do this unconsciously when we are concentrating on a conversation. (It would probably be impossible for Kathleen NOT to give verbal prompts in any language in which she is working.) If an interview or conversation is recorded, transcribing the uh-huh prompt can slow down the transcriptionist (Yow 1994). However, a transcription that detailed is not necessarily the goal in informal interviewing. The uh-huhs can be passed over, not transcribed, if they pose a constraint.

The following passage is from a semistructured interview with a woman in rural Kentucky talking about her childhood and her relationship with her younger sister. The "Really?" comment by the interviewer is an example of a word being used as a neutral verbal prompt.

Mrs. W: Yes, but I was older than her. Well, I'm 17 months older than her, but we started school together. When we got up to third grade, they wanted to pass me on to the fifth, and I can remember crying. I didn't want to, and my mom would tell me that I was older and I should . . . if I'd started I'd be in the fourth (grade). . . . I consented. Well, I didn't have much choice, I guess. So I went into the fifth grade, and left my sister in the third . . . and I cried! And we always took our lunch together. Mom fixed our lunch, in an 8-lb. lard bucket. That's what we took our lunch in, and although I was the oldest (I love to tell this on my sister!) . . . I was the oldest, but she was always bigger than me, after we got any size, and she always made me mad! So when it came lunchtime, she got the lunch bucket (I had to carry it to school!) and I had to carry it home in the afternoon. But when it came lunchtime, she got the lunch bucket and she got to eat what she liked best, and I ate what was left!

Q: Really?

Mrs. W: Well, this went on the first year. The second year we had a different teacher, and the teacher was kin (he was a cousin of my mother). So, he realized . . . it didn't take him long to realize what my sister was doing to me. . . . We started off the second year, and of course, we always had watermelons and cantaloupes and everything we raised in the garden . . . so my mother came by school and brought us a piece of watermelon for our lunch. And you know how that would look! Well, you don't . . . but I do! Oh, it would look so good, besides a biscuit and whatever we had, jam or jelly, that's what we would take, or a biscuit and sausage. Sometimes my mother would fry Irish potatoes for breakfast and we would take Irish potatoes on our biscuit, which was real good.

In a later segment of the interview with Mrs. L:

Q: Now that you have sold the cattle, you have some land which is idle, which is not being used?

Mrs. L: Yes, too much.

Q: And what are you going to do with it?

Mrs. L: Well, I really don't know . . . you don't rent to anybody. You know, there's nobody who wants to farm anymore. I don't have too much here. I have about 76 acres here, and then I have some more acreage, oh! it's just about half a mile from here. And you know, the hay wasn't even cut off of part of that last year . . .

Q: Yes?

Mrs. L: I lost my . . . something like 2000 bales of hay, it just wasn't put up. The people I had rented to, or my son rented to . . . they're good people. But it rained, and their tools were old, and they would break down and this, that and the other, and they just never did get it done. Now, they weren't liable, but they just . . . just didn't get it done.

In both of the examples above, the researcher is using a single neutral word to let the informant know that s/he is listening and is ready for the informant to continue.

An important caveat in using the "uh-huh" prompt is that the particular sound used may mean different things in different cultural settings. For example, it took Kathleen some time to realize that the "huh-huh" sound (the one that means "no" in English) is the correct prompt for "yes, continue" in Ecuador.

Repetition Feedback

Enelow and Swisher (1979) suggest a series of relatively nondirective ways of providing feedback to informants in order to facilitate further discussion and clarification, but not to direct or lead the conversation. The first is repetition feedback. Repetition is just that. The researcher repeats the last word or phrase uttered by the informant. Sometimes the phrase is given a questioning inflection. The following is an excerpt from a taped conversation in which the informant is describing breakfasts when he was a child. The interviewer repeats his last word to encourage him to continue with the description.

Mr. B: Well, when we was at home, we usually had some kind of meats and my mother always did fix some potatoes.

Q: Potatoes?

Mr. B: Uh huh. And then biscuits.

And later in the interview:

> Mr. B: Yes . . . see, they dried them . . . called them "shucky beans". . .
>
> Q: Shucky beans?
>
> Mr. B: What they would do, is all these beans had strings on them, and that string come off of them, you know what I'm talking about, then take twine and thread and a darning needle, and go right in the middle of these beans and string them on this string, and get a stringful and hang them up. And they could dry. (laughs)

And:

> Mrs. P: I put them (broccoli seeds) in my tobacco beds, and I put them out just like I would my cabbage. Of course, they're something you've got to spray every day. (laughs)
>
> Q: Every day?
>
> Mrs. P: Well, almost. You have to keep after them continuously. There's a little old white moth . . . they're coming to put an egg down and make a worm in your broccoli. And when I see one, I don't want anymore of it then . . . (laughs)

A danger with over use of repetition is the researcher begins to sound like a parrot. Used appropriately, however, it can facilitate the expansion of an idea or discussion.

Summary Feedback

Summary feedback is similar to repetition, but the researcher summarizes the last set of statements articulated by the informant. Again the goal is to let the informant know that the researcher has heard what was said, and to encourage the informant to continue and expand on the comments. Summary feedback also provides a check on the understanding developed by the researcher. It is an invitation to the informant to clarify any misconceptions held by the researcher.

In the following passage, Mrs. L says she cans a good deal of tomato juice, but cannot drink it. The researcher is puzzled so she summarizes what she heard, hoping for clarification:

> Mrs. L: Velveeta . . . that's not the best, I don't think, to cook with, but . . . either that or chunk cheese, I put it in macaroni or spaghetti and stuff like that. I still think cheese is great to cook with! There's several things that I buy now that I don't use to buy. I have plenty of tomato juice for juice. Now that's something that I can't drink. It gives me this (indigestion) . . .
>
> Q: So you have tomato juice put up that you can't drink.

Mrs. L: I can't drink it very often, although I use it for soups and all that and the other. I still love cream of tomato soup . . . I still love that. It's awfully good!

In this exchange, Mrs. L makes it clear that there are other uses of home canned tomato juice that the interviewer did not know about.

Summary feedback can be more elaborate. The researcher may take the opportunity to summarize a good deal of information to not only prompt the informant to add to the information, but also to check a series of event. For example in talking about her life, the interviewer said the following to Mrs. L:

Q: So before your father died your family lived on their own farm. When he died you were seven years old and your mother took you and your sister and brother to live with your grandparents. When she remarried, you stayed with your grandparents on their farm, while your younger brother and sister went with her and her new husband.

Mrs. L: Yes, I helped my grandmother on the farm until she died. I was 14 and then I took over the housework for my grandfather.

ASKING QUESTIONS IN INTERVIEWING

Even in conversations, and certainly in informal interviews, the researcher will occasionally be asking questions. All of us ask questions in normal conversation. We are interested in knowing more about what our companions are talking about; we need clarification when we do not understand a term or a concept; or the conversation has reached a natural conclusion and the opportunity comes to raise another topic. In conversations and informal interviews researchers, use questions for all of these reasons. Some techniques for effective use of asking questions follow.

Tell Me More

The "tell me more" question is as simple as saying "Then what happened?" "What did you do, then?" "What else?" and "That's interesting, tell me more." It is one step beyond the uh-huh prompt. The goal is to prompt the informant to continue with the same issue, not to introduce a new topic. In a slightly different form it is the "What did you think about that?" question. The "tell me more" question is short, succinct, and generally followed by the use of silence. In the following quotation Mrs. W is talking about her family when she was a child. She said that they moved frequently and described a home on the river bottom; the researcher is following up.

Q: When you moved away from the river bottom, where did you go then?

Mrs. W: We went to Monticello. I'm telling you about my home town. That's where I went to school at. Monticello. And Pleasant View, up above Monticello.

For Clarification

Questions are used to clarify words, ideas, chronologies, in short, anything that the researcher does not understand. Early in fieldwork, many things may need clarification. Actually, it is probably a good idea early in fieldwork to avoid asking for too much clarification. Asking for clarification breaks the flow of conversation and can end up in changing topics. Many things that are unclear or not entirely understood early in fieldwork will probably become clear just through experience. In the following quotation the researcher asks what the informant means by "not too good."

> Mrs. L: Yes, it's much better . . . much better. Or I always thought it was. I made some. I made about 12 half-gallon jars of kraut. It's not too good. I had some of it at dinner, and I didn't think it was too good.
>
> Q: What do you mean, it's not too good?
>
> Mrs. L: Well, it . . . I just didn't think it had the taste and the crispness that it . . . I like a good crisp kraut, and it looked like this is just not as crisp as I would like for it to be. But now, I tell you, they was a lot of hot sunshine on those cabbages, so I laid it to that. Although the ones I used seemed to be very tender, but now, that sunshine will do something to the cabbage. You know, the sunshine was unbearable, almost, for a while there, and I didn't get mine made hardly as early as I should. I don't recall what made me not get it done, but I didn't, and it's eatable . . . but . . . it could be better! (laughs)

Naïve Questions

A common problem for most people is that they become overzealous in trying to demonstrate their competence in their own cultural setting or in a different cultural setting. Rather than asking questions, these people make statements and then ask the person being interviewed for confirmation. Thus, they say, "People here make their living from farming, don't they?" or "Everyone here is Catholic, right?"

We are great advocates of asking dumb questions or naïve questions because, in our experience, some of the most interesting information that challenges our own assumptions about things have come as a result of feigning ignorance. During one of Bill's recent projects on shrimp farming in Mexico, his first evening in the state of Sinaloa he was eating dinner in a restaurant along the beach. Casually, he asked the woman seating customers (who was the manager) where they got the shrimp served in the restaurant. Although he expected a reply referring to some supplier or place, the woman replied that "This time of the year they come from the estuaries—or at least people tell us that they come from the estuaries." Although Bill had not been in fieldwork mode until that point, he began following up with other naïve questions. In the course of a few minutes, among other things he learned that: (1) shrimp come from the high seas, estuaries, or shrimp farms; (2) all farmed shrimp is exported, not sold locally; (3) there are different closed seasons for shrimp from estuaries and from the high seas; (4) fishing for shrimp during the closed seasons occurs, but there is little enforcement; (5) the marketing of shrimp is done by a very few people; and (6) several people who operated shrimp farms had been killed in the last few months, probably because of links to drug smuggling.

During the same project, Bill visited a number of different shrimp farms to talk with managers and owners. One of the topics in which he was interested was how much the farms were contributing to water pollution in the estuaries along which they were located. With many of these people, he used naïve questions like: "What happens to the water that is in the ponds?" "Do you have to change the water that is in the ponds?" or "Do you put anything in the ponds to make the shrimp grow faster?" At the time he was asking these questions, Bill knew enough about shrimp farming to make anyone's eyes glaze over within three minutes, but his purpose in asking dumb questions was to get a sense of the variability in technical operations on the farms and the degree to which those farms might be addressing pollution issues.

Our admonition to all of our students is to not be afraid to ask questions that may be seen to be naïve or dumb. In our experience, most people love to demonstrate and share their expertise. If you show yourself to be an interested "student" by asking questions, people will be patient enough to provide you with answers. Surprisingly, those answers will often expand your understandings or your knowledge far beyond what you thought you already knew.

AVOIDING CONFRONTATION

There are many times in our field research in which we have to bite our tongues to avoid getting into arguments or confrontations with people we interview. Invariably, we have found that these instances are generally with people from the elite or government sector who speak disparagingly about the characteristics of people in communities we have come to know. Bill recalls that, early in our field research in Temascalcingo, Mexico, he was ready to explode one day when a leader of a development project was talking about how uncooperative, stupid, and ignorant the small farmers in the valley were.

As much as we might want, in situations like that, to provide our contrary opinions and perspectives, our general rule is to treat all conversations as data. That is, we should be active listeners who are recording other people's perceptions and attitudes, so therefore we should avoid confrontations in most circumstances. There are times and places to engage in arguments and battles, but it is not wise to do this in the midst of field research. The good interviewer will avoid questions and comments that will provoke a confrontation with an informant.

CHANGING TOPICS

In both conversation and informal interviewing, the time comes when it is clear that one topic has been exhausted and there is a chance to introduce a new topic. Again, introducing a topic is something that is used sparingly in the kinds of interviewing used in participant observation. In more structured interviewing situations, introducing a new topic is a much more common occurrence. In changing topics, we believe that the key is to introduce a new topic with an open-ended question. The "tell me about . . . " question is an effective one. For example, the interviewer can use prompts like, "Tell me about what is was like growing up." "Tell me about the town." "Tell me what you think about X project." "Tell me what you do all day." The rules for asking direct questions in these circumstances include:

- Keep the questions as short as possible.
- Avoid editorializing as an introduction to a question, unless it is necessary. It is better to ask: "What did you do today?" than to say: "I know that you are a busy person and have a lot of things to do, can you tell me what you did today?"
- Ask open ended rather than closed ended questions whenever possible. A closed ended question is one in which the informant can answer with one word or a phrase. The following are closed ended questions that are unlikely to elicit much additional information: "Did you plant tomatoes?" "Did you go to the store today?" More information can be gained by saying: "Tell me about your garden" or "Tell me about where you get your food."
- Avoid "multiple-choice" questions. The multiple-choice question is rather like a closed ended question in which the informant is given the choices. "Did you buy the red tomatoes or the yellow ones?" "Did you go to work today or stay home or go out shopping or work in the garden or . . ." The multiple-choice question often trails off at the end, and the informant may never be entirely sure when it has ended. Some informants may not offer up other alternatives to those presented by the interviewer.
- Avoid "Chinese box" questions (questions within questions). An example of a Chinese box question is: "What time did you leave the house today and where did you go? Did you go to the senior center? Did you go to the grocery store?" Chinese box questions are exception-

ally confusing to the informant. By the end of the question, neither the researcher nor the informant may remember what was asked.

- Avoid leading questions at ALL COSTS! Leading questions are questions that suppose or suggest a specific answer. The most blatant types of leading questions are easy to spot. They often have the "did you/ didn't you" phrase in them: "You went to the senior center today, didn't you?" "You don't plant a garden anymore, do you?" "You never smoked cigarettes, did you?" Some leading questions are subtler, however. We recently heard a tape of an interview of Woody Guthrie conducted by ethnomusicologist Alan Lomax. Lomax is talking with Guthrie about his childhood and asks the question: "Where did you grow up? On a farm?" Guthrie's reply is "No, we lived in the city." Many of our informants will correct us when try to lead them, but not all are as confident as interviewee Woody Guthrie.

To improve interviewing technique, there is no substitute for practicing research conversations or informal interviews under conditions in which the interaction can be recorded. While it is helpful just to review the audio recordings alone, it is even more effective to do so with an experienced colleague. It can be a painful experience, but one that is very rewarding.

TALKING ABOUT SENSITIVE SUBJECTS

In the somewhat more natural settings in which conversations and informal interviewing used as part of participant observation take place, trying to pursue a topic that is very sensitive to an informant can be problematical. What is common is that the researcher creates discomfort, either because s/he wants more detail than the informant is ready to share, or because s/he unknowingly commits a blunder with a comment or question intended only to show participation in the conversation. The quotation from Whyte's key informant cited earlier in this chapter was prompted by a question Whyte posed during a conversation with several people who were involved in organized gambling (Whyte and Whyte 1984). He casually noted that the police were probably paid off. He reports saying this only to contribute to the conversation. The man with whom he was speaking denied that any police were involved and immediately changed the subject. Apparently talking about gambling was not a problem, but bribing police was. Whyte believes that he would have lost important contacts in the community if his sponsor, Doc, had not had such a strong position in the group and been willing to direct him in appropriate behavior. Hence Doc was willing to tell him to listen rather than talk about things he knows little about.

In more structured interviewing, in which the interviewer is trying to raise the same set of questions with a number of people, the problem of pursuing sensitive topics is a common one. For example, in a variety of research projects in Mexico, Honduras, and Ecuador, we and our students have carried out basic demographic surveys in small communities. As part of determining fertility, infant mortality, and other demographic indicators, we ask women how many children they have had, whether any of their children have died, and the age at which they died. The death of a child is obviously a painful subject to discuss and we and our students have several times stumbled into very emotional situations dealing with the health and death of children. Researchers doing social research must be prepared to deal with emotion and tears.

As important as dealing with subjects that prove to be sensitive to the informant is the problem of dealing with subjects that are sensitive to the researcher. It is not uncommon for informants and participants to talk about things that are very uncomfortable for the researcher. Bourgois (1995, 1996) writes about several instances in which he was made uncomfortable or even appalled by the conversation in which he was a part in El Barrio. In one case, the men with whom he was hanging out began to talk about the way they treated a kid with a physical disability when they were in school. Bourgois, whose son suffers from cerebral palsy began to weep. His reaction certainly had an impact on the flow of the conversation after that point.

In working with medical students over a number of years, Kathleen came to realize that many "bad interviews" were very frequently a result of the sensitivities of the medical students carrying out the interviews, not the willingness of the patients to share their experiences and thoughts. In one segment of the interviewing course, students, after practicing with each other and with actors playing the role of patients, were assigned an interview with a patient in the hospital. Students were to talk with patients about the chief complaints that brought them to the hospital, and conduct a social history. Segments of the audiotaped interviews were replayed and critiqued in small groups of students. Students were asked to characterize their impressions of the interview before replaying it for their colleagues. One young woman came into class saying: "This was a terrible interview. I couldn't get her to talk about anything." Review of the tape, however, revealed that it was the student who changed the subject every time the patient tried to talk about the problem that brought her to the hospital. In this case, the woman had just had surgery for a particularly serious cancer and clearly was interested in talking about it. After Kathleen pointed out several places where the student had cut off the patient and changed the subject, the student blurted out: "Well, I don't like to talk about cancer. It scares me." (This is not an uncommon response, cancer scares a lot of people.) Kathleen suggested that the student find someone with whom she could talk about her problem of talking about cancer. "Oh, no," she said, "When I'm really a doctor I'll be able to talk about it." Unfortunately for the student, getting the degree or even the grant does not magically make it easy for researchers to talk about subjects sensitive to them. It is the researcher's responsibility to deal with his/her own sensitivities. Sometimes they crop up when we don't even expect it.

In another instance, a medical student was assigned to interview a man who had attempted suicide with a shotgun, but had survived in relatively good condition. The student came to class angry. He felt this had been a difficult interview and that he had gotten little information. In fact, this was probably not a good patient to assign, but when he was asked if he would consent to be interviewed, the man had been eager to talk to a student and to talk about his condition. In fact, his interest in talking about what brought him to this act was evident on the tape. The student, however, continually changed the topic and avoided any discussion of the suicide attempt. In the debriefing discussion, the student acknowledged that he had changed the subject. The reason was, he said, was that he had no empathy or respect for the patient. The patient was clearly a failure. He could not even kill himself successfully. Ironically, the student said he would have had more sympathy and respect for the man if he succeeded in the suicide.

As these examples show, and as we have emphasized earlier, we are continually amazed with how willing people are to share sensitive information. For example, in research on women's social power in Ecuador, Kathleen and her colleagues became interested in learning about violence against women by their male partners. This was a topic they approached gingerly because they felt that it might be difficult for the women to talk about it. In fact, it was difficult for the women, but it was also clear that it was in many ways cathartic for the women to discuss their situations. After Kathleen and her colleagues got beyond their own reticence to raise an issue we thought would be sensitive, they found that many women in rural Ecuador were very interested in talking about their experiences.

CONCLUDING AN INTERVIEW

Finally, active listening takes a good deal of concentration. It is tiring and most of us cannot sustain the heightened awareness it requires indefinitely. This is true of the people we interview as well as the person doing the interviewing. When we do use survey instruments, for example, our general rule is that anything much more than an hour is difficult for our informants to bear. With participant observation and informal interviewing, longer conversations can be usually be sustained but there does come a point at which the quality of information being obtained diminishes or the researcher is just tired, or there is so much in the researcher's head that it will never be remembered for the field notes.

It is better to know when to "switch off" the high level of attention needed in active listening, or end the conversation rather than waste time after the researcher's (or informant's) attention begins to stray. When terminating conversation or interview, it is important to let the person know how much we enjoyed talking with them and how much we appreciated their time. We should typically indicate that we hope to continue the conversation another time. Learning the proper etiquette for leave-taking, the appropriate phrases and behaviors, is among the first things that one should try to learn when working in any setting.[3]

The good participant observer should know and observe the skills connected with good interviewing. In this chapter, we have reviewed the various kinds of interviews, emphasizing that different kinds of interviews are appropriate for answering different kinds of questions. We have indicated that there are many circumstances and questions for which informal interviewing and participant observation are particularly appropriate.

Being a good interviewer requires practicing the skills of active listening and sensitive silence. Prompts and several kinds of feedback can be used to encourage the informant to elaborate on, and extend, the information they are conveying. Informal interviewing also requires good techniques for asking questions. A good interviewer will ask questions in such a way as to be nondirective concerning the answers. Asking naïve questions, clarifying questions, and simple questions in nonconfrontational ways is important in eliciting information. We have to be prepared emotionally to deal with sensitive subjects, and to know when and how to conclude an interview.

NOTES

1. The quotations used in this chapter are taken from taped interviews and conversations carried out as part of the project, Nutritional Strategies of Older Adults in Rural Kentucky.

2. In chapter 11 we discuss the ethical issues involved in personal sharing information in the research setting. We believe the researcher should be willing to share information honestly when it is asked for. It is part of being honest, developing trust and is a form of reciprocity. However, the researcher does not need to insert personal information or opinions, when they are not asked for. After all, the goal is to understand the participants' opinions.

3. Bill has occasional periods, especially during sabbatical years, when he does a lot of consulting. Although most of this is done in Latin America, the appropriate form of saying goodbye is different in different countries or different regions of countries. Saying goodbye to female friends in most Spanish-speaking countries of Latin America requires one kiss on the right cheek; in Brazil it requires a kiss on each side. In rural regions, handshakes among men are usually elaborated in different ways. Bill is typically flummoxed the first day or two until he gets his bearings about the local custom.

❦ 9 ❧

Writing Field Notes

The primary method of capturing data from participant observation and informal interviewing is by writing field notes. While researchers can audio- or videotape more formal interviews and events in order to record words and behaviors for later analysis, and record more formally the results of response to formal elicitation, time allocation, input and output of energy, and so forth, the writing of field notes is virtually the only way for the researcher to record the observation of day to day events and behavior, overheard conversations, and informal interviews that are the primary materials of participant observation. A useful maxim that we have always used in training students is that: "If you didn't write it down in your field notes, then it didn't happen" (at least so far as being data for analysis is concerned). This chapter will consider the most important aspects of efficiently and effectively writing field notes. *Observation is not data unless it is recorded; and your brain is a poor recording device.*

HISTORY

Until recently, relatively little had been written about the nature of field notes and how researchers record observations. For example, the sixth and most recent edition of *Notes and Queries on Anthropology* (Seligman 1951:66–69), a book that for many years served as the major methodological guide for doing anthropological research, devotes only 1.5 pages to a discussion of "descriptive notes" as one of four essential types of documentation. (The other three are maps, plans, and diagrams; texts; and genealogical and census data.) In the discussion, *Notes and Queries* suggested that there are three kinds of notes. Its categories, which are still relevant today, include: (1) records of events observed and information given (based on researcher interviews or conversations with participants as events take place); (2) records of prolonged activities and ceremonies (in which interview is not feasible); and (3) a set of chronological, daily notes, which the committee called a journal, but that is distinct from the personal diary that a number of ethnographers keep (e.g., Malinowski 1967). Pelto (1970) and Pelto and Pelto (1978) provided approximately two pages of discussion of field notes in each edition of their book on *Anthropological Research*. Most of this space is devoted to examples of the level of detail (high) that they see as desirable in recording field notes. Field notes, like much of the art and practice of participant observation, have been mysterious, with few models for the new practitioner (Sanjek 1990a).

A recent edited collection addresses issues about field notes in more detail (Sanjek 1990c). In this volume, Jean Jackson (1990) summarized the responses that a sample of 70 fieldworkers, mostly anthropologists, gave to a series of questions about their relationships with their field notes. One of Sanjek's own contributions to the collection (1990b) reviews the historical changes in the nature of participant observation and field notes. The reader is encouraged to refer to Sanjek's volume for the best compilation of papers regarding field notes and a number of examples of field notes. Emerson, Fretz, and Shaw (1995) provide a useful book length discussion of writing, managing, and analyzing field notes.

Malinowski is not only often credited with developing the method of participant observation, but also the closely related method of recording information in chronologically organized field notes. Before Malinowski, field notes tended to be based on detailed and orderly interviews of informants conducted and recorded topically. When the primary activity shifted from collecting texts from informants to participating in daily life, the recording of observation got messier.

Experience and the literature suggest that there are several important points about field notes and their relationship to the participant observation method. The first is that observations are not data unless they are recorded in some fashion for further analysis. Even though it seems after a few months in the field that common events and their variations will remain indelibly etched in the researcher's mind for all time, memory is unfortunately more fleeting and less trustworthy than that. We lose the detail of observations and conversation all too quickly. The admonition in *Notes and Queries* that "it is unwise to trust to memory; notes should be written as soon as possible" (Seligman 1951:45), is still relevant today.

Participant observation is an iterative process, and, as we have noted, part of what occurs is the development of a tacit understanding of meanings, events and contexts by the researcher. Sanjek (1990b) notes that pioneering researchers like Malinowski and Mead knew this. They continually read and reread field notes, searching for things they did not understand, or on which they felt they had incomplete information (what Agar, 1986, refers to as "breakdowns"), so as to direct the flow of subsequent conversations or interviews. Mead and Malinowski recorded both observations and reflections on their fieldwork experience in field notes and personal diaries. If the researcher's daily reactions to events and contexts are not recorded, it will be virtually impossible to reconstruct the development of understanding, and to be able to review the growing relationship between the researcher and study participants in a manner that allows for reflexivity at the end of the process.

> The field researcher comes to understand others' ways by becoming part of their lives and by learning to interpret and experience events much as they do. It is critical to document closely these subtle processes of learning and resocialization *as they occur*; continuing time in the field tends to dilute the insights generated by initial contact with an unknown way of life. (Emerson, Fretz, and Shaw 1995:13)

The second important point is that field notes are simultaneously data and analysis. By this, we mean that they should be the careful record of observation, conversation, and informal interview carried out on a day by day basis by the researcher. At the same time, field notes are a product, constructed by the researcher. The researcher decides what goes into the field notes, the level of detail to include, how much context to include, whether exact conversations are recorded or just summaries, etc. (Clifford 1990; Emerson et al. 1995; LeCompte and Schensul 1999). Field notes are thus the first (or perhaps second, or third) step in the process of analysis. This inherent contradiction of being both data and analysis that is embodied in field notes is part and parcel of the continuing discussions surrounding the nature of anthropological inquiry and the nature of ethnography.

We believe that few anthropologists really ever believed that their observations were unbiased, or that eliminating bias was even possible or desirable in research. However, debates over the last two decades have made this point even more salient. Field notes are at least one more step removed from objective observation than the nonobjective observation in the first place. They are a construction of the ethnographer and are part of the process of analysis. As one of Jackson's ethnographer respondents said about field notes: "Each anthropologist knows it is dialectic. The informant creates it; you create it together. There must be a tremendous sense of responsibility in it, that is, a sense of political history, one version" (Jackson 1990:14).

Clifford notes that the view of the field note as "pure inscription"—that is, pure recording—cannot be sustained (Clifford 1990). Speaking of description (thick or otherwise) he writes: "Ethnography cannot, in practice, maintain a constant descriptive relationship to cultural phenomena. It can maintain such a relationship only to what is produced in field notes" (Clifford 1990:68).

Finally, the writing of field notes brings to the fore the inherent contradiction and ethical dilemma of participant observation for many fieldworkers. Jackson notes:

> The anthropological fieldworker frequently worries about intellectual exploitation. Having material in one's head is somehow less guilt-inducing than having it on paper. Some of this may be the two-hat problem: one is in some ways a friend of the natives, yet one is also a student of them, and one cannot wear both hats simultaneously. Writing field notes can make representing the contradictions in this balancing act more difficult. (1990:18)

It is undeniable that the writing of field notes is a central activity of the method of participant observation. Learning how to effectively write and analyze field notes may differ some with different theoretical approaches, but it is always done.

KINDS OF FIELD NOTES

There are several types and formats for notes taken during fieldwork, and any number of ways of keeping notes and managing them. Researchers jot down words and phrases, even whole sentences in a notebook during the course of a day or event; they write fuller more detailed notes during more quiet time, reflecting on the day's events; they review their notes regularly and write notes on notes; they keep a diary; they keep a calendar or log of events, listing activities in which they participated, events they observed, and people with whom they spoke. They even have some "notes" in their heads that never actually get written down. All of these acts of recording sum up to the body of stuff we call field notes.

There are also several "systems" for keeping and managing field notes (Bernard 2006; Emerson et al. 1995; Mead 1969 [1930]; Sanjek 1990b), and researchers following different theoretical traditions approach and value field notes differently. All of the systems share a few basic elements (Sanjek 1990a).

Jot Notes

Jot notes (Bernard 2006; Emerson et al. 1995) or scratch notes (Sanjek 1990a) are the words, phrases, or sentences that are recorded during the course of a day's events as primarily aids to memory. Most of us record them in as small a notebook as is feasible given the accuracy of the memory of the researcher (or his or her propensity to lose small things). Those with quite good memories can rely more on single words and short phrases, and hence, use smaller notebooks (LeCompte and Schensul 1999). Our jot notebooks have gotten somewhat larger as time goes on. Kathleen used to use one that was approximately 2" x 3". She later moved to a notebook the size of a 3" x 5" note card, and now uses a stenographer's pad. Bill increasingly uses a legal pad. The jot notebook and a pen or pencil are always with the researcher. Taking good jot notes is the first step to recording the detail that enhances the accuracy and the richness of observed events and activities. Jot notes may also include sketch maps, diagrams, and logs of days' events.

In Figure 9.1, we have included sets of jot notes for two days of work in Ecuador in 1998. At first glance, they are probably unintelligible to anyone but the writer. The first set was taken while attending a community meeting and includes short phrases describing the several items on the agenda. They contain the names of the officers of the association that sponsored the meeting. They include a small sketch map of the seating of men and women in the room and a count of the times men and women spoke in the meeting (in this project we were interested in male and female decision making in households and community meetings). The notes are dated. The second set was taken during a day of touring and meeting with the officials of several agencies that were to collaborate in a series of health fairs we sponsored for the communities in which we were working. Again, they include names and one or two word notes on the key issues discussed.

How much gets jotted down depends on the quality of the memory of the researcher and the circumstances under which s/he is working. When in doubt, jot it down. All numbers that have any significance should be recorded. Lists of items of relevance (or even the seemingly irrelevant), such as those used in an activity, or for sale in the market, or seen in a kitchen, should be noted. Text or comments that the researcher will want to reproduce verbatim should be recorded verbatim in jot notes. Local names and phrases, names of participants in events, and the names of people spoken to during the course of a day should be recorded. Words, phrases, or sentences that will provide enough contexts for the researcher to recall events and discussion should be noted. All entries should be dated and, if possible, the time noted.

Keeping even a small notebook close at hand can be a challenge. Kathleen now generally travels with a "fanny pack" or backpack, or big pockets in which we can fit a notebook, pen (and the other necessities such as a roll of toilet paper, bottle of water, etc.). Phyllis Kelly, working with Mazahua women in Temascalcingo, adopted their habit of wearing an apron with big pockets for all activities, and kept her notebook in the pockets. Powdermaker used a large purse to store her notebook (Bernard 2006).

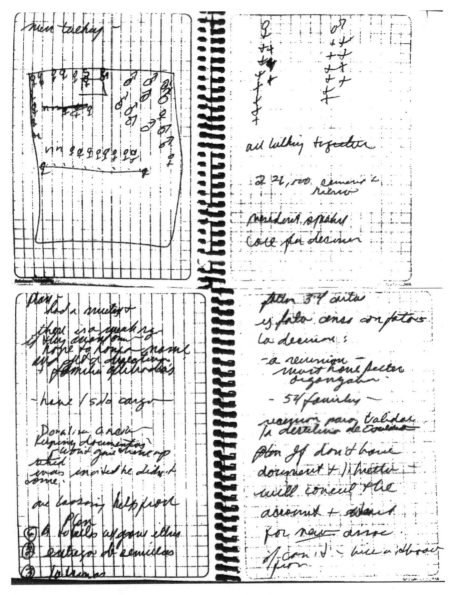

Figure 9.1: Jot notes for two days of interviewing in Ecuador, 1998.

The writing implement can be a problem. Bernard (2006) reports that William Sturtevant used stubby little pencils, which were easily concealed. We had on the job training in fieldwork technique from Bert Pelto, who, at that time, used a felt-tip pen. We have found, however, that felt-tip pens run badly when wet, and pencils are not much better. Soggy notebooks are not an uncommon event. Dentan (1970) recounts the effect on his notebook when the canoe in which he was traveling sank in a river in Malaysia. Waterproof ballpoint pens seem to work best for us but our tropical botanist daughter, who works primarily in rainforests, takes all of her field notes in moisture proof notebooks with a grease pen, not a bad idea in tropical forests.

Whether public note taking of jot notes (or longer transcriptural notes) has an impact on the flow of participant observation is a question that has been answered in a number of different ways by researchers. With respect to the impact of note taking during events, *Notes and Queries on Anthropology* suggests, "The investigator must sense the native attitude to note-taking in public. May peoples do not object to it, simply regarding it as one of the European's unaccountable habits" (Seligman 1951:45). This is still good advice.

On the other hand, the writers of *Notes and Queries* indicated that some people may become suspicious when the ethnographer takes notes, and a few people who are "otherwise friendly may never tolerate the practice." Jackson (1990) reports that a number of the ethnographers she interviewed found that taking field notes in front of participants was uncomfortable and objectifying. However, others found that participants were insulted when notes were not taken, suggesting that what they had to say was not important enough to record. Freilich (1970:193) found that pulling out a notebook in bars in Brooklyn stopped conversation. Whyte (Whyte and Whyte 1984) went to relatively great lengths to avoid taking notes in front of participants in his research in Cornerville. To gain accurate maps of interaction in a men's club, he would take trips to the bathroom or home in order to record events.

Philippe Bourgois (1995, 1996), however, openly taped both interviews and conversations as he hung out with crack dealers in El Barrio in East Harlem. Participants in his study even joked about "how the book was coming" (1995:27), an experience many of us have had with participants, who may even be anxious to see the finished work. Again, one of the strengths of using participant observation as a method is that the researcher is accepted as a participant in the setting. Taking notes will often serve to highlight the differentness of the researcher. On the other hand, our informants should know that we are also in the role of researcher and most of us have limits to our memories.

Finally, like some of the problems in interviewing concerning sensitive topics, a good deal of the success of overt note taking will depend on the discomfort of the researcher. If the researcher is very uncomfortable, then the discomfort will be transmitted to participants. Sometimes we are more uncomfortable with the process than our informants are.

In chapter 11, we discuss some of the challenges of dealing ethically with informed consent in participant observation. Occasionally taking jot notes overtly can serve as a reminder to people that research is occurring during informal interactions. The answer to the question, "How overt should I be in note taking?" is one that is relative to each research setting and each researcher. Whether jot notes are taken overtly, or are recorded out of sight of informants, they must be recorded as soon as possible (if simultaneously is not possible). When we say as soon as possible, we mean within minutes.

Some researchers are successfully able to audio or video record naturally occurring conversations and events (see Bourgois 1995). Recordings can be transcribed, or they can be summarized in field notes. Clearly, recording events and conversations provides a highly detailed set of observations. The use of recording is limited by its effect on situations. In our experience, recording can be more threatening than note taking. However, we have seen this tactic used effectively. One of our Ecuadorian colleagues always kept a tape recorder in view and running, with little impact on the fieldwork. While we always try to record semistructured and structured interviews, we find that we are sometimes uncomfortable ourselves with recording less formal interactions and activities, and we often avoid it. However, it may be our discomfort that limits our use of recorders, not the concern of the participants.

Back in the day when recording was done with rather large tape recorders the issue of conspicuousness was much greater. As tape recorders got smaller and then very small digital voice recorders with excellent built in microphones became cheaper and more available, the ability to have a small inconspicuous device recording events and conversations became more feasible. Even good MP3 players with an external microphone can be successfully used to record. Several of our colleagues record video with either "flip" cameras or conventional digital cameras set on video and then strip the audio portion off electronically for transcription (more on transcription in chapter 10). We prefer a small audio voice recorder with a built-in stereo microphone. We use an external microphone with a noise dampening feature when we are at events with background noise and want to capture conversations with a small number of people. We are always careful to request permission to record; however, we find that the participants in our research seem to feel more comfortable with the current smaller devices and the quite familiar MP3 players. They tend to forget that the recording device is there.

Expanded Notes: Field Notes Proper

Bernard (2006) identifies three different kinds of expanded field notes: descriptive (or ethnographic) notes; notes on methods; and notes that discuss issues or represent the next level of analysis (meta-notes or analytic notes). We will come back to the second two later after discussing what most anthropologists commonly think of as field notes. As Sanjek (1990a) points out, the practice of recording chronologically organized descriptive field notes was one of the innovations developed by Malinowski as he developed the participant observation approach. The descriptive, detailed chronologically organized field notes are as important to the method of participant observation as are participating and observing.

The expansion of jot notes into complete field notes is a painstaking, time consuming activity. In general, we budget at least an hour of note writing for every two hours engaged in fieldwork. In fact, the time budget is often closer to one-to-one, fieldwork to field notes. We have heard other researchers report that they spend several hours of work on field notes for every hour in the field. Because the goals in writing field notes are detail and completeness, there can be (and is) a wide variation in the dedication of a researcher in writing them. It is the detail and completeness of the record that provide the richness and texture of the written product. Aneeta Minocha (1979:213) writes:

> During my talks I scribbled key words on a small notebook. Later I wrote extensive reports of my conversations, and also recorded my explanations and interpretations as they occurred to me at the time. I also recorded the contexts in which particular conversation took place, as well as the general physical and emotional condition of the informants, their appearance and behavior, and the gestures they used. Usually it took me three to four hours to put on paper five to six hours of field work. It was because of such immediate recording of my field experiences that I was able to recreate the atmosphere in which each conversation or event took place. Even now, as I write, I can vividly feel the presence of the participants.

Minocha's comments highlight several key points concerning the recording of field notes. The first is that the translation of jot notes into field notes should take place as soon as possible after the events take place. The notes get "cold" and detail is lost the longer the interval between jotting and writing. What seemed clear with only a few key words an hour after the event or conversation is much less clear a week later.

Second, the level of detail to which the recorder should aspire is high. It should include description of the physical context, the people involved, as much of their behavior and nonverbal communication as possible, and in words that are as close as possible to the words used by the participants.

Indeed, verbatim quotes should be included to the extent to which the researcher has jotted them down or can accurately remember them. Specific
words, special language, terms, and vocabulary should be recorded.

Third, impressions, thoughts, concerns, explanations should be recorded.
With this last point, as we will discuss below, there are differing opinions
as to whether these observations and self-reflection should be recorded
along with the detail of observation, or recorded separately in a journal
or as analytic notes. Finally, we applaud that the detailed record made by
Minocha does indeed allow her to recapture "vividly" the presence of the
participants, and her description of her notes suggests that she is able to
articulate a good deal of "tacit" knowledge in written form. But we guess
that her field notes also act as prompt for memories not written down (see
"Headnotes" below). The extent to which Minocha is able to invoke that
presence for her readers is likely a combination of the detail of field notes
with the tacit understanding held in headnotes.

The quality of field notes relies on both the accuracy of the description
(of course, passing through the lens of the particular observer) and the level
of detail (Schensul et al. 1999). We have discussed the issues of accuracy
and objectivity in the recording of observations in chapter 3. To state the
main point again, the record of observations (field notes) should be as accurate, complete, detailed, and objective as possible. When the researcher
comes to understand that his/her description of events or conversations are
likely to be biased in some way, that should be noted in the field notes.
When a point is speculative that should be noted in the field notes or
placed in a separate document or file as a memo or meta-note (see below).
However, no matter how closely the description of an event or conversation
corresponds to the actual event, field notes are not the event.

Indeed, field notes are more accurately treated as a level of analysis. The
event or interactions have taken place within the presence of a specific observer, so there is an observer effect on the event. They have been observed
by a specific observer, who always brings subtle personal and theoretical
biases to bear on the observation, and they are recorded at some later time.
Even when the time difference is small, say several hours, the observer, now
recorder, has already begun to evaluate and integrate the observations into
the whole fabric of the fieldwork experience. Emerson et al. note that the
writer of field notes is creating a "version of the world" even at the point
of writing field notes (Emerson et al. 1995:66). As Jackson's (1990) respondent said: "I am a field note." Jackson further notes that the researcher
creates field notes, and, in some sense, the field notes create the researcher.
The act of attempting an accurate and objective record makes the observer
a researcher.

Field notes are better if the researcher has taken the time and introspection to anticipate the impact of personal characteristics and theoretical

approaches on the record. They may not be more accurate, but the direction of the inaccuracies can be assessed by the researcher and others. As we noted in chapter 4, all observation (in natural science, quantitative social science, and participant observation) is biased in some ways. All conclusions include interpretation and often speculation. All this said, the self-reflexive observer can produce a record that is *accurate enough*. In team research, we are often struck by how similar are the descriptions of the same event in the field notes of different researchers even though observers tend to focus on different aspects of the event.

Field notes are more accurate, and certainly richer the more detailed that they are. Schensul et al. (1999) remind the field note writer to record behaviors, "behaviorally rather than in terms of what they mean to the observer"; descriptions of people in as much detail as possible, including what they are wearing, what they are carrying, what their demeanor is like; and to record the physical environment "as if through the lens of a camera" (Schensul et al. 1999:115). It is probably impossible to have too much detail in field notes. The field note writer should record sufficient detail to bring the scene to life both in the field notes and in subsequent write-ups. Emerson et al. call this "creating scenes on the page" (Emerson et al. 1995:66–69). One of Jackson's (1990) respondents talks about the problems with notes that are not detailed enough: "I went back last year and they were crappy. I didn't have in them what I remembered, in my head, of his behavior, what he looked like" (27).

Although another respondent wrote:

> What the field is, is interesting. In Africa I [initially] wrote down everything I saw or thought, whether I understood it, thought it significant or not—300 photographs of trees full of bats. How people drove on the left side of the road. . . . Having sent [my advisor] back all that crap, he didn't say a thing. (27)

Both comments appear to be the reflections of experienced fieldworkers looking back on their first efforts. With experience, researchers do come to understand what can probably be left out of the written account. In addition, as a particular piece of fieldwork progresses, information that is well known will probably not be recorded over, and over, again. However, we would prefer the new researcher to err on the side of too much, rather than too little detail.

To give some idea of the difference between detailed and less detailed accounts, Pelto and Pelto (1978) provided a set of examples of brief and extended descriptions of events. Sanjek (1990c) reproduced several sets of field notes in his volume, *Field Notes*. Emerson et al. (1995) have a number of examples of good field notes in their volume devoted to field notes. We have included several examples of field notes from fieldwork in which we have been involved in the appendix. These examples include notes from research in Kentucky and Ecuador, and from a short-term consultancy that Bill did in Mexico. Because they are from three individuals, they give some sense of the individuality of field notes produced by different researchers as well as illustrating differences in the level of detail included. In part, the level of detail results from the distinct kinds of research projects illustrated.

Native fieldworkers (engaged in autoethnography) may have a particularly difficult time in recording a sufficient level of detail. Many events and activities that would be novel, and provide insight, are so commonplace to the native researcher that they are not recorded. While the native researcher has a depth of understanding and knowledge others may never achieve, they also bring the biases of their particular place in a well-established society and can mistake "conventional wisdom" for data. When we can get students working under these conditions to step back and observe and record with new eyes, they often develop completely new insights into the situation.

Methodological Notes

Bernard suggests keeping a set of notes that document the methods that are used in the project. Methodological notes can contain information on new ways to do things discovered by the researcher, in addition to what methods were chosen, on what basis they were chosen, how they were implemented, and what the outcome or problems with the methods were. Methodological notes can be kept with descriptive field notes, in separate files, or in the log. Methodological notes provide an important record of choices made that will be an aid in analysis and interpretation. They can also be easily transformed into the "methods section" of the report or a methodological paper. What we are calling methodological notes here are included in the notion of "audit trail," which is characteristic of the tracking of analysis in qualitative research in the health sciences. We will return to the audit trail in chapter 10.

Diaries and Journals

Journals and diaries are written documents that record the researcher's personal reactions and concerns throughout the course of fieldwork. Sanjek (1990b) and Bernard (2006) refer to the more personal account of the researcher's thoughts, concerns, and frustrations as a diary. Perhaps the most famous (or infamous) published ethnographer's diary is Malinowski's (1967). Published a number of years after Malinowski's death, translated from the Polish, and edited by his widow, A Diary in the Strict Sense of the Term provides a unique insight into the daily life of the researcher, his frustrations, his frequent illnesses, his relationships with the Trobriand Islanders, and his frank dislike of many of them. While the diary has often been cited for its discussion of Malinowski's rather limited sex life and frustration with the Trobrianders, it is most remarkable for its view of the ethnographer and his role in the village. It puts a personal face on the life of the lone researcher in a field site far from home, particularly in terms of the ways in which he coped with illness, depression, and loneliness.

Mead (1970b, 1977) kept a diary, but also wrote long letters to people at home that contained a good deal of self reflection that might be included in a diary. Her diary and letters also included materials that might be headnotes for a less prolific letter writer. Mead used her letters to others as material for understanding her own relationship to various field sites and peoples (e.g., Mead 1970b). Boas did not keep a diary, but while on Baffin Island, wrote long letters to his fiancée, even though he had no way to send them. The letters served the role of a diary.

While Malinowski's *Diary* is a valuable chronicle for understanding fieldwork, and should be read by new fieldworkers, it is not clear that Malinowski would have wanted his diary to be published. The diary or similar document is a place in which the researcher can vent frustration and record personal reactions to the field situation, successes, and failures. It probably works best if the writer intends it to be a completely personal record. One of the most important functions of the diary is provide a private outlet for the researcher. However, diaries are also part of the fieldwork record. Ottenberg (1990) notes that some of his headnotes would have ended up in a diary, if he had kept one, because at the time he did not see these reflections as a legitimate part of the "objective" field note record. However, diaries are also part of the research record and some contemporary ethnographers use the diary as tool in developing a self-reflexive account.

Now to 'fess up, we do not keep diaries in the field. While we believe that keeping a diary can be important for both personal and analytic reasons, neither of us has felt that we had the time to keep a separate diary. Some of what would ordinarily go into a diary is recorded as part of our field notes. The advent of computers has made it easier to manage written records that contain several "genres" of field recording in a single document or file. Miller, whose notes are included in section 1 of the appendix, includes diary-type materials in her field notes. Should it become necessary, the contemporary ethnographer can "sanitize" their field notes by expunging personal or other details. Although it was once common for anthropologists to deposit copies of their field notes in libraries for consultation by other researchers, this practice is unfortunately being lost.

Logs

Journals (Sanjek 1990b) or logs (Bernard 2006) are chronologically organized records that provide a calendar of events, thoughts on fieldwork, financial accounts, and other matters. Sanjek refers to the journal as providing a "key to the information in field notes and records" (1990b:108). Bernard suggests keeping the log in a large lined notebook (even if the field notes and diary are recorded electronically), devoting two facing pages to each day. On the right-hand page the researcher will keep track of where s/he goes, the events observed, people with whom s/he has spoken, meal times, weather conditions, expenditures, and so on. On the left-hand side of the double page, the researcher begins to record unanswered questions and hypotheses, and the things to do and people to interview to answer them. While Bernard appears to be committed to the paper log, the log or journal can also be kept quite easily in electronic form using one of several calendar/daybook programs that allow for extensive daily notes.

Either the diary or more likely the journal may also be the place in which the researcher records, or at least indexes, thoughts and ideas taken from reading or notes or references to other documents, such as official records and local histories. Sometimes meta-notes or methodological notes (see below) are recorded in the journal. They can then become part of the audit trail.

Meta-notes/Analytic Notes

Meta-notes or analytic notes are those notes that represent some level of inference or analysis. Some are generated during the recording of expanded notes, others are written upon further reflection on events and the notes that record them. They include comments on notes, summary of the evidence for a particular argument collected to that point, preliminary interpretations, hypotheses, and questions for further research. Fieldworkers writing field notes often find that they are already making inferences. Pelto and Pelto (1978), Schensul et al. (1999), and Emerson et al. (1995) all argue that the inclusion of even low level summarization and inference should be kept out of descriptive field notes. We agree. Summarization, inference, and new hypotheses form part of the body of analytic or meta-notes that are central to the enterprise, but sufficiently different from the more descriptive materials that should be the stuff of field notes that they should be recorded differently. As we note below, the use of computers to record field notes makes this separation easier as speculation and inference can be recorded on separate files, or put in memos attached to a field note file.

Researchers should be reading their own field notes, and commenting on them in the field (while there is still an opportunity to fill in gaps, etc.). These reflections are included in meta-notes and represent an intermediate stage in analysis. They are clearly analysis, even interpretation. But they are preliminary and incomplete, as the researcher is still in the field and still collecting information. While in some sense, field notes become fixed at the moment at which the researcher completes an entry; meta-notes can be mutable and temporary. As more information is collected, understandings and interpretations shift and change (like headnotes), and the meta-notes are expanded, amended, superseded. Meta-notes contribute to the planning of the next stages of research, and as chronicles of insights developed while in the field. Just as we forget the details of events after time, we also forget the moments of insight we have in the field. Later, meta-notes become the focus of analysis, and analytic notes and memos become critical in the development of coding schemes (Bernard and Ryan 2009; Saldaña 2009).

In olden times (precomputer) meta-notes were recorded as a separate set of notes. They might even have been incorporated in the journal. This approach is still used, even common, although the documents are now frequently separate text files. However, the availability of programs for the electronic management of textual data makes it possible to record and organize meta-notes within these programs. Most available programs allow the researcher to attach memos to documents, such as field notes and transcripts. Shorter comments and reflections on notes can be organized in memos and indexed for easy retrieval. Keeping and dating meta-notes also allows for the construction of an intellectual history of the stages of analysis and interpretation—the audit trail.

Headnotes

Finally, some materials never get written down. In some cases these are the tacit understandings and impressions that are difficult to record. (But that should be recorded if one is "setting the scene" in one's field notes.) In other cases they are just things that don't get written down. Headnotes (Ottenberg 1990; Sanjek 1990b) refer to this type of information that is "in the mind, the memories of . . . field research" (Ottenberg 1990) and not written down. All researchers have headnotes. Sometimes researchers have to rely exclusively on headnotes when writing because they have lost their written field notes. Cautionary tales of the loss of years of field notes in the Sepik River or on the voyage back home have become part of the lore used in training new researchers.

Losing one's field notes is one of the chief fears of researchers. The importance of field notes to researchers is clear in the ways in which they prioritize them. When fire threatened the village in which David Maybury-Lewis was working, he grabbed his notebooks and pencils; Pia Maybury-Lewis grabbed the camera (Maybury-Lewis 1965; Sanjek 1990e). In fieldwork in Ecuador, both of the graduate student ethnographers, living in two different hamlets, experienced a moderately strong earthquake, which shook the whole region. Each made the same decision: they grabbed the field notes and the computer (with the hard drive archives of field notes) as they ran from the houses in which they were living, leaving behind other personal goods.

For some, the fear becomes reality. Srinivas (1976) lost all of his field notes collected and processed over 18 years of work in Rampura, India in a fire in his office at Stanford University. He wrote the book *The Remembered Village* completely from headnotes. Leach (1954) lost a good deal of his notes and a manuscript as a result of enemy action in Burma. His ethnography *Political Systems of Highland Burma* was in part rewritten from memory and other materials he had gathered (Sanjek 1990e). Losing field notes is one of the great fears of researchers and many of us take precautions not to have all of the copies of notes in one place, and in these days, not have all of the electronic copies in one place either. Most of us hope never to have to rely on headnotes exclusively for our reporting of research results.

However, there is a way in which we all use headnotes. Tacit knowledge, the things we come to know without even knowing that we know them, the knowledge that is hard to put into words, often exists only as headnotes. No matter how diligent we are about writing up field notes, things we know and remember, are never really recorded. Ottenberg (1990) writes:

> As I collected my written notes, there were many more impressions, scenes, experiences than I wrote down or could possibly have recorded. . . . But the notes are also in my head. I remember many things, and some I include when I write even though I cannot find them in my field notes. (144)

Ottenberg also points out an interesting relationship between headnotes and written field notes. While we may reassess the meaning of field notes over time, as our experience grows and our theoretical perspective matures, the notes themselves remain unchanging. Headnotes, however, change and mature with us. Ottenberg describes his view of the Afiqpo, developed in the field, as based on democracy and much less devious than his wife's view of them. With time and experience with university politics, he came to see the Afiqpo as less democratic, and more manipulative. He notes that as his theoretical views matured, so did his headnotes (and his reading of his field notes to some extent) concerning the Afiqpo.

> the words in my written notes stay the same . . . the notes have not changed. But my interpretations of them have as my headnotes have altered. My headnotes and my field notes are in constant dialogue, and in this sense the field experience does not stop. Things that I once read in my field notes in one way, I now read in another. Evidence that I thought was excellent, I now question. I don't believe that I am more objective now than then, only that my interpretations are more accurate. (146)

Ottenberg notes that some of the impressions (headnotes) that he did not record in written form could have been recorded in a diary or personal journal. He reports that he was dedicated at the time, however, to "objectivity" in his field notes, which he interpreted as keeping himself out of the fieldwork record, and he did not keep a diary or journal. Even if the researcher keeps a journal, or incorporates journal-type entries in field notes (see below), there are still understandings that are hard to put into words, but form part of the equipment with which we interpret our recorded "data." It is also important to point out that Ottenberg does not indicate that he is repudiating his "data," but he interprets them differently, in a sense reanalyzing them over time.

Understanding that reinterpretation and reanalysis can and will take place over time suggests that an even greater attention should be paid to the capture of detailed field notes that will stand up to those activities. As one of Jackson's (1990) respondents wrote:

> Are memories field notes? I use them that way, even though they aren't the same kind of evidence. It took awhile for me to be able to rely on my memory. But I *had* to, since the idea of what I was doing had changed, and I had memories but no notes. I had to say, "Well, I saw that happen." I am a field note. (21)

In the sample field notes contained in the appendix, section 1, we have included a description of a party that was attended by one of the project ethnographers, Loren Miller, who worked with Kathleen in Manabí, Ecuador. In her description, Miller includes so much detail and describes her own reactions—material that could be included in a diary—that she captures part of the spirit and essence that often does not get recorded, but exists only in headnotes. We think that while headnotes will always be the only way some information exists before write-up, attention to recording rich field notes and keeping a diary can capture some of the feeling of the tacit knowledge that is so hard to verbalize.

FIELD NOTES IN VIRTUAL RESEARCH

Research in virtual or online settings has the distinct advantage that much of the text generated through interaction is recorded electronically and archived. This is true whether the research is in a virtual world setting (Boellstorff 2010; Guimaraes 2005) or is based on participating in and observing online chat groups, list serves, and blogs (Constable 2003; Hine 2000; Kozinets 2010). In some sense "nothing escapes the panoptic gaze" (Stone 1995:243) of the computer. This is a terrible temptation to let the technology do the recording. However, online researchers argue strongly that online participant observers need to write field notes in much the same way in which face-to-face researchers do. For Kozinets (2010), the role of field notes as a first level of analysis, and especially field notes that capture the researcher's description of her role and response to the field site, is critical in the process of online ethnography, or "netnography" in his terms. He reminds the online researcher that the researcher IS a participant observer and is making decisions and interacting in the research setting in ways that are not fundamentally different than in face-to-face research. Since he acknowledges that much of the text of interaction is capture, Kozinets focuses on the need to keep reflexive notes that explore the interaction from the point of view of the observer. Other researchers (e.g., Boellstorff 2010; Constable 2003; Hine 2000) discuss their approaches to recording field notes in virtual research in very similar terms to the ways in which face-to-face researchers do.

HOW TO RECORD

First, we cannot overemphasize the need to budget enough time to record sufficiently detailed field notes. Participating in the community on a 24/7 basis will do the researcher little good if there is no time to record observations, keep a diary, and reflect and write on what is being observed. The researcher needs a place to which s/he can retreat to write. It is better to have a place with sufficient light at night (since field note writing is often an end-of-the-day activity). Researchers in the contemporary world still sometimes conduct research in settings in which electricity is not available. Here the recording of field notes may be virtually indistinguishable from the conditions Margaret Mead encountered in New Guinea or Malinowski found in the Trobriands. One of our students working on an atoll in Melanesia, for example, spent the last year without access to electricity. However, if possible, it is preferable if the researcher can find accommodations with access to electricity both for adequate light in the evenings and for the use of the now ubiquitous personal computer.[1]

In our very first field experience in Temascalcingo, Mexico in 1970, personal computers were still the stuff of science fiction (even Captain James Tiberius Kirk didn't have a *personal* computer). In fact, we didn't even have a portable manual typewriter. Our field notes were hand written in notebooks in the fashion used for the first century of professional anthropological fieldwork. By our second field trip in 1973, we owned a portable manual typewriter and typed our field notes on Indecks brand cards—cards about the size and consistency of 5" x 8" note cards, or a half sheet of standard typing paper, with two rows of holes punched around the perimeter. We made two rather poor carbon copies on half sheets of plain typing paper behind the cards (so that they could be stored in different places). We diligently used these cards in Mexico as well as in research we did in southern Honduras in the early 1980s. The cards were "coded" by punching out the holes such that when a "knitting needle" was inserted into a particular hole in a stack of cards, and shaken, the "coded" cards would fall to the floor. You could search for two codes simultaneously by using two knitting needles.

By the 1980s, in research in Mexico and Ecuador, we could get access to computers in the field, either using the newly available "luggable" computers, or renting computers in-country. In addition, it was possible to find accommodations with electricity. We happily shifted to the electronic capture of field notes. However, the coding of notes was not much different, except that we could use the searching features of the available word processing programs to assist in locating text and codes. Much of the coding, however, was still done on the hard copies of notes. By the time we were involved in fieldwork in Kentucky in the late 1980s, the first-generation Ethnograph program was available and the process of coding and retrieval of data became electronically based for us. Over the last decade, the number of programs for assisting with the coding and retrieval of textual data has burgeoned. We find that the ease of management of textual data through the use of computer programs is so compelling that we recommend the computerization of all kinds of field notes.

Even if the researcher eschews the more sophisticated programs, even using the features available on most word processors is better than punching holes in cards. Kathleen uses the NVivo program for coding field notes. A number of our colleagues have switched to the program ATLAS.ti. As we noted above, some of our colleagues work in research settings in which the use of electronic capture of field notes is not feasible. When good quality typed notes can be produced, the notes can be scanned into a computer file. When the only option is handwritten notes, we strongly suggest that the researcher budget time or money for the transcription of notes either during the fieldwork or upon return.

As suggested earlier, computer-assisted management of field notes has one large drawback. One of the most important activities in the analysis of field notes and transcripts is reading and rereading the materials. To the extent that computerization allows the researcher to bypass frequent rereading of notes, it can limit the process of analysis. Because it has become easy to retrieve materials without rereading, this does not mean that the researcher can get away without doing it.

We are often asked about audio recording (dictating) field notes. Our advice is that this is fine way to capture a good deal of detail in a short period of time. It takes much less time, initially, to describe events verbally than to do so in written form. There are times driving or walking to and from places when notes can be dictated. However, we have found that dictating field notes only works effectively if the researcher has someone to transcribe the recordings. Material stored in audio files is hard to access effectively. While the files can be marked and coded electronically, and the marks recorded in a program such as NVivo or ATLAS.ti, recorded field notes are most easily used if they have been transcribed. There is a great temptation to assign the transcription of material on tape a low priority (after all, it is already recorded and won't go away like your memory will).[2] We find that voice recognition software is still not quite good enough to eliminate a lot of editing of the text files it produces, but the technology is improving rapidly. We anticipate that in the near future audio recording will be good enough and voice recognition software powerful enough to turn voice into text with little loss of time in editing, when the resources for electronic capture of data (electricity) are available.

In the study of older adults in Kentucky in which Kathleen participated, however, there were a number of hours of driving between sites and between Lexington and the study communities. Furthermore, we had sufficient grant support for transcription. In this case, we often dictated field notes while driving. We have also used the taping of a running description of a community or an area while walking or driving as an aid to memory in the writing up of field notes. In this case, our goal is not to transcribe a tape, but to use the taped comments to create a summary of the material in field notes.

Using a computer to capture field notes has one further advantage we should mention. It is very easy to either keep several files open at the same time, or to enter a stream of material that covers several genres (e.g., diary, field notes, meta-notes, methodological notes) and separate them out into distinct documents later. In the days of typewriters, there was much more of a barrier to shifting gears in the middle of a recording session. Even with jotting notes as reminders of what should go into the other document we believe that many ideas were forgotten, at least temporarily.

A final note on field notes: participant observation can be a very stressful experience (i.e., culture shock). It is sometimes comforting and helpful in assuaging guilt on those days when we just need to be out of the scene to say to ourselves: "Well today I MUST stay in and catch up on my field notes." And, as it is almost always true, it is the perfect excuse. However, do note that it is for just this reason that Agar (1996) is critical of time spent in recording field notes, time that he sees as more profitably spent in interviewing.

RESEARCH INTEGRITY: WHO OWNS THE FIELD NOTES

One of the consequences of keeping written field notes as compared with headnotes is that they can be accessed by others. Some researchers, who recorded relatively few written notes, appear to regret that their data will die with them (Jackson 1990). Some researchers provide for the curation or management of their notes after their deaths. Others appear to want these data to remain out the hands of others. However, it is possible for field notes to forcibly leave the control of the researcher. They can be subpoenaed, for example, and it does not appear that any existing laws protecting confidentiality apply to the researcher-informant relationship. In some cases in which agencies or other organizations contract for research the contracting organization may claim ownership of all data including field notes.

Recent approaches to research integrity have made the format and availability of field notes a more problematic issue than in the past. For those of us in academic settings it now appears that for many American universities, all data collected while affiliated with the institution, including field notes, are deemed to be the property of the institution. The University of Pittsburgh policies are not different from many other university policies. The policy states that all "recorded data" (including "notebooks, printouts, computer disks, slides, negatives, films, scans images, autoradiograms, electrophysical recordings, gels, blots, spectra . . . ") are property of the university, and can be made available for review by other researchers if the researcher is accused of research misconduct. The University of Pittsburgh requires that all data be archived for a minimum of five years, and that all data be available to the university. In the event that a researcher leaves the university, the university still owns the data generated by researcher carried out while the researcher was at the university. While the researcher can take the data, the university retains right of access. While the rules surrounding challenges to research integrity were developed with the quantitative data of the lab sciences, epidemiology, clinical trials, psychology, and survey research in mind, it appears that they can be applied to all phases of field notes (jot notes, field notes, logs, maps, etc.) as well. In addition, the policy appears to apply to students as well as faculty researchers.

While we have not heard of any instance in which a university has exercised its right to access to field notes, researchers should be aware that it is possible and know the research integrity policies of their institutions. Appropriate steps should be taken to protect the anonymity of informants. It is in part for this reason that we suggest that researchers with data captured electronically change the names of individuals, or assign them numerical codes, create a single identification key at some point in the analysis process, and then destroy materials that have the original names included.

This chapter has focused on the various methods of recording data from informal interviews and participant observation. Generically, these can be labeled as field notes, although we reviewed a number of different kinds of notes. The critical point to emphasize is that field notes are essential to qualitative, ethnographic research. As we indicated in the introduction, if we don't record observations, conversations, events, and impressions in our field notes, then it is difficult to document that these actually occurred. Field notes are simultaneously both data and analysis. In this chapter, we have focused on recording of field notes as data. The chapter that follows focuses on the next steps in the analysis of field notes.

NOTES

1. It is also becoming economically and practically feasible to use solar power for computers in the field.

2. We still have a few audiotaped notes from 1973 hanging around that were never transcribed. They resurface, un-analyzed, in the same Pampers box, every time we move. They represent data that were never fully incorporated into our writing.

✜10✜

Analyzing Field Notes

The goal of all data analysis is the summarization of large quantities of data into understandable information from which well-supported and well-argued conclusions are drawn. In other words, this is a process of reviewing, summarizing, cross-checking, looking for patterns, and drawing conclusions (Bernard and Ryan 2009; LeCompte and Schensul 1999; Wolcott 1994). LeCompte and Schensul (1999) agree with Michael Patton (1987) that

> analysis does three things:
>   It brings order to the piles of data [in this case, field notes] that an ethnographer has accumulated.
>   It turns big piles of data into smaller piles of crunched or summarized data.
>   It permits the ethnographer to discover patterns and themes in the data to link with other patterns and themes. (LeCompte and Schensul 1999:3)

Like much of the rest of the activities related to participant observation, the analysis of field notes is an iterative process. The fundamental techniques are reading, thinking, and writing; and rereading, rethinking, and rewriting. Frankly, there is no substitute for reading and rereading field notes and transcripts, each time with a particular question in mind. Despite several recent, quite good discussions of coding qualitative data (e.g., Bernard and Ryan 2009; Saldaña 2009), of all of the somewhat mystical activities associated with the method of participant observation, analysis of data is the most mysterious. In this case we think it is for good reason. While one aspect of analysis is the logical, sometimes tedious, building of descriptions and arguments by reviewing and organizing materials into categories and themes, some of the connections between observations and the insights that form part of the process of analysis take place subconsciously. What we experience is a "hunch," an "aha!" or "eureka!" moment, an insight into connections among various events. In a flash, things make sense, or, in a flash, what we thought seemed straightforward just yesterday becomes crooked and we see a new configuration. One of the important points we wish to make in this chapter is that behind the flashes of insight is the careful categorization, organization, summarization, and review of materials. Once an insight surfaces, it should be treated like a hypothesis with a return to the data in order to build the clear and logical argument to support it, often with recategorization, organization, and review.

PROCESS OF DATA ANALYSIS

The process[1] of analysis of qualitative data, including field notes, interview transcripts, and documents is not fundamentally different from the analysis of data from surveys, experiments, and formal elicitation, although the specific techniques used may be different. Experiencing flashes of insight, developing hunches, leaping to conclusions, and amassing documentation to support the argument characterize all scholarly research endeavors. The goal of analysis is to develop a well-supported argument that adds to the understanding of a phenomenon, whether the understanding is phrased in descriptive, interpretive, or explanatory terms. Survey researchers capture data on questionnaire forms or interview schedules; code data using categories created by the researcher; enter the data into computerized data bases; decide what questions will be asked of the data, and what ways of asking those questions (statistics) are most appropriate to the objectives of the research and the data; ask the computer to perform the calculations; examine the results and interpret them; and build an argument and body of evidence to support their conclusions. There are three sets of activities taking place in this process (Miles and Huberman 1994a): *data reduction* (focus on specific questions, coding, preliminary analysis into scales and indices); *data display* (tables and statistical tests); and *interpretation and verification* (getting hunches, leaping to conclusions, building the argument). The same activities of analysis apply equally to both quantitative and qualitative data, including field notes. However, the specific techniques applied may be somewhat different.

MANAGING QUALITATIVE DATA

Although new researchers often fear they will not get "enough data" for their study, the real problem with the management of textual data in field notes, transcripts, and documents is that it can quickly mount up to phenomenal levels. It is truly amazing to the new researcher how quickly the piles of text can get away from you. It is not hard to amass literally thousands of pages of field notes and interview transcripts. The wise researcher develops a strategy for dealing with these documents before beginning collection. The use of computers to record and organize data has made the management of data much easier.

As we noted above, we suggest that even researchers who have to record notes by hand should arrange to transcribe materials into electronic files. There are a number of programs available for computer-assisted qualitative data analysis (CAQDAS, pronounced "cactus"). The program that the researcher chooses should reflect his/her theoretical orientation, the kinds of data that s/he has, the degree to which s/he intends to use "memo-ing" features for tracking intermediate stages of analysis, and the degree of flexibility in indexing, coding, and moving text from different types of files s/he wishes to have. Several reviews of the features of programs are available (e.g., Lewins and Silver 2007). The extremely useful website of the Computer Assisted Qualitative Data Analysis Networking Project (caqdas.soc. surrey.ac.uk/) summarizes information from Lewins and Silver and several other sources and compares common software programs (CAQDAS 2010). The CAQDAS Networking Project site also reviews several program for working with audio and visual files. The program that a researcher chooses may also be influenced by cost and availability. All of the commonly used programs we know of have advantages and limitations. Several allow free trials of the software for limited periods of time. Check out which ones will work for your style. Whatever program or approach to data management you choose, keep in mind that the programs help you organize data. They do not "analyze" the data. Your brain does that (through reading, coding, writing, rereading, recoding, rewriting, and developing insights).

DATA REDUCTION

As we noted above, Miles and Huberman (1994a, 1994b) suggest that all data analysis includes three fundamental activities: data reduction, data display, and interpretation and verification. Further, all three activities are iterative. The analyst is constantly moving among the three activities during analysis. In some cases it continues after publication as new insights surface for the researcher.

Data reduction refers to "the process of selecting, focusing, simplifying, abstracting, and transforming the data that appear in written-up field notes" (Miles and Huberman 1994a:10). In some sense the process of data reduction begins long before data collection begins, even before fieldwork begins. The theoretical approach taken by the researcher influences the kinds of phenomena that are deemed important to the enterprise. The researcher focuses on a particular set of issues and places others in a lower priority. The process of choosing a specific question to study, in a particular place, developing a conceptual framework, using a particular design, limits the data that will be collected. Choices made about what events to observe, what activities in which to participate, and with whom to speak limit the amount and content of data that will be collected and is part of the process of data reduction.

It is for this reason that a carefully thought out and justified research design is essential to a good project. Analysis is not only planned for before data collection begins, the analysis itself has already begun by the time data collection begins. The development of a formal research proposal both allows the researcher to construct a coherent approach to a particular problem making explicit the particular theoretical and design choices and allows others to judge the extent to which the decisions made by the researcher before the project has begun are feasible, justified, and likely to move the field of scholarship forward. (Now, it is true that in ethnographic fieldwork the issues to be examined are often fairly broadly defined, and in the real world of community based ethnographic research the research questions change in the field. However, the universe of possible data to be collected is always limited by the time the researcher leaves for the field.)

Once in the field, the researcher continues to make decisions about who, what, when, and where to observe and participate. Phenomena not originally included in the design may be added. In the process of participant observation especially, researchers discover new angles to the research question and design in the field. Some phenomena identified beforehand may turn out to be impossible to include, or just not very interesting. While this process is also true of all other forms of research, it is explicitly built into the method of participant observation. These kinds of decisions and how the researcher arrived at them should be recorded in methodological notes as the research progresses.

Data reduction also takes place during the act of recording field notes. The observer reduces the observed phenomena to a finite number of pages of field notes. Even at the highest level of detail, it is not possible to capture the actual event on paper. Furthermore, consciously or unconsciously the researcher makes a series of decisions about what to report and how to report it. The researcher consciously or unconsciously includes some aspects of phenomena, and reports these aspects in a particular way. For this reason, we believe it is important for the researchers to be conscious of the fact that they are reducing data at the point of writing field notes and reflexive about their approach to the data.[2] As we noted in the previous chapter, we treat field notes both as a product of the researcher and as data. The self-reflexive researcher has some notion of what his/her particular biases and emphases in recording will be.

Once field notes (as well as other textual data) are recorded, the process of analysis becomes more formal. Thousands of pages of text must again be reduced to manageable descriptions of patterns of activities, ideas, and behavior, the exploration of meaning interpreted, and written up. There are two approaches to reducing the data in field notes with the production of a well-supported written summary argument in mind—indexing and coding.

We use the term *indexing* to refer to the use of "etic" or *a priori* categories drawn from the initial theoretical framework and applied to the text in order to aid in the retrieval of material for further analysis. What we mean by indexing is very close to the use of "descriptive codes" discussed by Miles and Huberman (1994a). We use the term *coding* to refer to the development of categories that emerge from the data (emic) as a result of reviewing the data for inherent concepts and patterns. Some writers refer to these as themes (see Bernard and Ryan 2009). Miles and Huberman's notion of "pattern" codes is also similar. In coding, the researcher is often attempting to identify themes that emerge directly from the observations and conversations captured in field notes. At the point at which categories and codes are developed, the researcher is reducing data to ideas and concepts and looking for patterns. While indexing is a step in data reduction, it is an activity that draws on *a priori* and design issues established early in the development of a project even if they are modified as the project continues. It is responsive to the initial theoretical approach that guides the fieldwork.

For us, "coding" is more closely tied to the development of new theoretical propositions, understanding of meanings, or patterns and ideas that emerge in the process of data analysis. In part it is a process of abstracting and interpreting ideas contained in the data themselves. It is closer to the notions contained in the grounded theory approach (Glaser and Strauss 1967; Strauss and Corbin 1990, 1998). While we believe that these are two distinct intellectual activities, we do not want to draw too strong a line between them. In practice both indexing and coding take place simultaneously and in similar ways as the researcher is reviewing field notes. Finally, researchers may also want to establish index entries for the *characteristics* of the people, places, and event included in field notes. Bernard and Ryan call these *structural codes* (2009). Indexing for characteristics allows for the retrieval of text associated with different categories and codes sorting by characteristics such as gender, age, and occupation.

Both indexing and coding are, in essence, the attaching of names or labels on pieces of text describing events and incidents, parts of conversations, words, sentences, or phrases recorded in field notes (Strauss and Corbin 1990, 1998). The labels refer to a more abstract concept, or a hypothesized pattern for which the piece of text is an example. Attaching labels draws us into the next level of conceptual abstraction and summarization. It also physically organizes materials that can be marshaled to support arguments in the interpretation and writing phases.

Approaches to Indexing

Traditional ethnographic field notes, aimed at a description of a particular "culture," "society," or community, are often indexed following the categories included in the *Outline of Cultural Materials* (OCM)—a set of categories developed to index ethnographic accounts for the Human Relations Area Files (Human Relations Area Files Inc. 2000, 2010). They are available online (www.yale.edu/hraf/) with operational definitions of the codes and direct references to coded text in ethnographies. When we were beginning fieldwork in Temascalcingo, Mexico, we started with the categories of the OCM, which we further refined with subcategories to fit the particular setting in which we were working. The OCM provides coding for the categories of social life that have traditionally been included in ethnographic description: history, demography, agriculture, exchange, material culture, housing, marriage, kinship, sickness, death, sexuality, religion, etc. It represents a set of etic categories developed to allow for comparisons among descriptions of diverse cultural systems. The OCM is a good starting point for the parts of field notes that deal with descriptions of cultural systems. When the ethnographer anticipates writing a description of family structure, marriage rules, and so forth, using the *Outline* can be effective. However, while the OCM can be presented as an atheoretical list of categories, no list of categories is atheoretical. The OCM reflects a particular approach to description that emphasizes a view of cultures as composed of a number of identifiable subsystems that can be compared one with the other. It assumes that there are universally applicable categories (etic) that can make such comparison feasible. While we don't think this is a particular problem for organizing materials for most holistic descriptive studies, the researcher should be aware of the inherent bias in the materials. As less of the work of qualitative researchers and even ethnographers is conceived of as broadly descriptive of whole cultures, the types of categories of interest for indexing field notes have become more specialized and focused on the particular problem at hand, and the OCM less applicable for many researchers. Bernard and Ryan (2009) discuss several different approaches to coding, with examples from research coming from several different theoretical perspectives.

Under any circumstance, one of the first activities of indexing and coding textual data such as field notes is to establish a *codebook*. Codebooks are documents that become part of the analytical record and the audit trail. They include the codes (labels) that are assigned to the categories and ideas for which the text is coded, the conceptual definitions of the codes, and the operational definitions of the codes. By conceptual definition we mean just that. What is the underlying concept that is being identified? It can be a social institution (marriage), an activity (cooking), an idea (*machismo*), or anything else. But the conceptual definition should be as clear as the researcher can make it. The operational definition refers to the specific situation under which the label will be attached to a section of text. What characteristics of text will result in the attachment of the code? Sometimes this is pretty straightforward. In other cases, especially as themes emerge from the data, both the conceptual definition and the operational definitions for codes shift over time, and the researcher may have to revisit codes and text several times as the codebook is built and rebuilt over time. Most of the CAQDAS programs allow for the evolution of codebooks through the use of memos and a log of the revisions of both conceptual and operational definitions. These also become part of the audit trail.

In our study of the nutritional strategies of older adults in rural Kentucky, part of our interest at the outset of the project was to describe the particular pathways that older adults used to procure food, and the resources they needed to use particular pathways. Our interests then were much narrower and in greater depth. Our preliminary indexing system included categories for the venue in which the observations or activities took place; pathways of food procurement (we called them nutritional strategies); food preservation; food consumption; food preferences; preparation of specific foods, etc. Part of the codebook used to index the field notes and interview transcripts is reproduced in figure 10.1. There are several points that we would like to illustrate with this list.

The listing is hierarchically arranged. While not all indexing and coding schemes are hierarchical, creating hierarchies where they seemed appropriate, here, was part of our further organizing, conceptualizing, summarizing, and, in the end, analyzing these data. We were continually looking to see where new information fit, both in the set of hierarchies and in our conceptual framework.

We started with a preliminary list drawn from our general knowledge of food acquisition in rural Kentucky, some came from our theoretical notions regarding the strategic nature of food getting and consumption, the existence of alternate pathways and how to access them; some came from existing literature on the rural South; and some from our previous experience in Kentucky. However, in the course of the project we identified a number of types of crops, gardening techniques, food preservation techniques, and programs that we had not known about. The list of categories grew as we progressed, and we occasionally had to go back and review previously indexed materials and reindex them. We also moved items around the categories when it seemed to us that they fit better under another heading. (How did we know they "fit better" in one place as compared with the other? This

Figure 10.1. Selected indexing codes from the study of nutritional strategies of older adults in two Kentucky counties.

1. Venues in which the observation or activity took place
    1.1   Senior center
    1.2   Senior picnic
    1.3   Informant's office
    1.4   Informant's home
    1.5   Store
    1.6   Church supper
    1.7   Homemakers club meeting
    1.8   Restaurant

2. Nutritional Strategies
    2.1   Food production
            2.1.1   food crop   information on field crops grown at least in part for food, such as corn, wheat, cornfield beans, orchards
            2.1.2   garden   information on garden crops such as sweet corn, fresh vegetables, tomatoes, beans, cabbage, greens, etc.
            2.1.3   milk   information on milk and other dairy products especially for home consumption
            2.1.4   eggs   egg production especially for home consumption; information on laying hens
            2.1.5   livestock   production and slaughter of all animals
            2.1.6   huntfish   information on hunting and fishing for food
            2.1.7   gathering   information on gathering wild plant materials for food or medicinal purposes
    2.2   Food purchasing
            2.2.1   fpwhere   information on where food is purchased including what is purchased
            2.2.2   smallstore   information on shopping in small neighborhood country stores
            2.2.3   supermkt   information on shopping in supermarkets in the county or outside of the county
            2.2.4   delivery   information on the delivery of groceries
            2.2.5   restaurant   information on food taken in restaurants, or on restaurants in the county

    2.3   Food gifts   information on food obtained as gifts or sharing with friends and relatives

    2.4   Food programs
            2.4.1   seniormeals   meals at the senior center
            2.4.2   foodstamp   information on the availability and use of the food stamp program by older adults
            2.4.3   commodity   information on the availability and use of foods from the food commodity program
            2.4.4   otherpgrms   information on other programs that relate to food distribution

2.5	Food preservation		
	2.5.1	canning	information on and observation of canning and jarring foods
	2.5.2	drying	information on and observation of drying foods (meat, beans, apples, etc.)
	1.5.3	curing	information on and observation of curing foods with salt or sugar, including making sauerkraut
	1.5.4	smoking	information on and observation of smoking foods, usually pork
	1.5.5	sorghum	information on and observation of making sorghum molasses
	1.5.6	sulphur	information on and observation of sulphuring apples
	1.5.7	porkpresrv	information on and observation of preserving pork products
	1.5.8	freezing	freezing foods
	1.5.9	rootceller	information on and observation of making root cellars and keeping food in them
	1.5.10	holing	information on and observation of "holing" foods, that is, putting food in holes in the field in order to keep them over the winter
	1.5.11	storepit	information on and observation of the construction and use of pits for keeping potatoes and other foods
	1.5.12	meatstore	information on and observation of the storage of meats
	1.5.13	miscstore	information on and observation of other methods of storage, including storage on the cellar floor, in the attic, in the barn, etc.
2.6	Food-related equipment		
	1.6.1	stoveoven	availability and use of stoves or ovens
	1.6.2	microwave	availability or use of microwave ovens
	1.6.3	refridge	availability and use of refrigerator
	1.6.4	freezer	availability and use of freezer
	1.6.5	presscanner	availability and use of pressure canner

Food Ideology

2.7	beliefs	information on beliefs about food
2.8	healthyfood	information on what foods are considered healthy and the relationships between food and health
2.9	preference	information on food preferences and preferred foods
2.10	fknowledge	information on knowledge about food and where it is acquired
2.11	statusfood	foods associated with particular statuses (e.g., low class; white trash; country foods)
3. County Information		
3.1	employment	employment in the county; jobs, industries, etc.
3.2	agriculture	agriculture in the county

(Continued)

Figure 10.1. Selected indexing codes from the study of nutritional strategies of older adults in two Kentucky counties. (*Continued*)

3.3	mining	mining in the county
3.4	transportation	transportation available in the county
3.5	churches	churches and religions in the county
3.6	restaurants	restaurants used by county residents
3.7	extension	Agricultural Extension Service
3.8	homemakers	Homemakers Clubs

4. Health Issues
    4.1   doctors
    4.2   hospitals
    4.3   medicines

was part of our insight from listening and reviewing the data.) We eliminated some categories as we found they did not fit or were not important.

Even if they were added after the initial round of indexing, the categories we used were drawn from our original conceptual framework and were conceived of as mainly descriptive of the various pathways and experiences around them. In other words, we were still in indexing mode here, not yet identifying themes and developing codes for them.

Even though the categories were pretty straightforward and inherently meaningful to us at the time we developed them, we wrote brief conceptual definitions of the codes. Each code is, in fact, a label (Bernard and Ryan 2009; Miles and Huberman 1994a) for an idea or concept that characterizes a number of pieces of text that have something (meaning) in common. Part of the process of analysis is making those concepts explicit and developing a set of rules for applying them to pieces of text. Many times, as in our example here, the conceptual and operational definitions are fairly obvious and easily understood. However, even when they are not particularly conceptually complex, several years later they may not be as immediately comprehensible as they had been at the outset. Even if it seems pretty obvious at the time, it is wise to write operational and conceptual definitions of categories and codes. Again, this is part of the summarizing and conceptualizing of the materials—that is, analysis. Computer assisted coding makes this a good deal easier. Definitions are stored with the codes and retrieved at any point.

We used words or phrases as labels. In part, this is a logistical device; it is easier to remember the meaning of a real word name than it is to remember what a number means. Also, it is part of the analysis. Naming the categories makes us articulate the commonalties and patterns that tie words, phrases, and sentences together and ties them more clearly into the original conceptual framework, and keeps us thinking about connections and abstractions.

Finally, making the initial list and then expanding it (and contracting it, in some places, where we saw new connections) as we continued through the project formed an important part of the analysis. We fleshed out and concretized our conceptual framework. We recategorized ideas and topics. We adjusted our ideas about the salience of particular activities and pathways as we gained a better understanding of how people managed food resources. Managing the list itself was a conceptually based analytic activity. Once the researcher begins to develop a set of categories for indexing text, it is quite easy to develop literally hundreds of them.

Coding for Themes

In addition to the *a priori* categories in which we were interested as a result of our particular theoretical approach and the design of the project, we were also looking for understandings and interpretations that arose from the materials as a result of the interaction of the ideas and concerns of the participants (older adults in rural settings) and the researchers.[3] As we talked with people and read and reread our materials, several sets of patterned responses that seemed to capture the concerns of the participants emerged. These represented both values that seemed to influence the lives of participants and the participants' characterizations of how their lives were organized and influenced. Identifying these themes and coding the materials for them is another type of data analysis. This is not *a priori* in the sense that, even though we expect themes and patterns of thought and concern to emerge, we usually don't know what they will be like. It is in this type of looking for patterns and developing codes that we discover the mechanisms as viewed by the participants. It is part of what Strauss and others (Glaser and Strauss 1967; Strauss and Corbin 1990, 1998) refer to as the development of grounded theory. It is the source of new hypotheses and a better understanding of the phenomenon from the point of view of the participants.

Coding for themes takes place iteratively as well. The analyst reads and rereads notes and interview transcripts on the lookout for recurring ideas and patterns of concepts. Gradually (or quickly in a "eureka" moment), the analyst begins to abstract a number of ideas and words contained in text into a single concept or a small set of related concepts (they might reflect the participants' view of internal relationships for example). In practice, the words of a particular informant or the description of a particular event provides an idea about at set of ideas. It is tentatively named and the analyst then goes back to the data to see if it can be applied to other individuals and events. This becomes a "theme," an idea that characterizes and ties together materials from different people or people in different settings. A label is created and pieces of text that appear to reflect that idea are coded and reviewed, and rereviewed. The ability to attach memos (meta-notes) to text, including codes allows for easy retrieval of materials on the evolution of codes. It becomes part of the audit trail, but is also part of the analysis itself.

The theme of "a woman has to feed her family" came initially from an interview with Mrs. L, a woman who was describing how throughout her life she was in charge of the cows and chickens and managed her garden in order to be able to feed her family. She negotiated with her husband to grind some of the corn he grew in the fields into meal for the kitchen. She described how she sold eggs and butter and used the money to buy sugar, flour, and other goods that were not produced on the farm. Then she talked of how her husband had the responsibility to produce tobacco and corn to pay the mortgage and buy clothes. It was her responsibility to provide the food. We had been thinking of the farm as an enterprise in which the farmer (read "man") took the primary responsibility for production and the "farm wife" maintained the household, cared for children, and provided some labor on the farm. After reviewing materials collected from Mrs. L, we returned to our notes and transcripts looking for other instances in which women were responsible for providing food, as well as preserving it and cooking it.

The development of codes follows a path of organization, abstraction, review, and frequently, further abstraction and organization (Bernard and Ryan 2009; Saldaña 2009; Strauss and Corbin 1990, 1998). A series of pieces of text are reduced to a few central concepts. However, the richness of the original text is not lost either. The central goal of coding is to make it easier to return to the original text in ways appropriate for building an argument and presenting it to others in as rich a form as possible to do efficiently and effectively. This may seem like the mysterious part, and in part it is. It is the analyst's mind and nothing else that makes the connections and sees the patterns. However, it is the reviewing and comparing of materials and writing explicit definitions that make it work. There is nothing mysterious about reading, and thinking, and making meta-notes.

The process of creating the code name is also part of the analysis. A code name can reflect what the analyst sees as the central concept. One frequently sees code names that come directly from the words of participants—*in vivo* codes (Glaser 1978; Strauss 1987; Strauss and Corbin 1990, 1998). Kathleen (K. M. DeWalt 1977) used the term "the illnesses no longer understand" to refer to an idea expressed by a number of informants that the illnesses that afflicted people had changed such that they no longer "understood" traditional herbal remedies, but now only responded to biomedical drugs. For Bourgois (1995), the concept of "respect" and the search for respect became the organizing theme of his ethnographic study of crack dealers in New York. In our study of nutrition of older adults another common theme was the value placed on self-reliance, which we coded as "We have to make it on our own." Figure 10.2 has codes for several of the themes we identified in this project.

Figure 10.2. Themes emerging from the study of nutritional strategies of older adults in two Kentucky counties.

T1 A woman has to feed her family	Statements and materials pertaining to the role of the woman as the food provider for the family. Includes the idea that it is the woman's job to provide food for her family through direct food production or using "butter and egg money" to buy staples.
T2 We have to make it on our own	Statements and materials pertaining to the value placed on self-sufficiency, people should produce their own food, home produced food is better.
T3 The younger generation doesn't know how to make it on their own	Statements and materials about the concern expressed that the "younger generation" has lost the skills to make it on their own. Less self-sufficient.
T4 Men are helpless	Statements and materials pertaining to the notion that men, especially widowers, can't take care of themselves. That men are not supposed to be able to cook or garden.
T5 Lard is fattening, Crisco is not	Statements and materials expressing the notion that margarine and vegetable shortening are less "fattening" than lard and butter. Also includes the ways in which people have changed their diet as a result of this belief.
T6 "I don't hardly eat what I used to"	Comments on changes in appetite with aging. Belief that appetite has declined.
T7 "Hardly worth cooking for myself"	Comments that cooking for oneself alone is not worth the effort.

In the development of codes for themes, writing and documenting the operational and conceptual definitions for codes is even more critical for analysis. It is the definition that contains the essence of the meaning of the theme; it is a critical part of the analysis.

When is the development and application of indices and coding over? Probably never. As Ottenberg (1990) has observed, ideas and concepts related to a particular piece of fieldwork continue to develop even after publication of the materials takes place. However, at some point, either the time runs out (the paper is due, the publisher's deadline has arrived) or more properly the analyst comes to see that s/he is experiencing "diminishing returns"—not many new ideas are coming to the fore—and the analyst starts to write. The bulk of coding is probably over (for the moment). Typically, though, we find that we continue to go back to text and "code" during the writing process. Again, as we will note again later, all of these activities are iterative and the analysis that can only take place as the researcher writes the argument sometimes requires a return to the data, even recoding materials.

Finally, again, the goal of data reduction is to take a large amount of textual data: written summaries of observations and conversations, and identify and describe patterns of activities, behavior and ideas; and describe the range of variation in these phenomena. The identification and application of codes and indices are one of the ways in which we organize data in order to find patterns, identify diversity, and develop descriptions.

Coding for Characteristics

If the analyst is using a computer-assisted approach to indexing and coding, it is easy, and a good idea, to code field notes for the characteristics of the venue, the people involved in the activity (age, gender, status, etc.), the type of activity (e.g., conversation, interview, observation, participation), and any other characteristics that will make it easier to sort materials later. Bernard and Ryan call this "structural coding" (Bernard and Ryan 2009:76). It is extremely easy to do with computerized qualitative data analysis programs. Because in the study of older adults we had some initial hypotheses regarding gender differences, differences between people who lived in town as compared with the unincorporated areas of the counties, and between people from different counties, we also coded field notes for the characteristics of people and areas where that was possible and appropriate. In this particular project there were three ethnographers, and, as we were using computer assisted coding (primitive as it was in 1990), we also coded whole field note entries for the ethnographer who wrote them, and the county in which she was working. This allowed us to sort text retrieved from the notes by ethnographer, county, and so forth, to aid in data display and to allow us to compare across venue and person.

Managing Coding and Indexing

The physical act of coding and indexing can be carried out in a number of ways. In the days of handwritten or typed notes, categories and codes were noted in the margins of notes. Researchers often made several carbon copies of field notes. The pages of notes could either be kept in chronological order and shuffled through each time the analyst was looking for a code or s/he could make multiple copies and file them by codes. If a page of notes had several codes, it would end up copied into several folders. Alternatively, the analyst could cut up pages into pieces of text and file them that way. With multiple copies of notes, cross-coded text could be placed in different folders for major codes and categories for retrieval. Here, keeping a log of the notes and the codes assigned for a particular set of notes made retrieval more efficient. One of the variations in this procedure was the one we employed in our early fieldwork. Using cards with holes in the perimeter allowed us to code and retrieve text with specific codes (mainly based on the *Outline of Cultural Materials*) a bit more easily than shifting through pages of field notes. In our earlier work, the advent of Indecks cards allowed for limited cross coding and retrieval by punching out holes in the margins of cards and using needles to hold back the pages that did not contain data with a certain code.

Now most researchers code and retrieve data using one of the CAQDAS programs noted above. In the current versions of these programs, indexing and coding take place on the screen by blocking chunks of text and attaching categories and codes to them. The analyst can attach codes and create new ones simultaneously. Pieces of text are automatically retrieved when the analyst uses the program to search on the codes and categories. We have been longtime users of NUD*IST, and now NVivo. Figure 10.3 contains output of the NVivo coding of a section of text from the field notes found in the appendix.

Word Searches

CAQDAS programs also allow for searches for particular words or phrases. This has several advantages for the field note writer and analyst. First of all, when writing field notes the writer can imbed words or phrases in the notes to assist in word searches. Alternatively, the analyst can search on particular words and phrases that are likely to be near text with information of interest. In the study of older adults, we were able to speed up some parts of indexing by searching on the names of particular foods and on the word "garden." In research in Ecuador we used the term "machismo" enough that we can identify most of the text that refers to the concept as it is understood by *Manabas* in our field notes. Carrying out word searches can be a useful, quick, but not foolproof, first step to indexing and coding. We recommend word searches only for analysts who know their text well. First of all, unless the field note writer is careful when writing notes to use words that can serve as objects of searches, a word search may not yield all of the appropriate pieces of text. For example, it was easy to search on "green beans" and "canning" to find references to putting up green beans, but not possible to know what to search for to look for the idea that women are the food providers in rural Kentucky. Perhaps, more importantly, there

We walked about 8 min and finally got to a place which was so overgrown that we couldn't pass. We had by then given up, and we re standing around chatting, making jokes, saying we needed to come back with machetes. I took a photo of Rosa. Then Rosa said she didn't want to go back there, bcz 'the y'd rape us.' I asked who, we re there crazy people back in the forest? She said no but women alone in the forest -- "peligroso" (dangerous). I said the three of us together, no one will rape us. I'll hit them with my camera. We were all laughing and Juana said, you know we were raped. 'Uno nos ha violada.' I didn't quite get what she was talking about, and she kept repeating it, saying, 'we've been raped.' Finally Rosa whooped, 'con gusto.' Juana was talking about their husbands. We had a 15 or so min. talk about sex in marriage. How young Rosa had been when she married, 15, didn't know anything about sex. Freaked out when she saw her husband without clothes. But she kept saying that she liked sex. But Juana said that sometimes a woman doesn't have 'el deseo.' And she has to have sex anyway (with her husband). Because if she doesn't, 'he will go off and find someone else.' Juana finally said how the first time that 'yo fui con Juan,' [I was with Juan] it was really quick and she 'wasn't ready. Hadn't had any time to build up desire. It really hurt.' She had known about sex bcz she and her friends talked about what it was like, that sometimes it hurt sometimes it was fun. Rosa said that in the beginning she was horrified, what was that 'fea cosa'. Juana said that Juan has learned a lot that she and he have really come to understandings. Now when she doesn't want to 'have relaciones,' he waits until she does. She says that if he ever wanted to go to another woman she would say, 'Go. And don't come back.' She doesn't need any other man; she's already had experience with one. Broke n him in. Got him to understand her a little. She doesn't want to have to go through it again. It could be worse with someone different. You've no idea what you might get.

Rosa kept insinuating that she liked sex. Juana less so. Juana got Juan to be more considerate of her she said when she started to 'cuidarse' (take care of herself: use birth control) with what I think she explained as the rhythm method. She gave me a fairly detailed explanation of when were safe and unsafe times to have sex. She said that she got pregnant several times using this method, bcz there were times when Juan said, Oh I don't care. He wasn't at all as cautious or thoughtful as she regarding the number of children they might have. She said sometimes he just didn't want to wear a condom at dangerous times or her didn't want to wait. But she said that he has learned patience. She won't ever let him take advantage of her she said. She's had too much experience. I asked them what does a woman do if she wants to have sex and her man doesn't? Does she force him or go out looking for someone new too? They laugh. Rosa says no, no. Juana says she wouldn't go for another man bcz adultery is a sin. Isn't it a sin when a man does it, I ask? Well, they say. 'El hombre hace lo que desea.' The man gets to do what he wants. But with Juana and Juan, Juana tells me, they have arrived at a point where they respect each other and won't go with anyone else.

The light is so pretty where Rosa sits and I tell her I want to take her photo. Just as I am about to click it she opens her legs wide in a wildly raucous gesture and screams with laughter. She and Juana think its hysterical and they both want to take photos of ourselves in somewhat comprising positions. I snap Juana's photo while she is laughing hysterically. They laugh even harder at that. As if there is something risqué about her laughing uncontrollably, letting loose perhaps. Then they scream, and you and you. Juana takes the camera and I show her how to do it and as I go to crouch down at the hillside and gather the bottom of my dress together, she snaps

Figure 10.3: NVivo coding of a section of text.

is a strong temptation to use word searches rather than read field notes and examine text in its original context. Again, the REAL analysis takes place as the analyst reads through materials in context in a thoughtful and questioning way. Pulling out 33 chunks of text that contain the word "bean" is not a substitute for examining and reexamining the text in context.

To be clear, what the CAQDAS programs do is ensure that the researcher makes the categories and codes explicit, assist in the management of codebooks and indexing systems, and streamline the retrieval of text. The programs do not find patterns, provide insights, or "build theory." These are the activities of analysis that take place in the mind of the researcher.

it. With who knows what exposed. The ye rupt in peels of laughter and I am laughing too bcz I am a little amazed at these 'reserved' women whooping it up deep in the forest where no one will find us.

We talked about man/woman relationships more generally. Juana says that she really works at open communication with her husband and her children. She always tells them she wants them to tell her if they are in love with someone. And if she can help in any way, or give advice, she will.

Juana tells us that Clara Espinoza, from Guayaquil, married to a man turned Evangelist, has just finally separated from him. She took a job in a factory and lives with some siblings. She has visiting rights to her son every weekend. The breakup was amable enough, and the door is open if she wants to return. And convert from Catholicism. Juana says that Clara is thinking about going to Quito. She doesn't want to stay in Guayaquil. Rosa can't believe that Clara left her man, Juana only just found out from Lydia yesterday. I don't know how the Espinoza's feel about it. I wonder aloud how Clara feels about leaving another of her children. Juana says that when Clara had Marisol with Paulo the couple had lived together 6 mos. But it didn't work out. Then Clara moved with baby Marisol to Quito, where she worked as a maid in a home. Marisol burned herself badly and it was difficult for Clara to take care of her there. Marisol went back home to live with her grandparents in La Colonia. Paulo never really recognized Marisol as his child - I think her surname is Espinoza.

Marisol knows he is her birth father but they don't have any kind of special relationship. She just considers him like 'any other guy in the street.' When Clara married the current/separated husband, and wanted to take Marisol with her to Guayaquil, her own parents wouldn't let her. 'They had grown accustomed to raising Marisol.' They wouldn't give her up and Marisol calls them, her grandparents, mom and dad.

As we walked out of the planta, I tried to get Rosa to talk a little bit more about her relationship with her husband. She told me that when she was young and newly married, she new nothing about anything, sex or otherwise. She knew how to cook and iron. She never spoke with her own kids about sex. But she and Juana said that they always talked amongst themselves, in groups of women, about any kind of sexual thing. And now Rosa said her kids and she are more open. I asked Rosa what she considers her husband, ie is he a friend, her best friend. She said claro that he is an amigo, but a particular kind bcz he lives in my house. I said, oh. 'El es un particular.' We all laughed and she said no, not a particular because he is the only one who shares my bed. So I asked, more like a socia, and she agreed.

We passed two little girls up in a tree and Juana called out to them, 'pajaros!' and said to me, 'why don't you take a photo of these precious little birds.' One of them didn't want her photo taken and Juana kept coaxing her to look at the camera with stories of witches and bigger birds. Juana was acting so freely. It was really something.

Figure 10.3: NVivo coding of a section of text. (Continued)

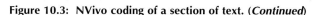

CAQDAS programs are not unlike the programs for the statistical analysis of data that perform the calculations for the tests designed by the researcher and provide summaries for data display. Even in statistical analysis using packaged programs, the researcher decides what data will be used, designs the coding scheme, codes data, chooses the specific tests to be used on the basis of theoretical and conceptual decisions made early in the project, reviews the data displays, and draws conclusions and interprets the data.

A final note on indexing and coding of participant observation materials: because of the nature of field notes, as summaries of the experiences in which the researcher has engaged during a particular day, indexing is probably going to be more important than coding in the analysis of field notes. Coding is a more common activity when the researcher is working with interview transcripts and other documents. Coding and indexing can (and should be) fun. Perhaps not as much fun as doing the participating and observing in the first place, but the process of reviewing and abstracting is intellectually rewarding. Developing and applying categories and codes is not an aid to analysis, it is analysis. It is the principal tool we use to build theories and arguments drawn from our data.

DATA DISPLAY

The second kind of activity involved in analysis is the display of data. Organizing and presenting data visually in an effective format allows the analyst to review a large amount of data efficiently, make comparisons, summarize patterns, draw conclusions, and present an effective argument. It is also the way in which the data supporting arguments will be presented to a wider audience in written reports and publications. The researcher could review all the field notes in chronological order, anytime s/he wants to write an argument and include all of the field notes (or transcripts, etc.) as appendices to the written product, but this is not very efficient or effective. There are a number of more efficient and effective ways to display data from field notes for further analysis and presentation. In general, the researcher uses direct quotations from notes or transcripts, development of vignettes or cases drawn from the data, tables, matrices, or flow charts to aid in organizing materials and developing conclusions.

Quotes

When coded textual materials are retrieved, either as slips of paper (ouch!) or as text on a computer screen, they are quotations. Pieces of material from field notes are quotations from the text created by the researcher or, when the researcher has captured conversations verbatim, the words of participants and informants. When the analyst retrieves text associated with particular codes, the first display the analyst looks at is a series of quotes, all of which have been assigned to the same categories and code(s). Sometimes this is as far as data display will go. Depending on the amount of material, the researcher may be able to see patterns and draw conclusions from organized pieces of text. The materials are summarized in written form and the researcher may reproduce a series of representative quotations to illustrate a summary concept or conclusion. Using quotations is more effective if they are drawn from the words of participants. Hamilton (1998) has very effectively used the quotes of informants in her work in highland Ecuador. She writes that:

> In my attempt to identify relevant behavior and discover its meanings . . .
> I found that the most reliable information often emerged from sustained

observation and from thematic conversational currents that reappear throughout the course of personal relationships. Rather than abstract this information, I have attempted to place readers literally on the scene to experience concretely, as I did, the interplay of cooperation and conflict within marital partnerships; the balance of power between women and men in household, kin group, and community; the valuation of women in these groups; and the perpetual constructing of valuation from material and ideational bases. In framing narrative passages that are relevant to gender-and-development policy issues, I have allowed a great deal of space for my informants to express themselves and for the unfolding of daily life. (Hamilton 1998:32)

She quotes extensively from her informants, but puts these into a context that explores the issues in which she was interested. Philippe Bourgois (1995) also uses extensive quotations from informants very effectively to support his arguments.

Quoting passages of field notes in publications is rarely seen, unless the notes include verbatim quotations from informants. Field notes, as we have noted, are themselves already several levels of analysis removed from the events. Just writing them up as descriptive passages is usually sufficient. Quoting one's own unpublished writing is not particularly effective.

Vignettes and Cases

A less direct, more abstracted way of presenting data is to develop vignettes or cases drawn from descriptions found in field notes. In the case of using vignettes or cases in analysis and presentation, the analyst builds a description of an event, activity, or person drawing the description directly from field notes (or other materials if other methods are also used). For example, sample 1 in the appendix contains a description of a dance. There are several descriptions of events in these notes that could be used as vignettes illustrating the relationships between men and women in the community. In sample 2, the description of a meal served at Mrs. L's house could be reproduced as a vignette in an ethnography.

Researchers frequently use descriptions of individuals and households drawn from a variety of materials to summarize common features and illustrate variation within communities. When coupled with survey data, cases or vignettes can be selected to flesh out or illustrate the variation found in quantitative data. Vignettes or cases are built by reviewing all of the material regarding a particular event, activity, or individual, listing it in a table, and then writing a summary description.

Studies of legal systems frequently include detailed descriptions of cases as their outcomes drawn from observation and documentation. Bailey's classic study of political activity and change in a region of India uses cases to build much of the argument. He reported that "whenever possible I have tried to present a case or a dispute, and to use it as a text, to comment upon it, and from the commentary to extract regularity and structure" (Bailey 1960:15). From Bailey's perspective, the advantage of this method is that "it allows the reader some kind of check on these abstractions, not by the test of internal consistency only, but also by relating the analysis to what goes on" (1960:15).

Bourgois (1995) builds his argument principally on the basis of case studies of individuals, vignettes, and quotations drawn from transcripts of audiotaped interactions (both informal and more structured interviews). In describing how young people are pulled in drug dealing, he draws on several years of observation of a young man he calls Junior:

> Candy's son Junior was the first boy I watched graduate into crack dealer status. When I first asked him at age thirteen what he wanted to be when he grew up, he answered that he wanted to have "cars, girls, and gold chains—but no drugs; a big roll [of money], and rings on all my fingers." In one of those conversations Junior even dreamed out loud of wanting to be a "cop."
>
> As the years progressed, Junior became increasingly involved in Game Room activities. Literally, before he knew it, he became a bona fide drug courier. He thought of it as simply "running errands." Junior was more than eager to be helpful, and Primo would send him to pick up ten-dollar packets of powder cocaine from around the corner, or to fetch cans of beer from the bodega two doors down. . . . Before his sixteenth birthday he was filling in for Caesar as a lookout. . . . Soon Ray promoted him to working . . . as a permanent lookout on weekends. . . . Although Junior had dropped out of school, by this time . . . he was a strict teetotaler. . . . By the time I left New York, Junior had begun dabbling in substance abuse, primarily smoking marijuana. (265–67)

Bourgois's description of Junior's progression into drug dealing provides a rich template for understanding the process for many young men and women in El Barrio. He is then able to contrast Junior's case with several others that share similarities and show some differences, to illustrate both the commonalties and the variations in the process.

Tables and Matrices

Tables and matrices are developed from the descriptions in field notes arranged into cells and categories. For example, in the study of older adults we were interested in differences between men and women. We were able to summarize our observations of men and women by creating a table with columns for men and women, with the rows representing various categories, such as attitudes and work associate with gardening, food preservation, and transportation.

In work that Bill and others have done, they essentially constructed a series of categories relating to development among indigenous people in Latin America. From accounts of other researchers' experiences with these development projects, counts were made of those characteristics of projects that made them successful or unsuccessful (Roper, Frechione, and DeWalt 1997). In this case, the "field notes" being analyzed were actual published descriptions.

CAQDAS programs can generate summaries of codes and indices and the connection among them, including what codes occur together and how often. When the researcher includes characteristic (structural) codes, the occurrence of themes can easily be cross-tabulated by the characteristics of the venue, time, community, and the individuals with whom the researcher has spoken. Coding summaries are very helpful in the generation of hypotheses.

Charts

For activities and events, a time sequence flow chart that presents the tasks involved in a particular activity can be constructed. In our study of women's cassava processing cooperatives in Ecuador, we know that men and women's associations processed cassava into different products that required differing amounts of labor. We also knew that men and women had different goals for their associations. Men said that they wanted a market for their cassava and women wanted opportunities for wage labor. The differences between the kinds of activities carried out by men and women in cassava processing became very clear when we mapped what we had learned of the two processes into a flow chart, which can be found in Figure 10.4 (Poats and DeWalt 1999).

Time flow charts are also useful ways of presenting local histories and life histories. Reviewing our own notes over ten years and listening to women talk about their view of the history of the association we were able to develop a chart of the history of the association (Figure 10.5). Reviewing this chart, we would like to make several points:

- Each of the "phase names" is actually a code for a theme that was abstracted from our notes and conversations and seems to characterize the phase of development with which it is associated.
- The events listed under each phase are abstracted from a large amount of material on the activities taking place at each time period. Materials were drawn from observational field notes over a decade, but also from association documents and oral history accounts collected from members and consultants. We coded text for time and activity, and organized the material by retrieving text associated with them.

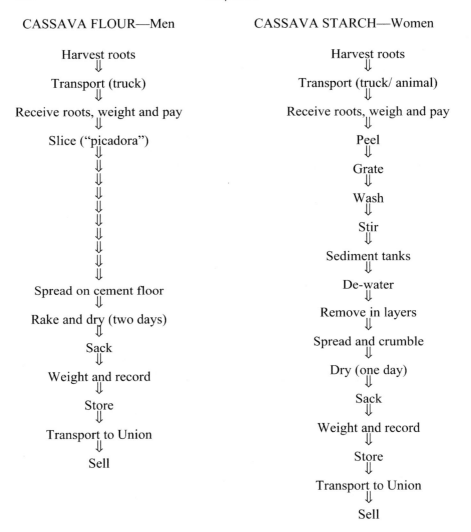

Figure 10.4: Comparison of processing steps for preparation of cassava flour and cassava starch.

- The flow chart provides a visual representation of the process for a reader. However, more importantly, the process of abstracting the materials into a chart helped us to see connections between different kinds of data, come to grips with contradictory materials, and place the materials in an overall analytical framework. The act of building the chart was part of the analysis.

Figure 10.5. Phases of development of the San Vicente Women's Cassava Processing Association.

Phase I: Organizing the Group

- Started with banana flour—small scale supported by Ministry of Agriculture
- External motivation by other women's groups and donors
- Membership: 45 women w/ little experience
- Members were older women, single mothers, daughters
- Organizationally was successful
- Economically was a failure—no market, credit, or income

Phase II: Joining the Cassava Union

- Half of members drop out
- Cassava union accepts women's petition to join
- Members make decision to process starch—requires adaptation of family-based production to a micro-enterprise
- Production was profitable
- Had difficulty in interactions with "socios" (men) in Union and technical team
- Had perfunctory participation as recipients, not decision-makers

Phase III: Disenchantment

- New industrial starch market volume up, quality down
- Union shifts away from consumption market to industrial
- Decrease in income/profits for women
- Men's associations begin to process starch and flour
- Women participate in identifying possible solutions to problem

Phase IV: The Pilot Plant

- Women received funding to develop a "pilot plant" for technified cassava starch production
- Objective: increase scale while maintaining quality (value per unit) and absorbing labor
- Members take on role of researchers in collaboration with local university students and faculty
- Year of learning—low profit but high interaction with Union leaders and outsiders
- Learning experience concentrated in leaders

Phase V: Scaling Up

- Starch demand increases
- Union economic difficulties
- External technical assistance ends
- Indonesia dumps cassava pellets in Columbia and destroys Ecuador market
- Women seek their own technical assistance and win prize and funds to invest
- Leadership changes—some of the long-term early leaders are replaced

Phase VI: Going It Alone

- Direct marketing independent of Union
- New projects and participants
- Re-shaping the Union

Decision Modeling

Creating formal models of decision-making processes abstracted from field notes and transcripts represents a specific use of the flow chart approach (Bernard 2006; Bernard and Ryan 2009; Gladwin 1989; Miles and Huberman 1994a; Werner and Schoepfle 1987b). In decision modeling, events are organized by the choices that must be made and the conditions that appear to affect those choices.

Young (1980), for example, drew on field notes and formal elicitation to construct a diagram of the factors he viewed as affecting the particular choices residents of the community of Pitacuaro made as they sought to alleviate illness. In developing an understanding of how decisions are made, constructing the model from observation, interview, and formal elicitation is usually only the first step. Initial decision-making models are better seen as hypotheses that need to be tested using data collected from a representative sample of informants engaged in really making the decisions. After developing the model, Young observed all of the health decisions for a sample of households over the course of several months to see if the case studies observed fit the model.

Figure 10.6 presents a combination of case study and decision flow chart. In a study of the factors that affect the ways in which mothers of young children make decisions about what foods to serve, carried out in a rural county in Kentucky, we interviewed a sample of mothers. Figure 10.6 is a decision flow chart drawn from an interview with a single family. In chart form, it depicts the factors that appear to influence this mother. From the chart, we see that her concerns include trying to meet the food preferences of her husband and children, concerns with the healthfulness of their diet, and concerns over the cost of food and maintaining a budget. This particular chart can be compared with causal flow charts drawn from other families. It is a causal flow chart drawn from a single case.

INTERPRETATION AND VERIFICATION

The third process in analysis of data is interpretation and verification. It refers to the development of ideas about how things are patterned, how they fit together, what they mean, and what causes them (description, interpretation, explanation), and then returning to the data to verify that those ideas are valid, given the data available. Drawing conclusions and attempting to verify them takes place at every stage of the research process. It begins when research begins. Early in the research process the researcher begins to have ideas (hunches) about how things fit together, what is important, what things mean. In participant observation, by its nature iterative, hunches become hypotheses for verification and even further investigation while

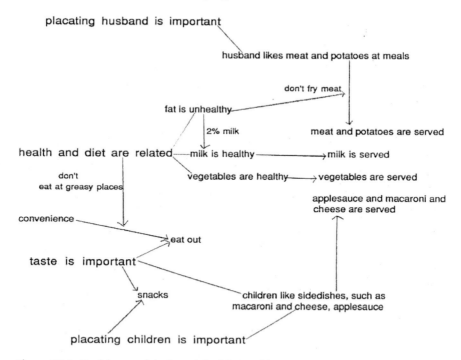

placating husband is important

husband likes meat and potatoes at meals

don't fry meat

fat is unhealthy

2% milk

meat and potatoes are served

health and diet are related——milk is healthy————→milk is served

don't
eat at greasy places

vegetables are healthy————→vegetables are served

convenience

applesauce and macaroni and
cheese are served

eat out

taste is important

snacks

children like sidedishes, such as
macaroni and cheese, applesauce

placating children is important

Figure 10.6: Decision model of meal decision making.

the researcher is still in the field. Researchers change research questions and design throughout the project in response to ideas and hunches developed. Developing new categories and codes for coding and indexing field notes is part of the process and also begins early, as new ideas and concepts surface, become clearer and can be supported by observation and texts.

Every new hunch or leap must be treated like a hypothesis. As ideas about meaning, cause, connection, and patterns develop/emerge, they are treated with skepticism (Miles and Huberman 1994a). They are also treated reflexively, with the analyst examining his/her ideas, not only against the materials s/he has collected and recorded, but also against his/her possible bias in both data collection and interpretation. While still in the field, this may be a prod to look for outlying cases that do not fit as neatly with the preliminary conclusions, or to expand the range of informants outside of the researcher's initial circle.

Where do hunches come from? Early in the research process, they come from theory. Most of us begin with research questions and hypotheses drawn from theory and previous research. Later, they come from the research experience and then from reading and rereading notes and

transcripts. Researchers begin to see (or think they see) patterns and connections early in the research process and they continue to look for these
patterns throughout the research process.

Hunches also come from the process of the constant validity check, or
in Agar's (1986) term, "breakdowns." In talking about breakdowns, Agar
is referring to those experiences in which the participant observer suddenly realizes that something is not what s/he expected. They are different
from the expectations that the researcher brings from his/her own cultural
background, or they are different from the model of the context that the
researcher has been developing. A bit like a paradigm shift in the Kuhnian
sense (Kuhn 1962), the breakdown experience requires the development
of a new view of the phenomenon. "Expectations are not met; something
does not make sense; one's assumption of perfect coherence is violated"
(Agar 1986:20).

In Agar's approach, the process of developing ideas and testing them
against experience is a process of developing interpretive or explanatory
schema, experiencing breakdowns and seeking new resolutions which result in the development of new schema. One of the dilemmas he and others
note is that when a resolution is reached, the issue tends to be relegated to
the "solved" pile, and our consciousness moves on to another issue.

As fieldwork progresses the ethnographer becomes less reflective about
earlier encounters. The informants may also become less informative because they assume the ethnographer knows more. To continue the process
of revising the conceptual landscape, every researcher has to continue to
try to see the world with new eyes. In part, this is accomplished by continually going back to questions and trying to fit in new information, and
again, looking for people and activities that are likely to challenge the
conclusions.

Researchers like Mead routinely reviewed their field notes and other
materials in the field looking for outstanding questions, inconsistencies,
and breakdowns. We believe that there is no reason NOT to begin to code
and index materials while in the midst of field research. The process of
developing and assigning codes and categories is also part of the process of
developing preliminary conclusions.

There are a number of caveats, however. As we noted above, it is common to lay aside a conclusion once it is developed and go on to newer ideas
without continually reexamining the first one. However, continual reexamination is an essential component of checking one's conclusions against the
real world data. First conclusions, often reached early, can be hard to throw
away in the face of new and contradictory data. Bernard (1995) cautions:

> Early in fieldwork, eagerness and observer expectations can lead to seeing
> patterns that aren't there. If you are highly self-critical, then as fieldwork

progresses your tendency to see patterns everywhere will diminish. But the problem can also get worse as research progresses if you accept uncritically the folk analyses of articulate and prestigious informants. (361)

He goes on to suggest a strategy he calls the "constant validity check," which relies on continually moving back and forth between emic and etic thinking, critically examining the researcher's conclusions in light of local understandings and local understanding in light of the overall data. It includes five elements:

1. Watching for disagreements among knowledgeable informants;
2. Checking informant accuracy whenever possible by checking against more objective data (logs, texts, records) and other informants' narratives;
3. Welcoming evidence that does not fit the pattern or the hypothesis in order to assess intracultural variation, identify "holes" in the data, and ultimately reformulate hypotheses;
4. Continuing to look for alternate explanations for observations, especially ones that seem to contradict "common wisdom"; and
5. Trying to fit negative cases into theory and hypotheses by reexamining and reformulating theory. (This usually requires reexamining the data to "test" the new hypotheses.)

During data collection, it implies that the researcher is continually looking for materials that challenge as well as support preliminary hypotheses and early conclusions. After data collection has ended, it means carefully considering all of the collected materials and building an argument that accounts for the greatest part of them. It also implies the continual reflexive examination of the researcher's original ideas, probable biases, and the limitations placed on comprehensive data collection by the characteristics of the researcher.

AUDIT TRAILS

The concept of the audit trail has become popular in writing about the analysis of qualitative data in several disciplines, especially in educational and health related research. It apparently entered the literature on qualitative research methods through the writing of Guba and Lincoln (Cutcliffe and McKenna 2004). They were concerned about the issue of "confirmability" in qualitative research. Their concern included a desire to reduce the amount of observer/researcher bias in research. In order to assess confirmability and the extent of observer bias they argued that a third party should be able to examine the data and the ways in which it was analyzed in order to:

> ascertain whether the findings are grounded in the data—a matter easily determined if appropriate audit trail linkages have been established . . . reach a judgment about whether inferences based on the data are logical, looking carefully at analytical techniques used, appropriateness of category labels, quality of interpretations . . . the auditor will wish to make an assessment of the degree and incidence of inquirer bias. (Lincoln and Guba 1985:323)

An audit trail is a detailed description of the research design, data, codes, coding strategies, changes in codes, and application of codes to text, which would allow a third party to make an assessment. The Robert Wood Johnson Foundation (2010) has been promoting the development of audit trails for qualitative research in health. They define an audit trail as "a transparent description of the research steps taken from the start of a research project to the development and reporting of findings. These are records that are kept regarding what was done in an investigation." Audit trails are roadmaps to all of the decisions made in collecting and coding textual materials.

The inclusion of an audit trail has become standard practice in proposals for qualitative research in health disciplines. In part we believe it is the result of a need to assure confirmability to review panel members in funding agencies who are unfamiliar with evaluating research that proposes qualitative research methods. Cutcliffe and McKenna (2004) suggest that the adoption of audit trails in nursing research may have come from a kind of "physics envy" in nursing. Just as nursing research began to come into its own, it also began to incorporate more qualitative research methods. "In the middle of this paradigmatic struggle, some qualitative researchers sought to convince their quantitatively oriented peers of the value of qualitative methods" (Cutcliffe and McKenna 2004:129). They argue that rather than trying to eliminate bias from research, which we have argued is impossible, that researchers should acknowledge their biases. Cutcliffe and McKenna conclude that the use of audit trails, especially by expert qualitative researchers, may be an "exaggeration of the case for method" (126) in nursing research.

We actually take a middle ground here. We agree with Cutcliffe and McKenna that the detailed audit trail called for by the Robert Wood Johnson Foundation and others is an overformalization of a process and method that contains many tacit subjective elements. We know that all research is biased, and attempting to establish a highly formalized approach to documenting analysis seems to us to deflect attention from the very nature of qualitative research as an approach that relies on intersubjectivity for its strengths. However, several of the steps in data analysis that we and other researchers recommend do regularize the way in which we, as qualitative researchers, approach our data. We strongly recommend formal analysis of textual materials, including the development of codes and codebooks with conceptual and operational definitions, which are updated regularly. We recommend the tracking of updating. We recommend the keeping of meta-notes, whether this is done in a type of field note file or using the memo feature of the programs for the analysis of qualitative data that document ideas, hypotheses, changes in coding procedures, etc. All of these are elements of audit trails. We also see the usefulness of record keeping when more than one researcher and/or coder is working with data.

In the analysis of qualitative data, the development of an audit trail is sometimes related to the establishment of interrater reliability in the coding and analysis of textual data. In chapter 7 we discussed the issues of reliability and validity in participant observation research. While there are issues of reliability in the over design of research, in the collection of materials and the writing of field notes, there is an additional and some-what separable issue related to the analysis of field notes. Once notes are recorded and codes established with both conceptual and operational definitions, different coders using the same codebook and the same set of data should be able to attach the same codes to the same pieces of text and come to the same conclusions about the data. One can compare the coding of two or more coders and calculate the extent to which they agree. This is a measure of "interrater reliability." While solo researchers rarely have a second or third person code their data to establish interrater reliability, projects with multiple researchers and multiple sets of data often do so. In the Two County Project in Kentucky there were three researchers contributing field notes to the project. In this project we did hire coders who worked from our established codebooks, and we did examine interrater reliability by double coding samples of the field notes. The calculation of interrater reliability is also more common in health related research. Again, it is, in part, the result of the need to provide a more detailed description of how qualitative research will take place and how the reliability (and hence the validity) of a set of methods will be established when seeking funding from agencies more used to assessing proposals using only quantitative data. The examination of interrater reliability in the coding of textual data has a long history and should be considered even when a solo researcher is conducting research.

WRITING UP

When does the process of drawing conclusions and verifying them end? Again, the real answer is probably never, but at some point there are fewer new "breakdowns," the data support the conclusions, or the remaining questions are either not so important or will form the basis of the next research project. Now is the time for writing up.

The goal of all research is reporting results. That is, writing the arguments and presenting the supporting materials to the best of the researcher's ability, in ways that respond to theoretical and practical concerns of the researcher and the discipline. In fact, a good deal of analysis takes place during the writing process. It is in the building and supporting of written arguments that much of the organization of materials takes place. So, at what point should writing begin? Wolcott (1999) says "it is never too early to begin writing" (200). Wolcott has presented an excellent summary of four possible indicators for when to start writing. Because he says this far better than we could summarize, we have quoted his four indicators verbatim. He writes:

> It is time to start writing if you have not begun to write, yet you feel that you are not learning anything sufficiently new to warrant the time you are investing. Start writing up what you already know. Such writing should not only test the depth of your knowledge but should also help you to identify areas requiring attention or warranting study in greater depth. That is also why writing is best initiated while you are in the field or still have easy access to it.
>
> It is time to start writing if you have not begun to write but you realize that you will never get it all and the possibility has crossed your mind that you may now be using fieldwork *as an excuse for not writing*. You would be better off to begin making sense of data already gathered than to bank on suddenly becoming a more astute fieldworker. If you are serious about turning to writing, this very moment is the time to begin, not tomorrow or the day after that.
>
> It is time to start writing if you have not begun to write, but you have convinced yourself that after attending "only a couple more" big events, or investigating "only a couple more" major topics, you will begin. If you feel that you are that close to getting started, then there must be certain topics about which you are already well informed. Start by addressing those "comfortable" topics, rather than putting the writing task off for a few more days (or weeks, or months). Remember that the point at which you begin organizing and writing need not mark the end of fieldwork. Far more likely, turning attention to organizing and writing may help you focus your fieldwork efforts during whatever time remains.
>
> It is time to start writing if you have not begun to write, yet you realize that you are now at the midpoint of the total time you have allocated for completing the study. (Wolcott 1999:199–200)

Years ago, Rosalie Wax offered cogent counsel about apportioning time for writing in *Doing Fieldwork: Warnings and Advice* (1971):

> It is a horrid but inescapable fact that it usually takes *more* time to organize, write, and present material than it takes to gather it. . . . The sensible researcher

will allow as much free time to write his (sic) report as he spent in the field. If he is really astute and can get away with it, he will allow himself more. (45)

Some researchers do feel that it is hard, in fact almost impossible, to start writing in the field (e.g., Ottenberg 1990). They feel too close to the material, too enmeshed in the scene to step back and take a more objective stance. We believe that reestablishing an objective stance is one of the reasons to begin writing. Part of what Wolcott and Wax mean when they talk of writing and organizing is to begin the process of analysis. In our terms, we call this coding, displaying, and interpreting data. When possible we begin the process of writing as we begin to develop codes for themes, index categories and sort by characteristics, develop preliminary ideas and conclusions and fit pieces of data together. We take advantage of the closeness of the field to begin this process, and fill in gaps. However, even when writing begins while fieldwork is still underway, the bulk of writing will take place after the researcher leaves the field. For the final analyses, it probably is necessary to have the added objectivity of being away from the field in order to finish analysis and write the most objective and balanced account possible.

Writing up materials, whether the write-up takes the form of conventional published books and articles, or reports to those who commissioned research, is not only important to the development of one's career as a professional, but is also part of the ethical conduct of research. When we bother people for information (and they agree to be bothered), we are also making the commitment to make that information available to the scholarly and policy communities. We told our informants we would do this, we promised the granting organization we would publish, we own our employer a report, so we have an obligation to do so responsibly.

We have emphasized in this chapter that, as with many of the other activities related to participant observation, the analysis of field notes is an iterative process. We find ourselves constantly reading and rereading our field notes. Each time we do so, we find new themes, new questions, and we are reminded of events, places, and perspectives. In addition to emphasizing the constant rereading of field notes, this chapter has also presented a number of methods for helping to organize, categorize, and review field notes. Just as with any other type of data analysis, three sets of activities occur in analyzing field notes—data reduction, data display, and conclusion drawing and verification. We have presented various schemes for indexing and coding field notes so that data retrieval is easier and quicker. We then moved on to means by which field notes can be used to further analyze data. We provided examples of using data displays, using quotes, presenting cases, and decision modeling. All of these are means to take the data from participant observation and to begin to put it into a published format. We have also discussed very formal ways of documenting analytic decisions in the development of audit trails. In the next, and last, chapter we will again examine and expand on some of the critical ethical issues related to participant observation.

NOTES

1. The analysis of interview transcripts and other documents follows the same three kinds of activities, and is similar to the analysis of field notes. In this discussion we will emphasize those aspects of analysis that are more closely linked to field notes.

2. It is for this reason that we also believe it is important to audiotape and transcribe interviews, even informal interviews if at all possible. While the act of interviewing also is an act of data reduction, as the researcher is always influencing the content and flow of the interaction, it is preferable to capture people's real words, rather than recording the researcher's further reduced summary of the interaction.

3. For us, thematic codes are codes for ideas that come more directly from our observations and the words of our informants. For Bernard and Ryan (2009) thematic codes include both of the activities we call indexing and thematic coding.

❧11❧

Ethical Concerns in Participant Observation

Ethical considerations span the life of every ethnographic research project. Researchers must be aware of the ethical considerations of research from the point at which they choose the question to be asked, through the choice of a population in which to study it, the methods to be used to collect data, the recruitment of informants, and publication. Fluehr-Lobban (1998) reviewed the overall ethical issues relating to ethnographic research, and that publication is recommended to the reader. In addition, the American Anthropological Association and the American Sociological Association both have comprehensive statements concerning the code of conduct for research, including qualitative and participant observation research (American Anthropological Association 2009; American Sociological Association 1999). The full text of both of these statements can be found on the cited web pages.

Both the AAA and ASA codes use as their starting point the principle that the researcher must respect the rights, lives, attitudes, and opinions of the people they are studying. The AAA code makes it clear that the safety of people with whom the researcher is working has the highest priority, superseding any scientific goals. Codes of professional ethics not only point to the need to protect the rights of subjects, but also the reputation of the profession as a whole, and, for anthropologists, access to field settings by other anthropologists.

There are a number of specific issues in conducting ethical research using participant observation and we will discuss those that we feel are central to the method. The issues we want to address here are 1) the need for competency; 2) the meaning of informed consent; 3) protection of confidentiality; 4) maintaining relationships; and 5) ethical publication.

NEED FOR COMPETENCY

The ethical conduct of research (American Anthropological Association 2009; American Sociological Association 1997; Fluehr-Lobban 1998) requires that the researcher be sufficiently trained to carry out research not only ethically, but also competently. At the most basic level, the idea here is that we should not be pestering people with badly designed or poorly carried out research. As we will note below, a researcher has a responsibility to publish the results of research, and those publications should be accurate and fair. It seems axiomatic that badly done research is unlikely to be accurate. When participant observation is used as a method, and even more so when it is the principal method, the considerations of competence are heightened because the researcher is the primary research instrument. As Fluehr-Lobban, speaking to anthropologists, specifically, notes:

> If an anthropologist has had little or poor training for the field, it will be difficult for him or her to resolve the everyday dilemmas that are part of the practice of the discipline. For example, the anthropologist may not have been well prepared as to the social and political environments of the people to be studied. Or the anthropologist may receive funding from a public or private foundation without having fully considered the conflicting demands and responsibilities between funder and people studied. During the research, when the field situation changes and the anthropologist's position becomes ambiguous, the art of negotiating and repositioning oneself resolves to ethical principles and choices. (1998:173)

Competency for ethical research has several components. The first is to obtain adequate training before beginning an independent research project. At a minimum, before undertaking unsupervised or minimally supervised research an individual should

- Know how to formulate a worthwhile question;
- Know how to design an effective project, understand research methods, and know how to implement them effectively; and
- Be able to analyze and interpret the data collected.

For the use of participant observation as a method of research, this also means knowing how to enter a new setting and develop effective field relationships. As we noted when discussing the method, it also means being attentive to the situation, knowing when to step back a bit, and how to listen; and, finally, how to leave the setting in such a way that subsequent researchers would find a receptive community.

Ideally, new researchers should have the opportunity to carry out research under supervision in order to get their research skills to the level at which they can carry out a project competently (and, hence, ethically) without supervision. For those using participant observation, this means practicing getting into settings, participating and observing, and recording field notes under circumstances in which the new researcher can talk about problems and concerns, discuss ethical issues, and have their field notes reviewed. For those who train new researchers, this means not tossing a new investigator into a setting without adequate training and backup. It is not only bad practice to inflict an inadequately trained neophyte on a community, but also it puts the researcher, the community, and the discipline in jeopardy. The professional codes of both the AAA and the ASA recognize this as an important ethical concern.

Second, the researcher should have considered the basic principles concerning the conduct of ethical research before beginning the project. When choices have to be made, there is often little time or resources available to carry out an in-depth analysis of ethics from scratch in the field (American Anthropological Association 2009). As Fluehr-Lobban points out, "matters of ethics are an ordinary, not extraordinary" part of the research experience (1998:173). Working knowledge of ethical principles and how to apply them is as fundamental as theory and methods. They need to be considered in design. Researchers need to spend time reviewing professional codes of ethics, developing an internalized sense of the meaning of protection of human subjects, and considering alternative strategies for addressing some of the more common ethical questions that arise in fieldwork. Again, it is the responsibility for those who train new researchers to make such training available in a meaningful way.

Third, in order to be a competent researcher, the participant observer should have prepared him/herself to anticipate as much of the specific social and political issues that might arise in any particular research setting. Seasoned researchers returning to research sites draw on their previous experience. For the new researcher or an experienced researcher moving to a new site, this means reviewing previous research and other materials available about the site and similar sites. In general, we do this routinely as part of our scholarly preparation for research but we believe it is useful to stress there is an ethical as well as scholarly imperative to understand the field site as well as possible before getting there.

Finally, we will say it again: there is no substitute for feeling and showing respect for the people with whom the investigator is working. Participant observation works best when there is true rapport between the researcher and members of the community. The code of ethics of the ASA and the AAA both include the basic principle that researchers must "respect the rights, dignity, and worth of all people" (American Sociological Association 1999:4). A researcher who truly respects the people with whom s/he is working is more likely to participate in the research context in a way that maximizes the success of the project as a well-done piece of research.

THE MEANING OF INFORMED CONSENT
IN PARTICIPANT OBSERVATION

Participant observation as a method raises the greatest number of ethical questions with respect to informed consent and the right of people to
choose to participate in research of any of the methods usually applied in
fieldwork. While it may be clear to most individuals who are being interviewed using structured interview schedules, or whose interviews are being
recorded in some way, that the information resulting from these activities
will be used in the research carried out by the fieldworker, the activities carried out during participant observation are less clearly so. The fieldworker
is traveling alongside community members, participating in events, work,
leisure activities, hanging out. Community companions will probably not
be fully aware that the fieldworker will faithfully record an account of these
events as soon as possible and that this will form a set of data for analysis.
Even if a fieldworker makes it clear that s/he will "write a book" or report
on his or her experiences, informants may not realize that what they share as
"gossip" during informal conversations may form part of this report. Fieldworkers rarely recite their informed consent script during an afternoon's
conversations carried while swinging in hammocks, or while drinking a beer
in the bar after a day's work, or while in bed with a lover. In fact, if informants were always consciously aware of our activities as ethnographers, the
information we acquire would be less rich. We want people to forget, for a
time at least, that we are outsiders. We want to develop sufficient rapport
and to have them become so comfortable with us as community participants
that they will trust us and share insights and information that only insiders
would know. We regard this as the strength of our method. It also requires
that we assume an extra burden for protecting our research participants. For
this reason Lugosi (2006) argues that ethnographic research is always in a
luminal state between overt and covert research.

Punch (1994) agues, quoting Ditton (1977), that participant observation
is inevitably unethical "by virtue of being interactionally deceitful" (Ditton
1977:10). That is, it is by its nature deceptive. We have all been impressed
by the degree to which our informants will suspend a conversation or
interaction to remind us that the topic about which they are speaking is
important, and to make sure that we will put it "in the book." But it is more
often the case that the informants "forget" that casual interactions may
form part of the data to be used in analysis. However, we would characterize participant observation as ethically challenging rather than suggesting
that participant observation is inherently unethical. We believe that we can
conduct participant observation ethically and within the guidelines followed by most Institutional Review Boards for the Protection of Human
Subjects (IRBs).

Respect for persons requires that subjects, to the degree that they are capable, be given the opportunity to choose what shall or shall not happen to them. This opportunity is provided when adequate standards for informed consent are satisfied. The 1991 version of Title 45 Part 46 of the Code of Federal Regulations defines informed consent as "the knowing consent of and individual, or a legally authorized representative, able to exercise free power of choice without undue inducement or any element of force, fraud, deceit, duress, or other form of constraint or coercion" (Code of Federal Regulations 1991).[1]

The basic concept is that people have the right to freely choose whether to participate in a research project or not. In order to make that decision, they need to have a reasonable understanding of both the risks and the benefits of participating in the research project. In addition, as we will note below, people have a right to privacy.

The most fundamental principle, then, is that people have a right to know that they are the subjects of a research project. In participant observation we actually hope that at some moments the research nature of the relationship can be made less explicit. However, as we have noted in previous chapters, we feel that there are important ethical considerations when the researcher takes on a covert role. Again, people have a right to know they are being studied, and they must have the right to refuse to participate. The notion of "informed consent" was added to the AAA code of ethics in 1995 (American Anthropological Association 2009; Fluehr-Lobban 1998). We believe this to be true even when the researcher is committed to complete anonymity of the people with whom s/he is working. This is not to say that in research there is no ethical wiggle room. The nonparticipating observer, standing on the street corner anonymously observing, does not have to wear a sign saying, "Be informed! I am a researcher." Observation in public places is generally not thought to be covered under informed consent. Observational research in educational settings is not usually considered to require consent.

Similarly, when a person responds to a questionnaire or formal interview, he or she is generally thought to be aware that they are participating in research. Respondents know that they do not have to answer questions, whether or not they are asked to sign a consent form or consent is obtained verbally. Under the Title 45, Part 46 of the Code of Federal Regulations (2009), research with minimal or no harm and for which the data collected cannot be connected to identifiable individuals is eligible for a waiver of informed consent.

In fact, at several different institutions, we have found that getting approval to use structured and semistructured interviewing using a spoken script and verbal consent has not been problematic. However, neither of these situations characterizes participant observation. Here the "interviews" are more like conversations. Even when individuals are in public places,

research participants are likely to view the nature of the interactions between themselves and the researcher as private. The Code of Ethics of the
American Anthropological Association directly addresses informed consent
within the context of ethnographic research:

> 4. Anthropological researchers should obtain in advance the informed consent
> of persons being studied, providing information owning or controlling access
> to material being studied, or otherwise identified as having interests which
> might be impacted by the research. It is understood that the degree and breadth
> of informed consent required will depend on the nature of the project and may
> be affected by requirement of other codes, laws, and ethics of the country or
> community in which the research is pursued. Further, it is understood that the
> informed consent process is dynamic and continuous; the process should be
> initiated in the project design and continue through implementation by way of
> dialogue and negotiation with those being studied. Researchers are responsible
> for identifying and complying with the various informed consent codes, laws
> and regulations affecting their projects. Informed consent, for the purposes of
> this code, does not necessarily imply or require a particular written or signed
> form. It is the quality of the consent, not the format, that is relevant.
> 5. Anthropological researchers who have developed close and enduring re-
> lationships (i.e., covenantal relationships) with either individual persons pro-
> viding information or with hosts must adhere to the obligations of openness
> and informed consent, while carefully and respectfully negotiating the limits
> of the relationship. (American Anthropological Association 2009:3)

Fluehr-Lobban (1994, 1998) following the AAA code of ethics, also argues that the spirit of informed consent can be met without the mechanis-
tic, formalist approach of getting a signed consent form from informants
during ongoing fieldwork. However, this dynamic, nonformal approach to
the spirit of informed consent places a heavier burden on the researcher to
be relatively sophisticated about analyzing situations and arriving at ethical
decisions about how research will be carried out in any particular setting.

It also raises the risk of a paternalistic approach to protecting the rights of
our informants. There can be a tendency to argue that the risks to communities and individuals are so small as to be negligible, and that the nature
of the relationships built up during participant observation are inherently
nonexploitative. Further, we can sometimes truthfully argue that obtaining
informed consent is a barrier between the researcher and the community.
There is a danger that we might take the position that we know the community so well, that we know what's best for our informants; further that
we can protect their rights, without full disclosure of the research. We feel
that this is a hang-over of the old "my village" thinking of colonialist social
science (Fluehr-Lobban 1994, 1998; Harding 1998). We certainly know
naïve and not-so-naïve researchers (see Whyte and Whyte 1984) who did
not anticipate the problems to be experienced by the people with whom

they worked after the materials were published. We also know that some informants and research communities cannot themselves anticipate the potential consequences of publication as well as the researcher.

In chapter 2, in the section on getting into a research setting, we discussed the need to make research goals clear to the community and to obtain community permission to carry out research. This is clearly the first step. However, we feel that the researcher should occasionally remind people of the research nature of the relationships. Taking notes in public at least some of the time may be a way to do this. Some researchers routinely audiotape interactions, even when they are informal and on the street. The researcher also needs to be continually aware of the ethical implications of what he or she is hearing and taking notes on.

The principal of informed consent not only includes disclosure of the goals of research, but also the honest assessment of the researcher as to the risks and benefits of the research to the people participating in it. How do we assess risks and benefits? The issue of benefits is, perhaps, the easier one to address. In general, in basic ethnographic research, the benefits to individuals and even specific communities are minimal. The main benefits accrue to the discipline and to the investigator. Our usual answer to people when they ask about the benefit to them, and they do ask, is that essentially there is none. We will tell their story as fairly and accurately as we can, but no material gain is likely to come from this research. However, the benefits are also generally not zero. We have noted that people generally like telling their stories. They often like having someone interested enough in their lives and their communities to spend significant time participating, observing, and listening. Just as we have heard anthropologists talk about "my village," we have heard people in some communities talking about "our anthropologist."

In some applied research settings there is the potential for direct benefit. The community will be included in a project, or specific resources will be made available, or the community can use the analyzed data group to its advantage. However, many case studies of programs or evaluations will have a much more important benefit for the design of future projects than to the participants in the current research. Under any circumstance, the potential benefits, or lack of them, should be clearly articulated to participants.

The risks of participating in research are a bit harder to assess; but the researcher has the responsibility to the best of his/her ability and knowledge to assess the potential risk. In general, in participant observation risks are also minimal. We are not "doing" anything to people in the way that a medical researcher, for example, might. We see the potential risks as (1) stress related to discussion of difficult or sensitive topics, (2) failure to protect confidentiality with respect to sensitive information, (3) disclosure of illegal activity or sensitive information to authorities, and (4) unanticipated results of publication.

All forms of interviewing have the potential for resulting in the experience of stress by informants, especially when the topics being investigated are sensitive. While fieldwork may include formal interviewing and questionnaire use, in "interviewing" in participant observation the researcher is usually following the lead of informants and engaging in a more conversational approach. The researcher does have the obligation to judge whether any particular line of conversation is causing discomfort or stress, but in general, our informants just stop talking about subjects they do not care to share.

Failure to protect confidentiality is very serious and we will discuss it in more detail below. However, breaches of confidentiality can be inadvertent when the researcher is "gossiping" with informants. Individuals can be harmed by the disclosure of sensitive information, even when the researcher does not actually name them in a conversation.

During the process of debriefing (for example, reporting at a national organization about the results of research) and publication, a researcher can disclose information that causes the intervention of local and extra-local authorities in a community or group. The researcher may not anticipate the negative impact of information. However, again this is an issue that needs careful consideration. The researcher needs to make the likely venues and types of publication known to the participant in research. Some researchers share materials with their communities before publication.

A final note about informed consent: it is often the case that participants in our research do not really understand all the potential for harm their participation might carry even when we explain it. There is a large literature from clinical research that shows that participants in clinical trials often minimize the risks of participation, even when the process of informed consent lists all of the potential risks in detail. One of the classic ethics cases provided by the American Anthropological Association tells the story of a researcher whose participants did not think it was important to use pseudonyms for the community or the individuals. They wanted people to know who they were! While the risks are usually mostly at the level of possible embarrassment, it may still be incumbent on the researcher to protect identities even when permission is given to use names of people and places, if s/he does not feel the participants can assess the full risk. While this sounds paternalistic, we would argue that it is wiser to err on the side of confidentiality (see below).

RIGHT TO PRIVACY

In addition to informed consent, federal guidelines for research with human subjects also recognize the primacy of the right to privacy of participants in research. This means that every effort possible must be made to protect the anonymity of people and sometimes of communities if they so desire. The Code of Ethics of the AAA says:

> Anthropological researchers must determine in advance whether their hosts/ providers of information wish to remain anonymous or receive recognition, and make every effort to comply with those wishes. Researchers must present to their research participants the possible impacts of the choices, and make clear that despite their best efforts, anonymity may be compromised or recognition fail to materialize. (American Anthropological Association 2009:4)

The code recognizes that anonymity can always potentially be compromised. Confidentiality is important at several levels. At the community level, the researcher often has information about people that the participants do not want shared with their neighbors. It is critical that researchers do not share information or gossip with community members, even when their informants are sharing gossip, or asking for some. We spoke of the need to maintain confidentiality for the sake of rapport. There is also an ethical imperative to do so.

Sometimes breaches of confidentiality are inadvertent. Recently a relatively young researcher, working in an indigenous community in the Andes, inadvertently compromised one of his informants with another community member. In this cultural setting, information about household resources and possessions is carefully guarded. People, in fact, attempt to deceive their neighbors about their possessions. The researcher was living with a family of informants in an urban setting. In the process of testing video equipment, and with the family's permission, he videotaped their farm, located some miles outside of town. The tape included views of their small sheep flock and dairy herd. Several weeks later he was testing out video replay equipment in another household and inadvertently popped the tape into the video play back machine in a neighbor's home. The neighbor became very interested in the tape, making comments about the size of the flock and herd and the size of the farm. He would not allow the researcher to remove the tape until it was finished. This was bad enough, but when the researcher returned to the home in which he was staying, his host noticed the tape and asked if the neighbors had seen it. The researcher acknowledged that they had. His host essentially threw him and his possessions out of the house for what he perceived to be a breach of confidentiality, effectively ending their relationship.

ETHICAL CONDUCT OF PARTICIPANT OBSERVATION IN ONLINE SETTINGS

The conduct of research in online settings, whether the research is carried out with CMC or as an avatar in a virtual world or MMORPG raises some of the same ethical issues regarding research as conventional face-to-face research; and some different ones. Researchers debate whether news groups, list serves, chat rooms, blogs and such are "public" places for which the participants might expect that their communication would be observed; whether the communications posted on the internet can be quoted directly; whether the online personas should be protected; and to what extent informed consent should be sought and how to do so (e.g., C. Allen 1996; Boehlefeld 1996; Boellstorff 2010; Constable 2003; Hine 2000; King 1996; Reid 1996; Sanders 2005; Thomas 1996; Waskul 1996).

Sanders (2005) conducted a study of the online sex industry in Britain. As part of the research she "lurked" covertly on several message boards used to connect sex workers with clients. She argues that revealing her presence would have altered the behavior of the participants and provoked hostility toward her. She also believed from observing the message boards that participants knew that "outsiders" were observing the site. She further argues that the anonymity of the Internet on such sites, on which most participants use pseudonyms, is already protected. The issue for Sanders arises when the researcher wishes to quote CMC without the authors' permission. Constable (2003), on the other hand, was overt about the nature of her research when participating in CMC. She was also careful to request permission for direct quotes from CMC sites.

Boellstorff (2010) was completely open with other participants in *Second Life* about his role as a researcher. He even had an online informed consent form and used pseudonyms for the avatars with whom he interacted, even though, even he acknowledges that to some extent, he was protecting the confidentially of fictional characters, who might actually be controlled by someone with a different gender, ethnicity, and experience than the avatar, and, even, might be controlled by more than one person. Reid (1996) reviews the concerns with informed consent on the internet and concludes that they are quite similar to those raised for non-internet-based research, with the caveat that internet participants may be even more likely to underestimate the potential harm to themselves with publication.

Hine (2000) argues strongly that researchers conducting research with CMC need to be full participants in order to truly understand the nature of the phenomenon they are investigating. Being a full participant for Hine means being overt about the research role. She writes:

> To participate in a newsgroup without revealing one's role as a researcher would, as in all cases of covert ethnography, pose a considerable ethical problem. Arguing that online interactions are sufficiently real to provide a context for an ethnographic study has an ethical corollary: online interactions are sufficiently real for participants to feel that they have been harmed or their privacy infringed by researchers. (Hine 2000:23)

While a number of writers suggest that the internet is a public place, it seems to us that we should carefully consider the ethical issues related to observing CMC as a lurker and participating in MMORPGs as a covert researcher. There is an ethical gray area here that will receive continued examination over the next few years. For us, these kinds of research activities are more similar to conventional, face-to-face research than they are different. The issue of downloading archived CMC materials for analysis in order to quote directly from CMC (which can be construed as published material) without attribution or citation is a problem, and requesting permission to quote would inevitably bring to light the research role (Hine 2000).

ETHICAL PUBLICATION

Decisions about what to publish, and how to publish, are also ethical choices. Whyte (Whyte and Whyte 1984) reminds us that once published, much of our work can be put to unintended use. That is, although we are interested in research questions for scientific and/or humanistic purposes, others may find the studies of use for other purposes. The lines between intended and unintended uses can, of course, sometimes become blurred. It has been alleged, for example, that some of the early research of anthropologists was done in the service of colonialism (Magubane 1971). In addition, during the days of the Cold War, there were many concerns that village studies being done by anthropologists could be used for counterinsurgency purposes (I. Horowitz 1967).

It is possible that, keeping in mind the primary priority of not harming participants in research, researchers might make the decision not to publish some of the data they have collected. We have often, for example, become privy to illegal activities of some individuals in communities in which we have worked. We are careful to never write about these activities in a way that could be tied back to any one individual, and generally do not include these activities in our publications unless the information is directly relevant to the research question.

Ethical publication should respect the general principal of doing no harm to our research subjects. In general, by maintaining anonymity of the people we study we are able to manage this fairly well. We do recall, however, reading an ethnography of a community near one in which we did research in which we were surprised to find a photograph with a caption that read something like: The Nastiest Woman in the Community. (For obvious reasons, we will keep the name of the ethnographer anonymous.)

It is important to emphasize that ethical questions surround not only the published information we provide but also relate to our field notes.

We would like to comment on two issues. First is the ethical question concerning the public taking of notes. Taking notes openly, at least part of the time, reinforces for participants that what is being done is research. The participants in Bourgois's crack research knew he was "writing a book," and his open taping of interviews and even conversations on the street made it clear to participants what was on the record and off. In fact, they sometimes suggested that he turn on his recorder when he turned it off. For us, openly taking notes, or taping events, alleviates some of the concern that participants lose awareness that they are participating in research.

The second issue has to do with preserving anonymity for participants identified in field notes. Not only is there the potential that can field notes can be subpoenaed, governmental funding organizations such as National Science Foundation and National Institutes of Health are becoming increasingly concerned with research integrity and falsification of data in funded research. They are demanding that primary data be available for review by others. Universities such as our own have developed policies concerning research integrity of nonfunded, as well as funded, research in which data, including field notes, would be available for inspection by review boards should allegations of a breach of research integrity be alleged.

Anthropologists have on occasion gone to jail to protect the identities of their informants. However, some concern with the protection of the identity of informants in field notes can help to alleviate these problems. While most internal review boards for the use of human subjects require that all questionnaires and transcribed interview data be stored without names, field notes have always constituted a gray area. With computerization, however, it becomes relatively easy to assign code names or numbers to participants and use these from the outset or use the global search and replace facilities of word processing programs to expurgate real names from field notes. The research integrity policy statement for the University of Pittsburgh, for example, now suggests that real names be expurgated from field notes against the possibility that they will be requested by others.

RELATIONSHIPS

Relationships developed in the field also present ethical dilemmas. Ethnographers actively attempt to become accepted into the research community, to develop close relationships, and to identify with the group they are studying. Although some anthropologists do continue to return again and again to the same research communities (see Foster et al. 1979), relationships with communities and people are almost always much more transient (Punch 1994). While many informants become true friends, such friendships are difficult to maintain when the anthropologist is thousands of miles away.

Anthropologists need to be aware of the implications of relationships and obligations that they incur in the field. Many anthropologists, for example, enter into fictive kinship relationships in order to find a place in a community. Katherine Lutz (1988) became a "daughter" to fit into Ifaluk society. She discussed the benefits and costs to her research of this relationship. Assuming this kind of relationship has a number of implications and adds a series of responsibilities for the anthropologists, these should be carefully considered before the identity is accepted. Becky Ross, whose story forms one of the ethical case studies published by the AAA (Cassell and Jacobs 1997), was "adopted" into a family as a daughter and granddaughter. When it became necessary to assume the responsibilities of a true granddaughter and care for an elderly "grandfather" she did it, at personal expense (loss of precious field time), until the biological grandchildren were available to take over.

Like many other anthropologists who have worked in Latin America, we have been asked on many occasions to become godparents for children of people with whom we have worked. Godparenthood in Latin America has been extended to many occasions, so that there are godparents chosen for confirmation, fifteenth birthdays of girls (an important coming of age celebration in many communities), marriages, school graduations, and so on. We considered being asked to be a godparent for any of these occasions to be an honor and a sign of our acceptance in the community. We also have come to realize, however, that it also implies a certain level of continuing responsibility to these children and their families. This is particularly the case when asked to be a godparent for baptism. Although we have made good efforts to maintain godparent relationships begun during our field research in Temascalcingo, over time it has become more and more difficult to do so. In subsequent research, we have generally declined to take on the role of godparent because we know that we will be unable to fulfill the obligations implied.

Even when the relationship is not intimate or familial, it may present ethical dilemmas. As part of research with older adults in rural settings in Kentucky, one of the places Kathleen and her collaborators "hung out" in order to get a better understanding of the problems confronting older adults was the senior citizens' centers. Here they chatted with the program participants, rode the transportation vans, and ate the meals provided by the centers. All of the participants and the program staff knew that the researchers were studying food and nutrition problems in the communities. When the regional senior picnic was planned for a recreation area near Central County, the researchers were invited to attend and arrived with the participants from the Central County Senior Center. They ate box lunches, participated in the auction for such goodies as fried apple pies and home canned vegetables and pickles. Much of the afternoon was spent in competitions among senior citizens, including walking races, baking contests, and other activities. One of the contests was an extemporaneous speaking contest. Judging was to focus on originality and eloquence of individuals who were given a topic on which to speak. However, there were no obviously unbiased potential judges. Most of the people at the picnic were participants or staff of individual centers. Kathleen and one of her collaborators were asked to be judges. Although protesting that they might be biased toward the contestant from Central County, they agreed. During the introduction of judges, the Central County Senior Center Director introduced Kathleen and her co-researcher by saying: "I would like to introduce two people to whom we have become very close over the past few months." Kathleen's heart sank because she realized that the project was nearing its end and that she was not prepared to maintain a long-term relationship with the center and participants after the project was over. Realizing the implied commitment to the community in the director's words, she began to develop a plan to put more distance between herself and the residents of the center. Avenarius (Johnson, Avenarius, and Weatherford 2006) found that after taking a particularly active role in the Chinese community, it was quite difficult to "leave the field" at the end of the research period.

Over the years we have developed strong personal relationships in different places and with different people. While we have tried to return as often as possible to communities we have studied to let individuals know we still think of them, this has not always been possible. Good intentions to correspond have rarely been possible to maintain. Whenever possible, we do make short visits to the communities in which we have worked previously. For both of us and for the people with whom we worked, these visits are always bittersweet. We, and they, realize that the daily interactions we once shared are not likely to occur again. The message is that while the fieldworker is almost always transient, we must recognize that this transience may not be the expectation of those individuals who become our informants.

ETHICS AND THE LIMITS TO PARTICIPATION

Another issue relates to the "limits to participation" that we have discussed in previous chapters. That is, to what extent should a researcher intervene in a situation in which their own ethical and moral codes are challenged? We noted that Good, while working with the Yanomama, chose at one point not to intervene in a rape and in a second instance did so. Scheper-Hughes chose to virtually kidnap a young man from "jail" in order to get him to medical treatment after he had been punished by the community in which he lived. In research with the Northern Kayapo of Brazil in 1976, at that time still a group of seminomadic horticulturists, members of the biomedical team with whom Kathleen was working were asked to provide a humane (medical) way to end the life of four-year-old child profoundly affected by Down's Syndrome. The physicians declined, even though they knew that the now again pregnant mother could not carry both a new infant and a disabled four-year-old with her. They also knew that infanticide was acceptable for severely handicapped children in that culture and the most likely outcome of their refusal would be that the child's life would be ended in a more painful manner.

There are no easy answers to these kinds of dilemmas. In fact, many ethnographic researchers believe strongly in some level of relativism in values and culture and, concomitantly, in some level of ethical relativism. And, as we have emphasized earlier in this book, we believe that the effective use of participant observation requires that researchers respect the culture and values of the communities in which they work. Researchers have to arrive at solutions through a process of careful thought and the weighing of the values of noninterference in community culture and values, and personal ethics. We believe that the researchers will have to live with themselves longer than with the study community.

Romantic relationships with our informants is another extraordinarily gray area in terms of the limits to participation. As we have emphasized earlier, because of the generally large differences in power, status, wealth, etc. of anthropological researchers and people in the communities they study, we do not believe that it is wise to enter into such relationships. The potential for exploitation is much too great.

The number of potential ethical dilemmas in doing field research is large. Review of the case studies and commentary by professional anthropologists available on the ethics page of the web site of the American Anthropological Association (American Anthropological Association 2009) can help in thinking through some of these issues, but the choice of action ultimately has to be that of the researcher.

Our discussion of ethics in doing participant observation has been intended to alert the researcher to the kinds of issues he or she might face. By no means have we tried to provide a prescription for solving every ethical dilemma, a task that would in any case be impossible. The AAA Code of Ethics makes it clear that no researchers can anticipate all of the possible ethical dilemmas that might arise, and that the key is to be trained sufficiently in ethics to be able to work through those that do arise.

Instead we have emphasized the need for competency of the researcher, being as well-prepared as you can be before beginning a study. This, of course, includes thinking through some of the potential ethical dilemmas that might arise. Among the most important concerns for someone doing participant observation is what we have called the meaning of informed consent. As we have indicated, this does not mean that we have to inform everyone with whom we speak that we are doing research. We should, however, not engage in covert research and take every opportunity to remind the community and the people in the community that we are doing research.

In terms of protection of confidentiality of the people we study, we need to be sensitive to the issue both in terms of maintaining confidences in the field as well as in our published materials and unpublished notes. Being alert to the kinds of problems and issues that might arise in terms of maintaining confidentiality is critical. Ethical publication, in particular, means that we need to attend to both the potential uses and abuses of our research results.

We close with a discussion of the ethical difficulties that arise from entering into and maintaining relationships. Participant observation is a method that opens up great potential for building strong and intense relationships while doing research. Just as we have to be conscious of appropriate ways of entering the field, we also must pay attention to leaving research communities. Once again, the principle of doing no harm is a good one to follow.

NOTE

1. A more comprehensive discussion of informed consent in the 2009 Code of Federal Regulations expands the basic definition into a number of components. The fundamental issues in informed consent are that the participants know:

- they are subjects of research, what the general aims of the research are, and what research methods will be used;
- what, if any, are the risks of participating in the research;
- what, if any, are the benefits of participating in research;
- that they are not obliged in any way to participate and can end their participation at any time;
- that the information collected about them is confidential and the researcher will take actions to ensure confidentiality and anonymity.

All of this must be in understandable language.

Appendix:
Sample Field Notes
from Three Projects

―――◈―――

SAMPLE FIELD NOTES 1

The first set of sample field notes[1] are drawn from the study women's social power and economic strategies in Manabí, Ecuador. They are the work of ethnographer Loren Miller. Here she reports on a single day of fieldwork in one of the four study communities. There are several points we would like to illustrate with these notes.

1. The discussion of sex and marriage related in the first part of these notes was experienced during a walk to visit the cassava processing plant. The ethnographer did not anticipate this particular discussion at this time and did not have her notebook handy.
2. The level of detail recorded regarding the conversation, the actions of the women, their reactions to each other, and their behavior and nonverbal communication allows the ethnographer, and even the noninvolved reader, to evaluate the meaning of the event.
3. In the description of the dance in the community of La Villa, Miller records a detailed description of the venue, the people who are there, the ways in which people are dressed, and the activities that take place. Even a reader who has not observed the event can derive a feeling of immediacy and "being there" from the description. Certainly, it will evoke a clear memory for the ethnographer herself. If this event is important in building an argument later, the description in the field notes will need little editing.
4. Miller describes her role in the event, as well. Later she may use this information to understand how her presence influenced the particular

227

way in which the events unfolded. She records the reaction to her outfit, especially her shoes, in such a way as to highlight the expectations people from the community have for appropriate dress for these events.

5. Miller mixes different types of notes in her field notes. While most of the text is descriptive, she includes some passages that could have been included in a diary, and she has inserted analytic notes in the text, as well. She could have put these different types of note in different files, but she can sort them out later should she choose to. Or she could assign "type of note" codes to them during analysis; or she could place the analytic notes into memos or meta-note files.

La Colonia
Loren Miller
22 August 1998
General gender; Sex talk with 2 socias; La Villa dance
Wrote field notes in the morning, took a post lunch break to ride horses and take photos with the family and Carlos's family. At lunch Susana sat down next to me with her bowl after everyone was served and had nearly finished, as is more and more our practice. She had the chicken feet in her caldo (soup). I asked her why the women always eat the chicken feet, because the night of the July La Villa dance Nelly Reyes ate the chicken feet at her brother's house, Rosa Vera also eats the chicken feet. And with relish. Susana told me because they're the best part. And those who prepare the food get to eat them.

Was supposed to go to the new cassava processing plant with a group of socias, Juana and I each thought the other would inform them. It wound up being just Rosa P., Juana and myself. I went without notebook, only my camera, as I'd had no intention of taking notes. We 3 wound up having one of the most frank discussions I've yet had. I don't know if it was bcz of the lack of pen and paper, or bcz we were out in the forest with no one at all around us, or bcz I've by now gained a level of confidence and people are feeling even more open since I'm leaving. Also the nature of the survey, ie reproductive history, also might have opened a door. In any case we walked up long the road through Valentine, passed the plant equipment. We finally came to the 3rd barbed wire fence on the right, with a wooden gate, and went in. The herbs [weeds] were really high but there was a path. Rosa said she had never been there.

We were headed to the well, to check out it's condition and see what sort of minga (communal labor exchange) would be needed to clean it. We passed a small stream; Juana explained that that was where the cassava runoff went to. We walked about 8 min and finally got to a place which was so overgrown that we couldn't pass. We had by then given up, and were standing around chatting, making jokes, saying we needed to come back with machetes. I took a photo of Rosa. Then Rosa said she didn't want to go back there, bcz 'they'd rape us.' I asked who, were there crazy people back in the forest? She said no but women alone in the forest—"peligroso" (dangerous). I said the three of us together, no one will rape us. I'll hit them with my camera. We were all laughing and Juana said, you know we were raped. 'Uno nos ha violada.' I didn't quite get what she was talking about, and she kept repeating it, saying, 'we've been raped.' Finally Rosa whooped, 'con gusto.' Juana was talking about their husbands. We had a 15 or so min. talk about sex in marriage. How young Rosa had been when she married, 15, didn't know anything about sex. Freaked out when she saw her husband without clothes. But she kept saying that she liked sex. But Juana said that sometimes a woman doesn't have 'el deseo.' And she has to have sex anyway (with her husband). Because if she doesn't, 'he will go off and find someone else.' Juana finally said how the first time that 'yo fui con Juan,' [I was with Juan] it was really quick and she 'wasn't ready. Hadn't had any time to build up desire. It really hurt.' She had known about sex bcz she and her friends talked about what it was like, that sometimes it hurt sometimes it was fun. Rosa said that in the beginning she was horrified, what was that 'fea cosa'. Juana said that Juan has learned a lot that she and he have really come to understandings. Now when she doesn't want to 'have relaciones,' he waits until she does. She says that if he ever wanted to go to another woman she would say, 'Go. And don't come back.' She doesn't need any other man; she's already had experience with one. Broken him in. Got him to understand her a little. She doesn't want to have to go through it again. It could be worse with someone different. You've no idea what you might get.

Rosa kept insinuating that she liked sex. Juana less so. Juana got Juan to be more considerate of her she said when she started to 'cuidarse' (take care of herself: use birth control) with what I think she explained as the rhythm method. She gave me a fairly detailed explanation of when were safe and unsafe times to have sex. She said that she got pregnant several times using this method, bcz there were times when Juan said, Oh I don't care. He wasn't at all as cautious or thoughtful as she regarding the number of children they might have. She said sometimes he just didn't want to wear a condom at dangerous times or her didn't want to wait. But she said that he has learned patience. She won't ever let him take advantage of her she said. She's had too much experience. I asked them what does a woman do if she wants to have sex and her man doesn't? Does she force him or go out looking for someone new too? They laugh. Rosa says no, no. Juana says she wouldn't go for another man bcz adultery is a sin. Isn't it a sin when a man does it, I ask? Well, they say. 'El hombre hace lo que desea.' The man gets to do what he wants. But with Juana and Juan, Juana tells me, they have arrived at a point where they respect each other and won't go with anyone else.

The light is so pretty where Rosa sits and I tell her I want to take her photo. Just as I am about to click it she opens her legs wide in a wildly raucous gesture and screams with laughter. She and Juana think its hysterical and they both want to take photos of ourselves in somewhat comprising positions. I snap Juana's photo while she is laughing hysterically. They laugh even harder at that. As if it there is something risqué about her laughing uncontrollably, letting loose perhaps. Then they scream, and you and you. Juana takes the camera and I show her how to do it and as I go to crouch down at the hillside and gather the bottom of my dress together, she snaps it. With who knows what exposed. They erupt in peels of laughter and I am laughing too bcz I am a little amazed at these 'reserved' women whooping it up deep in the forest where no one will find us.

We talked about man/woman relationships more generally. Juana says that she really works at open communication with her husband and her children. She always tells them she wants them to tell her if they are in love with someone. And if she can help in any way, or give advice, she will.

Juana tells us that Clara Espinoza, from Guayaquil, married to a man turned Evangelist, has just finally separated from him. She took a job in a factory and lives with some siblings. She has visiting rights to her son every weekend. The breakup was amiable enough, and the door is open if she wants to return. And convert from Catholicism. Juana says that Clara is thinking about going to Quito. She doesn't want to stay in Guayaquil. Rosa can't believe that Clara left her man, Juana only just found out from Lydia yesterday. I don't know how the Espinoza's feel about it. I wonder aloud how Clara feels about leaving another of her children. Juana says that when Clara had Marisol with Paulo the couple had lived together 6 mos. But it didn't work out. Then Clara moved with baby Marisol to Quito, where she worked as a maid in a home. Marisol burned herself badly and it was difficult for Clara to take care of her there. Marisol went back home to live with her grandparents in La Colonia. Paulo never really recognized Marisol as his child—I think her surname is Espinoza.

Marisol knows he is her birth father but they don't have any kind of special relationship. She just considers him like 'any other guy in the street.' When Clara married the current/separated husband, and wanted to take Marisol with her to Guayaquil, her own parents wouldn't let her. 'They had grown accustomed to raising Marisol.' They wouldn't give her up and Marisol calls them, her grandparents, mom and dad.

As we walked out of the planta, I tried to get Rosa to talk a little bit more about her relationship with her husband. She told me that when she was young and newly married, she new nothing about anything, sex or otherwise. She knew how to cook and iron. She never spoke with her own kids about sex. But she and Juana said that they always talked amongst themselves, in groups of women, about any kind of sexual thing. And now Rosa said her kids and she are more open. I asked Rosa what she considers her husband, ie is he a friend, her best friend. She said claro that he is an amigo, but a particular kind bcz he lives in my house. I said, oh. 'El es un particular.' We all laughed and she said no, not a particular because he is the only one who shares my bed. So I asked, more like a socia, and she agreed.

We passed two little girls up in a tree and Juana called out to them, 'pajaros!' and said to me, 'why don't you take a photo of these precious little birds.' One of them didn't want her photo taken and Juana kept coaxing her to look at the camera with stories of witches and bigger birds. Juana was acting so freely. It was really something.

We crossed Pedro and Carlos walking up towards Valentine with Machetes just before we got to the La Colonia river. As with everyone else I've run into the past few days, I asked them if they were going to the dance. Yes! Carlos was going in his car around 8 and Pedro walking at 7. I asked Carlos if I could go with him. No problem. Pedro told me, 'we are going to dance together.' I asked him who Maria (his wife) was going to dance with if he and I danced together. He was stumped. He said we'll all dance. They were all in good moods. As we walked on Juana told me that Pedro doesn't like to dance with Maria. I asked why not. She said, 'no se.' But he likes to dance with other women and never asks Maria. Well then, I said. I'm not going to dance with him. Like I told PC, I don't like to dance with married men. Juana said, dance with him one or 2 dances and then tell him to go dance with Maria.

Later Helena and her sister and brother and a friend arrived from Manta for the La Villa Virgen Saint dance. They got all decked out. Helena in a white satin short dress and stockings. One thing that was interesting about me asking people if they were going to the dance, the men if they were going, all said yes. Unequivocally. In fact I hadn't spoken to any men who said they weren't going. The women and girls said, 'no se' (I don't know) Or 'we'll see.' Or 'it depends.' Isabelle didn't know if she was going bcz she didn't know if her mother would go. I said I was going, and she and Susana both said that I could be the chaperon, as well as Tia D. Susana didn't know if she would go. She said she would have to wait until it was time to see if she was animated to go.

As I was ironing my clothes after dinner, and Paulo, Jaime, Susana gathered around to verify that I knew what I was doing; Margarita still didn't know if she was going. She was waiting for Manuel to come home, she couldn't find him. She said that, 'my papi still hasn't told me if I can go or not.' I asked Susana why they needed Manuel's consent if Susana agreed that she could go. Susana said that 'bcz here this is the way we do things. Not just one or the other can make a decision. Isabelle already has accord from my part, and now she needs the accord from the other.' In the end, everyone went except for Renato. He stayed to watch the house. And also to guard the school house for Paulo so that Paulo could go to the dance. It seemed sad bcz he had been looking forward to this activity. But he said it was ok. He gets to go out a lot and it would give the others an opportunity. Although Paulo and Raquel both went to the dance, Raquel went with Maria, Margarita stayed behind. I asked why if the kids were going too. They said, to watch the house. Particularly the chickens. Otherwise people would steal them.

The dance was actually really fun. Carlos's truck picked us up after 8. The back was filled with guys, boys and some men. Also a stroller for Ariel who was already there. The mothers sat in the front with Pedro and we solteras (single women) stood in the back. This is the first time I'd ridden in a car through the road to La Villa, it's only recently fixed. At the school yard where the dance was, 'Disco Movil' from Manta/Guayaquil set up on a big podium. There were flashing colored lights on the podium, and smoke. There were also two dancers on stage. Dressed in extremely short, black hotpants, halter tops and high-heeled boots. They were like the dancers on the evening television program where boys dance with the dancers and the best one wins. There were at least 200 people there, a big group of hiphop boys from Manta wearing their shiny baggy pants and slicked back hair. Women's entrance [fee] was 3000 sucres and men 5000 sucres. On the way in I was given a rose which I then offered to the Virgen. There was a fairly elaborate set up—A big ceramic stature of Christ, flowers and offerings on a table in a corner, seats around it, mainly women sitting perched there. Others came up and prayed to the Virgen, kissed the different idols, were solemn, gave their flowers. Junior Valeriano brought a plastic wrapped bouquet of carnations for the virgin and a wrapping paper wrapped bottle, of puro (cane liquor). Patricia climbed up on a step and put a folded written message in a big box marked something like 'sobreviivres [?]'

I sat at a table with Carlos, D, Susana, Paulo, P, Isabelle, a Ramirez girl, and JC and JD and another Moreno guy sat on the cement bleachers nearby. They filled the table with fantas, cokes, beer, and puro. When we first arrived Pedro was sitting uptop the bleachers holding Ariel, his son. I got up and said hello to ET and Felicia, and their daughters and family. By the time I left it was Maria who was sitting atop the bleachers near the food stand with Linda. She said she was going to help her sister in law sell in the kiosk.

Pedro was the first to ask me to dance. When I first saw him, he had just sat down at a table with some cousins nearby. They were drinking. He told me we're going to dance. But wait just a bit. I guess it was when he was sufficiently loosened up by the alcohol that he asked me to dance. He's a wild man on the dance floor. Has tons of energy. Bounces. Jumps around. We danced a set than I told him I couldn't dance anymore it made me so tired. I told him go dance with Maria. Yeah, yeah, yeah. He said. I'm going to. The short version of the dance is that I don't think Pedro ever danced with his wife. She said watching us dance at one point. I felt a bit uncomfortable, having had that talk with Juana. But Maria seemed to have a bemused expression on her face, as did Pedro's daughter who I met for the first time. She was dancing nearby at one point, she's really warm and friendly, and looks extremely New York hip. I danced with a few different guys, but mainly Pedro and Juan Carlos. Also EB—all my connections are with the community leaders. It was actually fun to whoop it up with them, and share a few drinks. I sat with Belinda a while, she was there with only her 2 oldest kids. Timoteo was home sick and she wasn't dancing. She lent me her sandals to wear as I had come in flip-flops, the only shoes I had, which was apparently a major faux pas.

I noticed EB's son point out my shoes on the dance floor to his sister, with a kind of smirk. I made a joke of it to Leana and Patricia, and also to Maria. They all looked at my feet and then said, 'no importa' (it doesn't matter). But in a way that made me think it was a big deal and they were trying to make me not feel uncomfortable. I didn't really care but I did wish I had some sparkly heels like the other chicks. E had lent me a shiny midriff blouse. Which I was glad to wear, and felt like I fit in more than I would had I kept on my stretched out cotton tank top. Patricia told me I should have asked her to borrow shoes. She sews and seems to be the big fashion authority. She had on gold nail polish to match her gold sandals. Isabelle wore a long black print skirt and matching top, with a triangular flap opening to reveal part of her stomach. It was elegant and fit her well. Margarita had made it. Interesting how so many women want to learn dressmaking while several already seem to do it quite well.

Back to dancing. The 3 times that Pedro asked me to dance, well didn't ask really but came to my table, increasingly more drunk and said 'LORENA MIJER VAMOS A BAILAR!' Somehow the DJ had gotten my name and kept making announcements about Lorena Mijer, Miyer, Mijet, Miter, the Norte Americana don't leave us. Throughout the night, my last name changed. The last time Pedro and I danced, I was sitting with Belinda and I think her brother in law and some of their kids, drinking beer and floratine with them, when he just stood at my table with his hands outstretched. We galloped across the dance floor to the front of the room and wound up dance a lot with Diana Espinoza and another EXTREMELY drunk on his feet guy, who looked a bit like a light skinned V. It was hysterical. We did square dances, switching partners, we skipped in circles, we all held hands and spun around really fast, we got in a line and spun each other around, we danced the hora, charged into the center of our circle with our hands raised yelling 'whooe!' We were creating such a huge raucous. But it was so fun. We were like children. At different points I'm sure we were obnoxious, banging into other people around us. Pedro and I held hands and skipped around the perimeter of the pista. Than the four of us in a line, supporting the drunk guy, who also I'm sure is a big community leader, by the shoulders. A lot of people were laughing, we were having so much fun and I'm sure the spectacle was fun to watch. But the men were really smashed, and the one especially kept bumping people. By our 2nd time around some people were looking annoyed. Betti had a look that it wasn't proper. Susana was holding her sides laughing. At one point, I mouthed to N "no mas" (no more). But she kept on dancing, she was having great fun too though it seemed that like me, there were moments when it was getting out of control. Yet she kept on going. Even when it seemed she was just getting pulled along. I tried to get the guy to sit down but he kept staggering up for more dancing. The set was long. And Pedro and I at least were dripping with sweat by the time it ended.

We all congratulated ourselves and each other and as the men went to sit down, a fight almost broke out between Pedro and some other guy. It got calmed quickly. I don't know what it was about. Then the long speeches to announce the Reina (queen) began. Each of the 5 contestants from diff parts of La Villa had to walk to music around the dance floor, pose like runway models, and then stand in a line while the MC, Don Criollo talked about their beauty of Ecuador.' And also something about them being beautiful virgins for the virgen celebration. Some one was there with a camcorder, filming the whole thing, trained on the girls as they made their round on the dance floor. One particularly curvy contestant, no more than 20, dressed in tight, tight gold pants, gold sparkle shirt, high gold heels, was a great dancer. The camera stayed on her ass as she sashayed to display herself. The contestants had to each dance, trying to follow the lead of the ballerinas. Then boys were called to volunteer to accompany each girl. Some guys literally raced up front to stand next to a girl. Helena was a contestant and seemed the most self-conscious about posing. She was also dressed the most conservatively, and at 23, older than the others. The boy and girl contestant walked around with dishes to collect money and funds from those attending the dance for the chapel. In the end, Helena collected 93,500 sucres and won. The others collected 60,000 and 80,000 sucres. The most bodacious girl, with lots of poise and a good dancer, won the least amount of money. All her enthusiasm had died as, to slow sad music, she and the others made the final tour of the floor with some compensatory red roses.

Interesting how the girls get paraded for their beauty, poise and dance ability, but then in the end it is the one able to collect the most money in order to help the chapel who wins. The outgoing Reina was MV, a catechist and Estella's cousin. Her speech was to thank everyone for their collaboration in building up the church, not only in mano de obra (work) but in materials. She hoped that the coming year would be even more successful for the community and seguir adelante (move forward). Helena is to be a representative of the La Villans from outside the community. She told me her responsibilities are to help out in all ways possible. When I asked if she would be coming more frequently to La Villa, she said, 'tal vez' (maybe).

COMMENTS: Without TV, radio, newspaper, much of the news outside of what is happening right in front of me, seems very remote. It's not that I feel cut off, or in a cloistered world, bcz we still are connected. Discussions daily have to do with market activities, and the road, and the foreign lending and aid, and government actions. News that I am interested in is what gets transmitted in daily conversation. This is the information that has directly to do with peoples' lives here. For example, yesterday when we were taking horse pictures Juan Carlos, 28, told me that though he had been trained to work the UOMA tractors, the tractors still sat in the shed in PV untouched. They were waiting for the 'Polish trainer' to come and instruct them in the usage. The trainer was supposed to come already, but they were still waiting 15 days.

Back to the news—I've no idea what Clinton's up to, no idea of what's in the papers about Africa, Asia, the middle East, Europe. I only know parts of what's being broadcast as far as international lending and aid goes.

SAMPLE FIELD NOTES 2

This second set of notes was collected as part of the study on the nutritional strategies of older adults in rural Kentucky. The notes were recorded on audiotape. The running description in the first section was audiotaped while driving through the county. The description of the visit with Mrs. L was taped immediately following the visit, while driving on to the next event of the day. The notes contain directions to places in Central County, descriptions of the road and the traffic on it. The visit with Mrs. L is summarized in the notes with as much detail as could be recalled immediately after. Some of it is summarized in synopsis form at the beginning of the section describing the visit. In these notes there is somewhat less of the overt presence of the researcher than in the notes by Miller. However, there has been an attempt to record exact words, both of the researcher and the informant.

Central County
Kathleen DeWalt
August 8, 1989:
Visit to Central County—Interview with Mrs. L

I stopped in at the Agricultural Extension office, talked to the secretary, and got directions to CC's house. You take Route 49 north from the courthouse, to the Atwood Chapel Methodist Church, then you take your first left onto a blacktop road. You go down about 1/2 to 3/4 mile and his house is the fifth house on the left. It's a trailer. I didn't actually stop at his house. I stopped at the home of a nephew and his wife, which is the fourth house on the left, and the first brick house down that road and off of Route 49. I introduced myself to CC, and said that I would like to talk with him, since Steve Davis said he was knowledgeable about agriculture in the county. He said to come anytime early in the morning or late in the afternoon or early evening, or at lunchtime, which is around 11:30–12:00, and that he would be happy to talk to me anytime that I can catch him at home. It sounds like he is out working most of the day, though.

I did find out from one of the children around, that he is not married and has never been married. He did say he has been farming for a long time in Central County and did know a lot about farming. His niece, or his niece-in-law, M, said "he taught me how to farm, but you better be careful because the way he taught me is he put me up on a tractor and said 'Go that direction..' " I explained that I didn't necessarily want to learn how to farm, but I wanted to learn about farming and food and what people did in the past and what they do now. After turning off Route 49, it's about half to 3/4 mile down that road, until you get to M's house.

From Liberty to the turn-off on Route 49, it's about 7 or 7 1/2 miles, to the courthouse. The turn-off to the Carr's place is in farming area. What you see along the side of the road are some houses and barns, a lot of pasture land, or land that looks like pasture land, and an occasional tobacco field. I passed several churches. The Atwood Chapel Methodist Church is the farthest one out. Many of the houses along Route 49 appear to be trailers, or converted trailers, and some very small houses. The C' house looks like one of the most substantial houses in the area.

One of the other churches along the way is the Bush Creek Christian Church, the Bush Creek Pentecostal Church. Going back down to town, I managed to get behind a truck hauling logs, and it is going very, very slowly up the hill, but the logs look pretty fresh cut and I am reminded that Steve Davis says that about half the county is in forest or in woods, and that logging, although we don't think of this as a mountain or a forest county, that logging is still an important economic activity here. The closer you get to Liberty on Route 49, the more prosperous things look. You see a little more tobacco and some houses with big lawns. A fair portion of the land right around the road is wooded.

I've come upon another logging truck. That makes two, one following the other, although it's some distance.

I then went to visit Mrs. L. she told me yesterday that she would be canning this morning, so I am kind of hoping to drop in on her while she is canning. I'll be getting there about 11 o'clock.

The land on Route 70, or the other side of the road north towards (no, west toward Mrs. L's house) looks undeveloped, at least for the first couple of miles. A lot of weeds, and it looks like on the right hand side, it looks like mostly forest up on the hillside up to the ridge, and down towards the valley it looks like land that's been left fallow, or has been left to go back to forest. There is a lot of brush and shrubs, and some areas are along the creek and are wooded. About two miles outside of Liberty, the land to the left of the road appears to be a meadow or open field, maybe hay fields. There are some barns in the background, and most probably, hay, because on the right side there is a field that looks like it's been recently mowed with hay rolls in it. Two miles outside of Liberty for the next couple of miles, it's pretty open land although the ridge tops are wooded. Mostly houses and some things that look like garages . . . there is a Ralph Mills Masonry Company on the left, an Ashland garage or service station which looks like it has a small store. On the left about 4 miles outside of Liberty, it looks like they are building a new service (gas) station. On the left and right, there are used car lots. There is a very big cornfield next to a couple of trailers that's hard to tell whether the trailers go along with that. There is a junkyard, down to the right, which may be the junkyard that Beverly has referred to earlier. On the right, Lee's Orchard, which looks like a salesroom, and on the left there are several good-sized cornfields, right across the street from the Citgo gas station, which is about 6 miles outside of Liberty. Hayfields, some corn, some tobacco, and some cattle being pastured . . . about six miles outside of Liberty. They look like dairy cattle, rather than beef cattle. To the left, about 6 1/2 miles outside of Liberty, is a small orchard. It almost looks like a backyard or garden orchard, there are only about 50–60 trees. Turning off Route 70 onto Route 206— there are a number of trailers along Route 206, right at the turnoff, with fields of corn with heavy Johnson grass infestation here.

Turn off Route 207 (?) onto Route 1640 and bear to the left, and I'm getting to Mrs. L's house right about 11 o'clock—

These are notes from a conversation with Mrs. L today. When I got there, we sat down for about 5 minutes, just with pleasantries, and I gave her some jars that I had brought, because she said last time a problem was she gives away a lot of the food she cans, and never gets the jars back. She had given me a jar of pickles, and I had a number of jars in the garage that Bill was wishing that I would get rid of, so I did that. I also gave her a fish with a magnet on the back, that I had brought from Ecuador. I came in about 11:00 o'clock and we sat down for about 15 minutes, and then she said, "I want to give you some lunch." And I protested that I hadn't meant to come in at lunchtime, but had managed to do so. And she said, "It's not going to be much, because I don't have anything really prepared, but do you like vegetables?" I said yes, I like vegetables. She said, well, we've got some vegetables and some other things, and so she sat me down in the kitchen and started to work on the lunch. I was trying to clarify a little bit her life history, and so a lot of the questions I asked her were backing up some of the information I had gotten from her last time, about her life history and what she had done, and who she had lived with, and when she had lived there. This is a little synopsis of what I know so far:

She is going to be 79 in October, which means that she was born in 1910. When she was eight years old, her father died of typhoid fever. He got typhoid fever, and was actually recovering from the typhoid fever, but it left him with Bright's Disease, (kidney failure), and he eventually died of kidney failure. He was 29 years old, and her mother was 27 at the time. She said that she had always been close to her mother's parents, the Crockett family. Her maternal grandmother's family name was Helms, and she said the Helms' and the Crocketts were among the first settlers in Central County, along with the Grants and some other families. All those families came from Tennessee. Her grandfather's grandfather was a first cousin of Davy Crockett. Much of the family was kind of "ornery" like Davy Crockett, although her own grandfather did not believe in drinking and swearing and gambling and all the other stuff some of the other families did, things that she associates with the Crockett family.

When she was a young child, she said her grandparents used to come to her parents home and say, "We're taking Mrs. L . . ." And they would take her to stay with them for a few days. She said her mother really couldn't say much about it, because they just really came and took her, but her father was always a little sore, because she was spending so much time with her grandparents. When her father died at age 29, she was eight years old, she had a six-year-old brother, she had a three-year old sister, and a five-month old brother. Eventually all of them went back to live with her mother's parents. Her mother tried to maintain the family on the farm where she and her husband had farmed, but the grandparents said, "No, you should come back and live with us . . ."

Mrs. L said her father, when he knew he was dying, had said to his wife, "I know you're too young to be alone and I know that you'll remarry . . . I just hope that you'll marry somebody who will treat you and the kids well . . ." Mrs. L 's mother lived with her parents (she and her children) for about two years, and which point in fact, she did remarry. She married a man who had been married before, and she took the two smallest children with her, and left the two oldest children with her grandparents. Mrs. L at this time was ten years old. She then (Mrs. L 's mother) had another child with the new husband, so that Mrs. L has one half-brother.

Mrs. L lived with her grandmother and grandfather (her grandfather was a blacksmith and a farmer); he did a lot of repair work and shoed horses. He was . . . apparently his "smithie" was a local hangout, and she said her grandmother used to say, "Now, fly down and see how many men are down there, so I know how much bread to prepare." Her grandmother would make lunch, or make dinner, and invite all the people who were hanging around the "smithie" at the time, to dinner. She said that they raised most of their food, and that they would take her grandfather, who also had a corn mill, and would take corn and grind it for meal, and crack it for the animals. When other people brought their corn to the mill, the way that they paid for it was by taking a toll, or giving a toll to the miller, and there would be a certain measure of each bushel of corn that would be kept aside for the miller, as payment. She said before that her grandfather had orchards, and that they produced a lot of apples, as well as the garden crops that her grandmother raised. She (Mrs. L) helped, and wheat, corn . . . they raised pork and they would smoke it, but that both in her grandfather's house and later, when she was married, until the time she had a freezer, they would very rarely eat beef. They would never raise or kill a beef until they had a freezer. Before that time, somebody would slaughter every week or two, and they would buy enough beef for a day or two, and use it that way. But for the most part, they had pork and chicken.

Her grandmother died when she was fourteen, and in Mrs. L 's terms, she "took over all the jobs of a woman" . . . she kept house, she cleaned and cooked and mended, she kept the chickens, and did a lot of farm work, the kind of farm work that women did, and she said that the reason she married so young, at 16 1/2, is just because she just wanted to get away from there. She didn't want to cook and clean for other people. She thought if she got married, then there would be two of them working together. So she married a man who was nineteen at the time she was 16 1/2 years, and went to live with her parents-in-law. She said she lived with her parents-in-law for 2 1/2 years, and "kind of didn't like it" because the parents-in-law were farmers and as soon as she and her husband moved into the farm, they started traveling and left all the farm work to their two sons and all the housework to Mrs. L . So, Mrs. L said she had all the housework for this extended family, including cooking and cleaning and mending and washing, as well as taking care of her own baby.

Her first child was born a year after she got married, the second one was born 22 months later, and the third one was born when the second child was three years old, and Mrs. L was not yet 22 years of age. I said, "Why didn't you have more?" She said, "Why, three was enough. I didn't think I could educate more than three, or raise more than three." And then she added, "Well, I guess it was to be . . ." I was kind of hoping she'd tell me how she managed not to have more children after she was 22 years old, but she didn't volunteer the information, and I didn't feel quite ready to ask, although I may, some time in the future.

Her three children are—the oldest boy is named R, the middle one is a girl named A, and the third one is a boy, and I think the name she has mentioned is "Albie," but I'm not sure that I've gotten it quite correctly. The boy (R), who is now himself in his sixties, is the son who lives across the street, and was farming the dairy farm with her, and still raises some tobacco, but they sold off the dairy herd about a year ago, and he has gone to work in the Oshkosh Factory. He says it is easier work, and it was getting too hard to do the farming, although he still kind of likes cattle, and he now has twenty-five (or they have, together) 25 head of Holstein cows that they are breeding to a Hereford bull, for beef cattle. They still have one cow that they keep because they are raising a few veal. . . a few small calves, with the milk.

She had a gallon jar of milk in the refrigerator, which she used to cook with. She says it's from the cow. I don't know how long that lasts, although she used milk in several dishes, in the lunch that I'll describe below.

After she and her husband left his parents' house, about 2 1/2 years after they were married, they moved (they rented a house), that she said was the house that she in fact had been born in. It was the same house that her parents had been renting when she was born, although they later had bought their own little farm. Her husband had a team, and he worked in road construction as well as renting farm land and farming, for a number of years. She said they moved to Ohio once to try out living in Ohio, and lasted there about six weeks. She said she didn't mind it, but actually her husband didn't like it and wanted to come back to Central County. They came back. I'm not sure about the timing of it, but I'm sure it was fairly early in their marriage. Later on, he continued to farm and work in road construction and other kinds of things and eventually they bought the farm that she is living on now. I don't know how many acres they started out with, but she now has about 100 acres. She was complaining that most of it was growing up, and that they are not cutting the hay and they are not farming it anymore. Her son isn't, in the way she would like to, and it kind of hurts her to see the farm go to weeds.

She mentioned a date of 32 years ago that she and her husband had gone into dairy farming. I'm not sure, from other things she said, (I need to pin down the date) I think they have been on this farm a little bit longer than that. They've been on the farm for around 40 years, and they had moved there in the 1940's. She and her husband operated the dairy farm together until eleven years ago, when her husband died. Then she and her son operated the dairy farm up until last year.

She has always grown a garden. She was telling me about the kinds of things she has in the garden. She showed me a pole bean (or she calls it a stick bean) that she has been raising for something like 40–45 years, that her husband had been working on someone else's farm and they fed him lunch, and he came home and said, "These are the best beans. I had the best beans I ever ate today!" So she went to that person and asked for the seed, and since then has been growing that particular kind of "stick bean" in her garden and saving the seed. She has given the seed to a lot of other people in the county. She thinks that pretty much anybody that has that particular "stick bean" has gotten the seed from her, and people will say, "You know I'm growing this bean. I think you gave that seed to my mother . . ." And she said, "Yes, I did . . . I gave it to your mother thirty or forty years ago." She doesn't appear to do much selection, although when she is shelling beans for seed, she selects out the best looking beans, the biggest ones, for seed.

These are the beans she had just canned, a total of about 100 quarts, although that includes 38 half gallons. She's been using half gallon jars. I asked if that wasn't a lot of beans, and she said, "Well, it's too much for her now, but in the past, she used to have to feed farmhands, and they usually had two or three farmhands, and they'd eat up a half gallon of beans at a time." So, now she's still sort of in the habit of canning half gallons, she likes the half gallons. The beans are cut into about inch and a half segments, and canned. The seeds are pretty big (I ate some for lunch), and they taste as though, in fact, they were probably at the point when a lot of the structural proteins are being laid down. They tasted almost like (they are fresh beans) they could have been dried before cooking. I need to know more about the nutrient content of that, but I think that, like corn at the "dough" stage, they had already started to lay down structural proteins. But the pods are still green and tender. She said that the advantage of this kind of beans is that they get nice and big and they still stay tender and they have good flavor. In fact, they did, to me, have a very good flavor. She also grows several kinds of lower growing beans. She grows two kinds of white runner beans, one that, from her description, sounds like half runners, because she said one is shorter than the other. She also grows another kind of runner bean (I've forgotten the name). I think she said it is a brown-seeded runner bean, but it didn't sound like a scarlet runner. She has got early crops and late crops. She has a late crop that is not yet ready to pick. Her early crop is at the height of the picking season, and she has been picking beans that morning, and in fact, had canned about four half gallons, or eight quarts, by the time I got there.

She grows several different kinds of tomatoes. She likes the Rutgers tomato for canning, because it has a little more acid. She was saying (she only grows the hybrid, and doesn't save seed for tomatoes) that the modern tomatoes have less acid, and while she knows that you're supposed to add lemon juice to the beans when you're canning them, to increase the acid content, she doesn't do that herself. She says she's never had a can of tomatoes go bad on her. She is growing Rutgers (tomatoes) for canning, and she also grows Big Girl, because she likes them better than the Big Boys, for example, and she mentioned another kind of tomato that she showed me, a very large slicing tomato (but I've forgotten the name of it). She has two corn crops, and there are two corn crops planted. She's got a white corn variety that is coming in right now, and actually it's just now ending. She says she has picked the last ears from this corn crop, and the next corn crop will be in a couple of weeks. She says that's her big crop. That's the crop that she is going to do—freeze, from.

She talked about the kinds of canning that she is doing. She says that the plums were ready, and that she had been canning plums. She showed me some jars. But what she has been working on for the past two or three weeks is mostly beans, because the beans were in and the crop was ready to can. She was just starting to work on tomatoes, and that for a while, since this crop of beans is over, she is going to be working on tomatoes and tomato juice, and had actually picked a bucket of tomatoes this morning, because she is going to can them tonight. Her canning for tomatoes—what she is planning to do with this particular batch—is to just section the tomatoes and put them in jars and process them in a cold water bath. She had processed the beans in a pressure canner. For the tomatoes, she said one way of dealing with the fact that the tomatoes have less acid, is that she processes them a little more than she used to. She used to use a processing time of about 28 minutes for a quart (which seems quite low to me, actually), but now that she was adding a little bit of time to that, because she was afraid the tomatoes needed more time, now that they were less acidic.

She has sauerkraut made and jarred, about 10 quarts. She said it looked good, and she said this batch was going to be pretty good. It was hard to tell this early. She said kraut was kind of tricky, but the color looked good. It was still sort of processing itself in the jars.

The other thing she talked about starting to put up now was peaches, and that she was buying peaches at the grocery store. She thinks they are from Georgia. Central County has some peaches, although she doesn't have any peach trees. Central County grows some peaches, but she thinks the crop was lost this year because of the late freeze.

Later in the visit, she took me down to show me the stuff she had already put up, and as I said, I saw about 10 quarts of sauerkraut, and what clearly looked like 100 quarts, or close to 100 quarts, of beans. Also 10–15 jars of different kinds of pickles, and she said she had quit pickling. She had quite a bit of stuff left over from last year, and she said she was going to pour out some of it. She said she would pour out the fruit juices. She had plum juice and apple juice, for making jelly, but she didn't make as much as she used to, because "nobody eats it anymore." She doesn't know why they don't eat it, but she guesses they use toast rather than other kinds of bread, and just don't eat the amount of jelly they used to. She said she might want to pour out some vegetables that are from two years ago, and she just doesn't use as much as she used to. She gives a lot of it away. In the past, when she had to cook for farmhands, she used a lot more. Now she only cooks for herself and her son. Her son R eats dinner with her everyday during the school year, because his wife is a schoolteacher, but during the summer, he doesn't eat with her. So she was saying, I need to start putting up some stuff, because in two weeks R is going to start to eat with me again. She did mention that she hardly wants to cook for herself. As a matter of fact, earlier, or during my visit, she was baking biscuits and the biscuits burned, and she said, "Oh, it's just because I'm so out of practice!"

She prepared a lunch for me, which she apologized about, because I think I kept her talking too much, and she wasn't paying attention to it, but she used some of the beans that she had prepared for canning. She had some still in a pot, and she cooked them with a pork chop, and basically cooked them the whole time I was there, or until we ate, which was about two hours. She took about five ears of fresh corn, and cut the kernels off, and then sort of scraped the corn to get the corn milk off, into the bowl, and then she put what looked like about two tablespoons of Crisco in a skillet and added the corn, and also cooked that for about an hour and a half or so. She started preparing this about 11:30, and we ended up eating at about 1:00, so that the corn cooked for about an hour and a half. She sautéed it for a while in the Crisco, and then towards the end of the cooking, she added some milk and butter so that it was a very nice creamed corn by the time it was served. She took four pork chops and dipped them into beaten egg and then flour, and put what looked to be about a quarter or a third of a cup of Crisco in a skillet, and fried them. They probably were fried for about forty minutes (they sat on the table a little while before we ate). She took some fried apples out of the refrigerator, and she said she was just going to warm them up. She put a little more Crisco in the bottom of another skillet, and warmed them up. She made some boiled potatoes. I think she peeled about 3 to start out with.

They were potatoes that she grew in her own garden, and had dug them up. She said she keeps them in the basement, but they don't last very well anymore. They don't last through the winter. They sprout. In the past, she said, that they had a root cellar, and then showed me a concrete slab in the backyard, which is apparently excavated. It is the roof of a root cellar, built into a little hillside. She said that the concrete slab had cracked, and that the root cellar leaked and so it didn't keep things anymore, and that she had tried patching it a couple of times, but it still leaked. She was needing to get somebody to help her get a new repaired, some new concrete or pour a new one, so that she could use the root cellar and keep her potatoes which she hasn't been able to keep. Then she said she thought she would do what they used to do, that when she lived with her grandparents, and then she and her husband would bury potatoes. They would hollow out a little bit in the ground and line it with straw, and then pile the potatoes up, and then cover them with straw and then cover the whole thing with dirt, and that would keep the potatoes through the whole winter without any trouble at all, in real good condition. She was talking about having her son help her bury the potatoes this year, so that she could keep them through the winter.

[This particular type of storage sounds very like the kind of storage that is used in parts of Ecuador, and that kind of straw and dirt burying method is called a "Yata." It sounds very, very similar.]

These potatoes were potatoes that she had just dug, however, and she said she also had several varieties. This was a white variety, with some very nice tubers. Very nice looking potatoes, and that she had another variety coming along in a little while.

At any rate, the first set of potatoes—we got to talking and forgot about them, and they ended up scorching, and she threw them all out and started over again, and peeled another 4–5 potatoes, and boiled them. She served them with what looked like a quarter of cup of butter poured over the top. She baked biscuits, and I was impressed because she, although I know that good cooks can do this, she didn't measure anything. She just sort of sifted flour until it looked like enough, and then she put in, kept adding Crisco until it looked like it was enough, and baking powder—and didn't measure that either—mixed it around, and then added milk, until it was the right consistency (added milk from the jar in the refrigerator. She kneaded them and rolled them out, and put them on a tray and put them in the oven, and eventually when she took them out, they were quite overdone. They hadn't risen very much, and dark brown, although not really burnt, and she apologized and said she had turned the oven up too high, and hadn't really looked at it, and had baked them at too high a temperature.

I asked her about her oven—it is an electric stove, with an electric oven—and I asked her if she had used electricity to cook with for a long time, and she said, "Yes . . ." She had used electricity for over 30 years because her husband didn't like to cut stove wood, so that they had electric. This was her second electric stove and it worked like a dream. She had to replace the elements a couple of times, and it had had a double oven and one of the ovens stopped working. Since she really didn't need the oven anymore, she had never had it repaired, but yes, she was quite used to cooking on an electric range.

When she took the pork chops out of the pan, she added some flour and browned it in the pan juices, and then added milk and made white gravy for the biscuits. Then she opened a jar of peaches, which was dessert, so that our meal consisted of pork chops, creamed corn, boiled potatoes, beans with some pork in them, fried apples, fresh sliced peeled tomatoes, and later, canned peaches.

While she did some cooking with real butter, I thought it was kind of interesting that she put margarine on the table. She said, "I don't usually put this on the table (she put it on the table in the tub), but I'm going to do it." She kept apologizing that she hadn't had time to cook a real, good dinner, because she had been canning all morning. So, I said, "Oh, don't you make your own butter anymore?" She said, "no, I put away the churn." So I asked if it was because they didn't have dairy cattle anymore, and didn't have enough milk. And she said, no, actually we get enough milk to churn, but nobody eats it anymore. "My children don't want butter anymore, they say it's got too many calories, and that they want margarine because it doesn't have as many calories." Then she said, "this one wants this kind of margarine, and that one wants that kind of margarine, so I just stopped using or making butter," although she did have some in the refrigerator, and used it too cook with. She said "I think they make too much of that, I don't think that it makes any difference, butter or margarine." Then she opened the freezer, and said, my one son will only eat this stuff, and she had Shedd's Country Crock. He said it has less calories. I said well, that one does have less calories, but the other margarines that she put on the table that she said her other son eats, was a sort of generic tub soft margarine. It was in fact, a corn oil margarine.

One thing I noticed about what Mrs. L ate, was that she did not eat any of the pork chops. She had beans, and corn, and biscuits with gravy, and several—at least three slices of tomato—and several helpings of the fried apples, but she did not have any of the pork chops. While I was there, she did not have any peaches. She made me coffee, but she did not drink coffee, or iced tea, although there was iced tea in the refrigerator.

I noticed that she had a microwave which she used to defrost the pork chops, and I said, Oh! a microwave! how long have you had that? She said she had had it for a couple of years, and that her daughter gave it to her for Christmas, and she was kind of mad because her daughter had given her several other things for Christmas. Then she said, "Why did you go and get me a microwave too?" And her daughter said, "Well, I had one, and I won one at a raffle . . . and so, I won this little one, so this one's for you." So she said, "I'm just going to give this one to you, Mother." What she said was, that she didn't think she wanted it, until she got it, and now, if it were to break down, she'd go out and get another one. She finds it real handy, especially defrosting. And also, she makes her oatmeal in it every morning. So I said, Oh! you eat oatmeal every morning? And she said, well, I really don't care much for it, but I heard that it's good for you. "Now I don't have cholesterol, but I've got that other stuff—triglycerides—and they say that's worse, and wouldn't you know it! I'd have the worst one, so I've been eating oatmeal because they say it's good for your cholesterol."

We got to talking a little bit about oatmeal and oat bran, and I said, well, I kind of like oatmeal, but I like the oat bran cereal better. That it tastes more like Cream of Wheat. She said, well, I don't like Cream of Wheat either. But she said, "I can eat it. I can eat any of those things, and I can eat the oatmeal, but I don't kind of care for it much."

We started talking about cereals, or breakfast food—and she said, well, when we were younger, or when I wasn't living alone, I'd make biscuits every morning, and we'd have biscuits and gravy. And I said, Oh! biscuits and gravy . . .! And she said, "Oh, you must be a country girl, if you like biscuits and gravy." So I said, "No, I wasn't . . . but my husband was . . . I grew up in the city and all I ever had was Cheerios. What I had most of the time was Cheerios . . ." She said, "Cheerios! I really still like Cheerios. They're my favorite! But you know, they've gotten so high. They are so expensive . . ." So we started talking about how expensive breakfast cereals were, and I said the other day I went to buy an oat bran cereal and I realized it was $3.00-something a box . . . and she said her daughter probably was trying to buy the same cereal, because she said she was buying a box of cereal that cost $3.00 a box, and she was sort of horrified! Mrs. L said, I don't think I'd buy it if it was that expensive . . . So I said, yes, well, Cheerios are getting kind of expensive too! But she said, yes, but a box of cereal lasts her several weeks. Recently she's been eating corn flakes, which she doesn't like that much, but she said, "You know, when I eat them it's not for breakfast. You know, I kindly don't sleep too well anymore, and I kindly want to stay up late, and I get hungry in the evening, so I have a bowl of corn flakes before I go to bed at night and that kindly satisfies me, so I can sleep."

Another thing that was on the table was a jar of homemade plum jelly.

She said that when she was younger, when she was a kid, that nobody had any money. People didn't have money, but they traded for the things they wanted, to some extent. They raised a lot of the things they needed. She said that their family was poor, but they always had everything they needed. She said the one thing she has always regretted, and she said this the last time I talked with her, is that she didn't have an education. She was in a one-room school until she was in eighth grade, at which she passed the eighth grade exam when she was thirteen, and then she would have had to have gone into town for high school, and the only way to get there would have been riding a horse, and her grandfather said she was too little a girl to ride a horse into town. She thought she probably would have had to leave real early and probably get back about sundown, but she really wanted to do it. She said a lot of the boys went to school, but very few girls went to high school. But there were a couple of girls up a little ways from her, that rode horses to school, but that not very many girls went to high school who didn't live in town. She said she's always been sorry that she didn't get more education, that she thinks if her father had lived, that that side of her family (the Davis') felt that education was important, and that if her father had lived, she would have gotten an education.

She talked about feeling that she didn't remember names and things too well anymore. Names "would just fly out of my head," she said, when she tried to remember them. She wondered if it wasn't the medication she was taking. She has had a flare up of bursitis in the last couple of weeks, and she has been taking steroids, which she said, seemed to have helped quite a lot. She also takes two high blood pressure pills a day. Then she says she's had some pains in her legs, so she takes quinine (?) for the pains in her leg. I'm not sure exactly what that is. She said the quinine gives her a headache. She said she needs to be careful about blood pressure, since she has got high blood pressure, and that it runs in her family. On her mother's side of the family, "all the women died of strokes, and all the men died of heart disease." She feels that it runs in the family. Her mother died of a stroke, although she was eighty-five. She says she thinks it has a lot to do with the diet that they used to eat, that everything was salted and smoked, all the meat. So, she thinks that kind of might contribute to the blood pressure problems, because she says, "Now they tell you you need to be careful about salt." I did notice that she did use quite a bit of salt in the cooking. She would add it to the food in what seemed to be very generous pinches, almost handfuls! As I said, she said that her son eats with her during the school year when his wife is working as a schoolteacher, but that during the summer, she eats by herself, and that she just doesn't cook that much for herself. Then she apologized, and she said that was one of the reasons why she burned the biscuits, because she's just not used to making biscuits.

She said that when she had farmhands, she always fed the farmhands. So I said, "Oh, is that part of a farmhand's wages around here?" And she said, "Not really, not too many give them lunch anymore, but James (her husband) always said I don't have a man working for me that I wouldn't eat with.." So that they would always feed the farmhands dinner. She mentioned before (and it is in other notes) that she would cook something like two chickens a day to feed her family and the farmhands. And, as I mentioned before, she said that she is so used to putting up half gallon jars of things, because they would use that much when they had to feed farmhands. She's not had any farmhands to feed, though, for about a year now.

She talked a little bit about what might happen when she got older. She said when her husband was quite ill, just before he died, he said, "Mrs. L , when I die, why don't you sell the farm and move into town? You'd be more closer to things and it would be easier to get around.." But she said she thought about it some, but she's never really quite gotten around to doing it, and she doesn't think she'd like living where she couldn't "feel the dirt under her feet." So, she has never done that, although she said, "If I got bad, maybe I would have to move to town, although I don't know what good it would do me, if I were in an apartment. It wouldn't be any different, I've got the electricity and the water and things here in the house.." She said she would kind of like to go to the Senior Center, but she doesn't have a way to get there. She's never been there. That's one thing she thinks she might do if she lived in town. She'd be able to go to the Senior Center.

She did say that she didn't have water in the house for many years. She would haul water from the well, just outside the house to drinking and haul it from the creek to wash. When they dug a well and piped it in she said it made her job a lot easier and her husband was kind of repentant that he had not put water in the house before, that he had made her do all that extra work.

She said that she had—she obviously tends this garden by herself—that she had picked several bushels of beans in the last few days, and she picked a bushel of tomatoes this morning, and she said, "Well, I can see that someday I wouldn't be able to do that, but for now, I really want to . . ."

By the way, her birthday is October 25, 1910.

Let me note that Mrs. L did say that she wasn't going to put up any more of those—at least this kind of bean—and my impression was any other kind of bean, because she now had enough, the 100 quarts would be enough.

Although somewhat later, she said she was going to get a late crop of beans, and I wasn't clear as to whether she was going to put up any of them.

———————◉———————

SAMPLE FIELD NOTES 3

Bill has done a number of social analyses and evaluations of development projects for the World Bank, Global Environment Facility, World Wildlife Fund, and other institutions. In general, Bill works with local investigators in the countries in which these analyses are done, and most of the evidence is gathered through rapid rural reconnaissance rather than intensive, long-term field research. Just as with research projects, he makes jot notes while speaking with people and then writes field notes as soon after as he can. Because his work is generally focused on a particular set of activities or evaluation of a project, Bill's field notes are often "sketchier" on other aspects of life. Bill does not formally code the field notes, but uses the word processor find options when he needs to recover specific information.

The following field notes come from a project to evaluate a World Bank community forestry project in Mexico (whose acronym is PROCYMAF; PRODEFOR is a Mexican government program to support the forest sector). Fernando Guadarrama Olivera was the local anthropologist who worked with Bill on this project.

13 July, 2000—Oaxaca, México
Billie R. DeWalt
Fernando picked me up promptly at 8:00 to go to San Sebastian de las Grutas. He was able to borrow a car from a friend, so it was an easy trip of about 80 kilometers. We had a bit of luck because, just when I suggested Fernando stop for some breakfast, we were at the turnoff to Sn. Sebastian. Otherwise we would easily have missed the turn. We had breakfast there in El Vado before taking the dirt road toward San Sebastian.

The fairly decent dirt road parallels a very pretty little river that is filled along the banks and in the river with sabinos, a very pretty, gigantic tree. It is an ecosystem of its own with lots of bromeliads and vines. The water was very clear and there were lots of little riffles and places where the river ran among huge boulders. (It reminded me a lot of Sabino Canyon that goes into the hills near Tucson.) There was a spot where there was a large flat spot by the river that looked well used by picnickers. It was surprisingly clean.

Sn. Sebastian has a huge, well-maintained church. The municipal and comunidad indigena offices are right in front of the church. Off to one side is a really large, well-maintained school. We were met by two young guys who said that the main officials were still up in the hills. They were expecting us, and apologized that the others were not there. We talked with them while waiting for the others. They were J. S. R., the Secretaria Municipal, and L. S. S., the Secretary of the Comisariado de Bienes Comunales.

They talked about their ecotourism project, saying that until the earthquake last year they had three cabins to rent. The earthquake destroyed two of these, so only one is left functioning. The cabins are made of adobe and they said that CEDETUR told them they could not use the two damaged cabins. One of the projects they have had with PROCYMAF is an ecotourism study, and they currently have an application pending to build three wooden cabins.

We talked a bit about the history of the place. They said that there were very old documents relating to San Sebastian that dated to the 1500 and 1600s. The church is old (they had no idea how old) and was reconstructed about 8 years ago.

They have about 5400 hectares of land in the community. There is also an area of about 2000 hectares that is under dispute with a neighboring community (Aldama). They said that conciliation talks have been held and that they hope this will be resolved soon. They said there are about 400 mayores de edad (adults) in the community who are comuneros. Total population is about 2000 in the main town and two rancherias. They said that there are some people in the community who do not plant crops, but most people earn their living from agriculture. They have very little productive forest because the Compania Forestal de Oaxaca had the concession in the 1970s and they took away all of the best trees. They are not exploiting the forest now; last year they did a "cleaning" of the forest to get rid of the diseased trees and they sold some of this. They vender madera en trozo (sell logs). They started selling their own trees in 1985 but they really sell very little. They don't have a lot of forest that can be exploited right now. What they sold last year was as a result of culling the diseased trees (saneamiento). They do have a 10 year plan for the management of their forest.

They were part of the Union Mixa but withdrew from it in May of 2000. They said it did not make sense for them to belong because they were not engaging in forestry activities. At one point, it sounded as though they had to pay fees for a technician to the Union, but then later they said this was not the case. It was not clear what the reason for their withdrawal really was. The Union Mixa (Miza??) was formed in 1982 or 1983.

They first began hearing about PROCYMAF in 1998 because of regional meetings that were held. They said the foros regionales were held in different places and that they had held one of the first meetings in San Sebastian. Last Thursday the latest meeting was held in Sebastian Jutanin. They had plans to send a representative but said that something came up at the last minute and no one could go, but they do attend regularly.

They have had several projects from PRODEFOR that have supported the community. In October 1999, PRODEFOR supported the preaclareos (thinning of trees). PROCYMAF has supported two studies for them. In 1998, they did a study that looked at the possibility of bottling water for the community to commercialize. This study showed that it was possible and could be a good business, but they were scared off because it showed they needed a capital investment of about 1 million pesos. They thought this was quite high, and kind of complained that it included new everything, including two new trucks. The community voted against getting into this because a) there were not funds to install the equipment and b) some people thought there would not be enough water left over to irrigate land.

The second study was done at the end of 1999 and was an ecotourism study. They now have a project to construct new cabins, using wood from the region instead of adobe like the last ones were. The Centro Interdisciplinario de Investigacion para el Desarrollo Integral Regional of the Politecnico in Oaxaca did both studies. For the ecotourism project the community will have to put up 25% of the cost and PROCYMAF will put up 75%. They are waiting to see whether this project will be approved in Mexico City.

They have also had people attend several courses for training. One was on environmental impact in Santiago Textitlan in November of 1998, another was about rural stoves (estufa lorena) in Santa Catarina in February of 1999. One young girl also completed a course on ecotourism, a guy dropped out of the same course because he left for working outside the community.

I asked about the course for rural stoves and its effects. They said that when they came back they talked with people about the stoves, but they could not convince anyone to really build them. The Comisariado de Bienes Comunales was one of the people who attended. They said that they thought that PROCY-MAF needed to do a course in the community before it would have much effect.

We talked a bit about the struggle to eliminate the concessions. They talked about the organization of communities that had done it. The people from San Pedro el Alto, Sta. Maria Zanisa, and others led the fight.

The Comisariado de Bienes Comunales, L. P. L. and the head of the Comite de Vigilancia, N. L. G., showed up about halfway through the interview. It was clear that they did not have a clear understanding of the difference between PRODEFOR and PROCYMAF. Their main contact with both programs has been through P. C. who is the technician working with them. They are very supportive of the projects however. They said the big problem they had was that there was no support given to them after they got the rights to their forests. This is the first real support and the regional meetings are what they see as the vehicle for support. They said the Comite de Recursos Naturales began in 1998.

I asked about cargos (community offices) and migration. They said that people chosen for cargos do come back to the community, but the mayordomo part of the system has really broken down. They said they used to have mayordomos for everything, but now just have collaboration of the community to have the fiestas. There are several people who belong to a Protestant sect, but they said this was not a problem. Those people participate in the tequios (communal work) and so are members of the community. Apparently there is little social conflict because of religion. They also said that the PRI had won their community by just a few votes, with the PRD coming in second and PAN third. Again, they said that the political differences did not split up the community. Those people who do migrate are employed as masons, drivers, machinery operators. Both boys and girls are migrating equally they said.

About 20% of their land is in cultivation, mainly in maize and beans. They have about 10% of land in pine, and the other 70% is a mix of pine and Encino.

They had tobacco up until about 10 years ago but the company went broke and they had no market for it. They also cultivated Zempozuche (I think this is marigolds) for a while.

The comisariado said that there were about 300 family heads and that about 50% of these had their own yunta (ox team). The average amount they plant is three hectares. Although he initially could not give an estimate of yields (porque no tantiamos), Fernando skillfully got the data in another way. The result was that he estimated that they harvested 40 cargas per hectare and this added up to about 1500 to 2000 kilos of maize per hectare and about 300 kilos of beans. They plant one kilo of frijol to 4 kilos of maize, interspersing them randomly. The 300 kilos of beans they thought would last a family a whole year, and they estimated that family consumption of maize was 56 kilos a week. The comisariado has quite a mixed enterprise with about 150 chivitos (both sheep and goats), and lots of chickens. He said others have even larger herds of chivitos. They have enough chickens in the community so there is no need to buy them outside. When they do look for work outside, they work as peons in the forest enterprise of San Pedro el Alto.

We returned to the theme of the projects. They said that most people were not very enthusiastic about the projects because they are studies, and that they have not received any actual resources for projects. They also have PROCAMPO that about 80 people are getting (a lot of people just don't want it) and PROGRESA in which about 60 families are left out with about 180 participating. They also get milk from the DIF program with about 90 people getting that—for kids between 4 months and five years. There is also a rural store (tienda). The comisariado said that all of them brought benefits to the community.

No one any longer speaks Zapotec in the community. They said it disappeared as a language about 20 years ago. INI has been there with programs but when Fernando asked if they participated in any of them, they said no, that people did not want to take on debt. They wanted gifts. As he so picturesquely said, they are interested in programs "dado y olvidado" (given and forgotten), not ones for which they have to take on debt. PROCYMAF is good because it is mostly dado y olvidado.

Services in the community—

They do have a telephone. There is piped water but it doesn't have much pressure so most people use wells. There is no drainage and most people use latrines. They have had electricity for about 30 years. There is no plaza so they have to go to Yocuso (Tuesdays) or to Zimatlan (Wednesdays). But most people just go to Oaxaca. The PROGRESA program makes the mothers go to the clinic in San Vicente which is supposed to be there for them. But they said that they could not count on the doctor being there, that the medicines needed were not available, and so most people went to Oaxaca for medical care. It costs 20 pesos to go to Oaxaca on the bus and there is service about every two hours. There are still a few midwives in the community. They do have a telesecundaria but have to go to Oaxaca for preparatory school. They also have postal service. It was interesting that they had a SKYTEL for television on the roof of the community building. People chipped in for it, although it apparently only gets a few channels.

They said that a travel agent in Oaxaca books the cabins for ecotourism. They did not know who it was. SEDETUR is also involved. They said the river always has water in it.

We then went to the springs in the community and the place where the cabins are located. The cabins are in a very nice spot, on a very level plain. Someone was occupying the one cabin that was still in good shape. The area around the springs was very well kept with no garbage around. They said the community made sure it was kept clean. We then walked up the hill to one of their caves. They have a guide who takes people through. They only have two large flashlights, so when the group is large, it is a bit difficult.

The tour consisted of the guide pointing out different formations and telling us what "form" these formations had. So, there were elephants, penguins, two people embracing, falcons, chickens, turtles, etc. The guide knew nothing about the geology of the cave. There were bats flying around, and a few pools of water. At one point we could hear an underground river. Apparently, by rappelling, you can easily get down to it. The guide said he had been there and that along the river it was sandy. A group from the polytechnic in Oaxaca was in the cave exploring one of the branches. We were neither able to see or hear them. The cave is nicely provided with both an entrance and an exit. The exit is a fairly steep climb, but they have done a good job of building steps both in the cave and at the exit. There is apparently another cave, but it only has an entrance and they have not discovered if there is an exit.

There was a group waiting for us when we got back to the entrance. It had eight people (mostly teenagers) in it. Another group of about eight came up the hill also – an extended family by the looks of it. They charge 7 pesos for entrance and the guided tour. Apparently there is only one guide.

Before we left, we bought lunch for the three guys who accompanied us. There is a small restaurant in the community that has built a really nice palapa over some tables. They had a chicken dish and beef steak. I had the latter which was grilled to be almost crisp. Fernando reported that the chicken dish was not any better. Some of them had beer and I and one of the guys had a mescal. They said the mescal was made in the community and was far better than the "artificial" stuff from Oaxaca. When we got back to the municipal building, we said our goodbyes. They gave each of us a handful of small peaches to eat on the road back to Oaxaca.

NOTE

1. All names used in the text of the sample field notes are pseudonyms.

❧ Bibliography ❧

Adler, Patricia A. 1985. *Wheeling and Dealing: An Ethnography of an Upper-Level Drug Dealing and Smuggling Community*. New York: Columbia University Press.

Adler, Patricia A., and Peter Adler. 1987. *Membership Roles in Field Research*. Newbury Park, CA: Sage Publications.

———. 1994. Observational techniques. In *Handbook of Qualitative Research*. N. Denzin and Y. Lincoln, eds. 377–92. Thousand Oaks, CA: Sage Publications.

Agar, Michael. 1986. *Speaking of Ethnography*. Beverly Hills, CA: Sage Publications.

———. 1996. *The Professional Stranger: An Informal Introduction to Ethnography*, 2nd edition. San Diego: Academic Press.

Allen, Christina. 1996. What's wrong with the "golden rule"? Conundrums of conducting ethical research in cyberspace. *The Information Society: An International Journal* 12(2):175–88.

Allen, Katherine. 1988. *The Hold Life Has: Coca and Cultural Identity in an Andean Community*. Washington, DC: Smithsonian Institution Press.

Altork, Kate. 1995. Walking the fire line: The erotic dimension of the fieldwork experience. In *Taboo: Sex, Identity, and Erotic Subjectivity in Anthropological Fieldwork*. D. Kulick and M. Willson, eds. 107–39. London: Routledge.

American Anthropological Association. 2009. Code of Ethics of the American Anthropological Association, www.aaanet.org/_cs_upload/issues/policy-advocacy/27668_1.pdf (accessed May 2010).

American Sociological Association. 1997. ASA Code of Ethics. www.asanet.org/members/ecoderev.html (accessed May 2010).

———. 1999. ASA Code of Ethics. www.asanet.org/images/asa/docs/pdf/Ethics%20Code.pdf.

Arhem, Kaj. 1994. Antropologins mening: En introduktion. In *Den antropologiska erfarenhetem*. K. Arhem, ed. Stockholm: Carlsson Bokforlag.

Ashkenazi, Michael, and Fran Markowitz. 1999. Introduction: Sexuality and prevarication in the praxis of anthropology. In *Sex, Sexuality, and the Anthropologist*. F. Markowitz and M. Ashkenazi, eds. Urbana: University of Illinois Press.

Atkinson, Paul, and Martyn Hammersley. 1994. Ethnography and participant observation. In *Handbook of Qualitative Research*. N. K. Denzin and Y. S. Lincoln, eds. 248–61. Los Angeles: Sage.

Babbie, Earl R. 1973. *Survey Research Methods*. Belmont, CA: Wadsworth.

Bailey, Frederick G. 1960. *Tribe, Caste, And Nation: A Study of Political Activity and Political Change in Highland Orissa*. Manchester, UK: Manchester University Press.

Barnouw, Victor. 1963. *Culture and Personality*. Homewood, IL: Dorsey.

Bastidas, Elena P., and Carlos A. Gonzalez. 2009. Social cartography as a tool for conflict analysis and resolution: The experience of the Afro-Colombian communities of Robles. *Peace and Conflict Studies* 15(2):1–14.

Becker, Howard. 1970. *Sociological Work: Method and Substance*. Chicago: Aldine.

Behar, Ruth. 1996. *The Vulnerable Observer: Anthropology That Breaks Your Heart*. Boston: Beacon Press.

Bell, Diane, Pat Caplan, and Wazir Jahan Karim. 1993. *Gendered Fields: Women, Men and Ethnography*. London: Routledge.

Benedict, Ruth. 1934. *Patterns of Culture.* New York: Houghton Mifflin.

Bentley, Margaret E., et al. 1988. Rapid ethnographic assessment: Applications in a diarrhea management program. *Social Science & Medicine* 27(1):107–16.

Bernard, H. Russell. 1995. *Research Methods in Anthropology: Qualitative and Quantitative Approaches*, 2nd edition. Walnut Creek, CA Altamira Press.

———. 2006. *Research Methods in Anthropology: Qualitative and Quantitative Approaches*. Lanham, MD: AltaMira Press.

Bernard, H. Russell, and Gery W. Ryan. 2009. *Analyzing Qualitative Data: Systematic Approaches*. Los Angeles: Sage Publications.

Boehlefeld, Sharon Polancic. 1996. Doing the right thing: Ethical cyberspace research. *The Information Society: An International Journal* 12(2):141–52.

Boellstorff, Tom. 2010. *Coming of Age in Second Life: An Anthropologist Explores the Virtually Human*. Princeton, NJ: Princeton University Press.

Bohr, Niels. 1963. Essays, 1958–1962, on atomic physics and human knowledge. In *The Philosophical Writings of Niels Bohr*. Volume 3. New York: Interscience Publishers.

Bolton, Ralph. 1995. Tricks friends and lovers: erotic encounters in the field. In *Taboo: Sex, Identity, and Erotic Subjectivity in Anthropological Fieldwork*. D. Kulick and M. Willson, eds. 140–67. London: Routledge.

———. 1996. Coming Home: Confessions of a gay ethnographer in the years of the plague. In *Out in the Field: Reflections of Lesbian and Gay Anthropologists*. E. Lewin and W. Leap, eds. 147–70. Urbana: University of Illinois Press.

Bourgois, Philippe. 1995. *In Search of Respect: Selling Crack in El Barrio*. Cambridge: Cambridge University Press.

———. 1996. Confronting anthropology, education and inner-city apartheid. *American Anthropologist* 98(2):249–65.

Briggs, Jean. 1986. Kapluna daughter. In *Women in the Field: Anthropological Experiences*. P. Golde, ed. 19–44. Berkeley: University of California Press.

Brymer, Richard. 1991. The emergence and maintenance of a deviant sub-culture: The case of hunting /poaching sub-culture. *Anthropologica* 33:177–94.

———. 1998. Hanging out with the good 'ole boys, gangsters, and other disreputable characters. In *Doing Ethnography: Fieldwork Settings*. S. Grills, ed. 143–62. Thousand Oaks, CA: Sage Publications.

Caplan, Pat. 1993. Introduction 2. In *Gendered Fields: Women, Men and Ethnography*. D. Bell, P. Caplan, and W. J. Karim, eds. 19–27. London: Routledge.

CAQDAS. 2010. Computer Assisted Qualitaitve Data Analysis Networking Project. caqdas.soc.surrey.ac.uk/ (accessed June 21, 2010).

Cassell, Joan. 1987. Oh no they're not my shoes!: Fieldwork in the Blue Mountains of Jamaica. In *Children in the Field*. J. Cassell, ed. 1–26. Philadelphia: Temple University Press.

Cassell, Joan, and Sue Ellen Jacobs. 1997. *Handbook on Ethical Issues in Anthropology*. Special Publication of the American Anthropological Association 23.

Cernea, Michael M. 1992. Re-tooling in applied social investigation for development planning: Some methodological issues. In *RAP: Rapid Assessment Procedures*. N. S. Scrimshaw and G. R. Gleason, eds. 11–24. Boston: International Nutrition Foundation for Developing Countries

Cesara, Manda. 1982. *Reflections of a Woman Anthropologist: No Hiding Place*. New York: Academic Press.

Chagnon, Napoleon. 1983. *Yanomamo: The Fierce People*, 2nd edition. New York: Holt, Rinehart, and Winston.

Chambers, Robert. 1980. *Rural Development: Putting the Last First*. London: Harlow.

———. 1983. *Rural Development: Putting the Last First*. London: Longman.

———. 1992. Rapid but relaxed and participatory rural appraisal. In *RAP: Rapid Assessment Procedures*. N. S. Scrimshaw and G. R. Gleason, eds. 295–306. Boston: International Nutrition Foundation for Developing Countries.

Chapin, Mac, Zachary Lamb, and Bill Threlkeld. 2005. Mapping indigenous lands. *Annual Review of Anthropology* 34(1):619–38.

Clifford, James. 1990. Notes on (field)notes. In *Fieldnotes: The Makings of Anthropology*. R. Sanjek, ed. 47–70. Ithaca, NY: Cornell University Press.

Code of Federal Regulations. 1991. Title 45, Part 46 (Protection of Human Subjects). Washington, DC: Government Printing Office.

Code of Federal Regulations. 2009. Title 45, Part 46 (Protection of Human Subjects). Washington, DC: Government Printing Office. www.hhs.gov/ohrp/documents/OHRPRegulations.pdf.

———. 1997. *Routes: Travel and Translation in the Late Twentieth Century*. Cambridge, MA: Harvard University Press.

Cohen, Ronald, et al. 1970. Entrée into the field. In *Handbook of Method in Cultural Anthropology*. R. Naroll and R. Cohen, eds. 220–45. New York: Columbia University Press.

Collings, Peter. 2009. Participant observation and phased assertion as research strategies in the Canadian Arctic. *Field Methods* 21(2):133–53.

Constable, Nicole. 2003. *Romance on a Global Stage: Pen Pals, Virtual Ethnography, and "Mail Order" Marriages*. Berkeley: University of California Press.

Coy, Michael. 1989. Introduction. In *Apprenticeship: From Theory to Method and Back Again*. M. Coy, ed. Albany: State University of New York Press.

Cromley, Ellen K. 1999. Mapping spatial data In *Mapping Social Networks, Spatial Data and Hidden Populations*. Volume 4 of *The Ethnographers Toolkit*. J. J. Schensul, M. D. LeCompte, R. T. Trotter II, E. K. Cromley, and M. Singer, eds. 51–124. Walnut Creek, CA: AltaMira Press.

Cupples, Julie. 2002. The field as a landscape of desire: Sex and sexuality in geographical fieldwork. *Area* 34(4):382–90.

Cutcliffe, John R., and Hugh P. McKenna. 2004. Expert qualitative researchers and the use of audit trails. *Journal of Advanced Nursing* 45(2):126–35.

Dentan, Robert K. 1970. Living and working with the Semai. In *Being an Anthropologist*. G. D. Spindler, ed. 85–112. New York: Holt, Rinehart, and Winston.

Desjarlais, Robert. 1992. *Body and Emotion: The Aesthetics if Illness and Healing in the Nepal Himalayas*. Philadelphia: The University of Pennsylvania Press.

DeWalt, Billie R. 1979. *Modernization in a Mexican* Ejido: *A Study In Economic Adaptation*. Cambridge, New York: Cambridge University Press.

DeWalt, Billie R., et al. 2000. *Shrimp Aquaculture, People and the Environment in Coastal Mexico*. Washington, DC: WB/NACA/WWF/FAO.

DeWalt, Billie R., F. Guadarrama Olivera, and J. L. Betancourt Correa. 2000. *Mid-Term Evaluation of the Mexico Community Forestry Project: World Bank Latin America and the Caribbean*. Section Units: Washington, DC.

DeWalt, Kathleen M. 1977. The illnesses no longer understand: Changing concepts of health and curing in a rural Mexican community. *Medical Anthropology Newletter* 8(2).

———. 1983. *Nutritional Strategies and Agricultural Change in a Mexican Community*. Ann Arbor, MI: UMI Research Press.

———. 1999. Women's income, social power and child welfare in Manabí, Ecuador. Paper presented in the symposium Women's Associations, Social Power and Child Welfare in Manabi, Ecuador. In *Annual Meetings of the Society for Applied Anthropology*.

Dillman, Don A. 1978. *Mail and Telephone Surveys: The Total Design Method*. New York: John Wiley & Sons.

Ditton, J. 1977. *Part-time Crime*. London: MacMillan.

Dohrenwend, Bruce S., and S. A. Richardson. 1965. Directiveness and nondirectiveness in research interviewing: A reformulation of the problem. *Psychology Bulletin* 63:475–85.

Dreher, Melanie. 1987. Three children in rural Jamaica. In *Children in the Field*. J. Cassell, ed. 149–71. Philadelphia: Temple University Press.

DuBois, Cora. 1951. Culture shock. In *Mideast Regional Meeting of the Institute of International Education*. Chicago.

Dubois, Rene J. 1968. *So Human an Animal*. New York: Charles Scribner and Sons.

Dwyer, Kevin. 1982. *Moroccan Dialogues: Anthropology in Question*. Prospect Heights: Waveland Press.

Emerson, Robert M., Rachel I. Fretz, and Linda L. Shaw. 1995. *Writing Ethnographic Fieldnotes*. Chicago: University Of Chicago Press.

Enelow, Allen J., and Scott N. Swisher. 1979. *Interviewing and Patient Care*, 2nd edition. Oxford: Oxford University Press.

Fernandez, Renate. 1987. Children and parents in the field: Reciprocal interests. In *Children in the Field*. J. Cassell, ed. 185–215. Philadelphia: Temple University Press.

Finnström, Sveker. 2008. *Living with Bad Surroundings: War, History, and Everyday Moments in Northern Uganda*. Durham, NC: Duke University Press.

Firth, Raymond. 1985. Degrees of intellegibility. In *Reason and morality: ASA monographs # 24*. J. Overing, ed. 29–46. London: Routledge.

Fluehr-Lobban, Carolyn. 1994. Informed consent in anthropological research: We are not exempt. *Human Organization* 53(1):1–9.

———. 1998. Ethics. In *Handbook of Methods in Cultural Anthropology*. H. R. Bernard, ed. 173–202. Walnut Creek, CA: AltaMira Press.

Fluehr-Lobban, Carolyn, and Richard Lobban. 1986. Families, gender and methodology in the Sudan. In *Self, Sex and Gender in Cross-Cultural Fieldwork*. T. L. Whitehead and M. E. Conaway, eds. 182–93. Urbana: University of Illinois Press.

———. 1987. Drink from the Nile. In *Children in the Field*. J. Cassell, ed. 237–256. Philadelphia: Temple University Press.

Foster, George, Thayer Scudder, Elizabeth Colson, and Robert Kemper, eds. 1979. *Long-Term Field Research in Social Anthropology*. New York: Academic Press.

Freeman, Derek. 1983. *Margaret Mead in Samoa: The Making and Unmaking of an Anthropological Myth*. Cambridge, MA: Harvard University Press.

Freilich, Morris. 1970. Mohawk heroes and Trinidadian peasants. In *Marginal Natives: Anthropologists at Work*. M. Freilich, ed. 185–250. New York: Harper and Row.

Frisch, O. R. 1967. Niels Bohr. *Scientific American* 216:145–48.

Gearing, Jean. 1995. Fear and loving in the West Indies: Research from the heart. In *Taboo: Sex, Identity, and Erotic Subjectivity in Anthropological Fieldwork*. D. Kulick and M. Willson, eds. 186–218. London: Routledge.

Geertz, Clifford. 1973. *The Interpretation of Cultures: Selected Essays*. New York: Basic Books.

———. 1995. *After the Fact: Two Countries, Four Decades, One Anthropologist*. Cambridge, MA: Harvard University Press.

Gittelsohn, Joel, Anita Shankar, Keith West, Ravi Ram, and Tara Gnywali. 1997. Estimating Reactivity in Direct Observation Studies of Health Behaviors. *Human Organization* 56(2):182–89.

Gladwin, Christina H. 1989. *Ethnographic Decision Tree Modeling*. Newbury Park, CA: Sage Publications.

Glaser, Barney G. 1978. *Theoretical Sensitivity*. Mill Valley, CA: Sociology Press.

Glaser, Barney G., and Anselm Strauss. 1967. *The Discovery Of Grounded Theory; Strategies For Qualitative Research*. Chicago: Aldine Publishing Company.

Gonzalez, Nancie L. 1970. Cakchiqueles and Caribs: The social context of fieldwork. In *Marginal Narratives*. M. Freilich, ed. 153–84. New York: Harper and Row.

Good, Kenneth. 1991. *Into the Heart: One Man's Pursuit of Love and Knowledge among the Yanomama*. New York: Simon and Schuster.

Goodenough, Ward. 1992. Did you? In *The Naked Anthropologist: Tales from around the World*. P. DeVita, ed. 112–15. Belmont, CA: Wadsworth, Inc.

Green, Jesse, ed. 1978. *Zuni: Selected Writings of Frank Hamilton Cushing*. Lincoln: University of Nebraska Press.

Green, Jesse, Sharon Weiner Green, and Frank Hamilton Cushing. 1990. *Cushing at Zuni: The Correspondence and Journals of Frank Hamilton Cushing 1879–1884*: Albuquerque: University of New Mexico Press.

Grills, Scott. 1998 "An invitation to the field: Fieldwork and the pragmatist's lesson." In *Doing Ethnography: Fieldwork Settings*. S. Grills, ed. 3–18. Thousand Oaks: Sage Publications.

Guimaraes, Mario J. L. 2005. Doing anthropology in cyberspace: Fieldwork boundaries and social environments. In *Virtual Methods: Issues in Social Research on the Internet*. C. Hine, ed. 141–56. Oxford, New York: Berg.

Hader, John J., and Eduard C. Lindeman. 1933. Dynamic Social Research. New York: Harcourt, Brace and Company.

Hall, Edward T. 1959. *The Silent Language*. Garden City, NY: Doubleday.

———. 1966. *The Hidden Dimension*. Garden City, NY: Doubleday.

————. 1974. *Handbook for Proxemic Research*. Washington: Society for the Anthropology of Visual Communication.

Hamilton, Sarah. 1998. *The Two-Headed Household: Gender and Rural Development in the Ecuadorean Andes*. Pittsburgh: University of Pittsburgh Press.

Harding, Sandra. 1998. *Is Science Multicultural?: Postcolonialisms, Feminisms, and Epistemologies*. Bloomington, IN: Indiana University Press.

Harris, Marvin. 1979. *Cultural Materialism*. New York: Random House.

Hecht, Tobias. 1998. *At Home in the Street: Street Children of Northeast Brazil*. Cambridge: Cambridge University Press.

Hine, Christine. 2000. *Virtual Ethnography*. London, Thousand Oaks, CA: Sage Publications.

————, ed. 2005. *Virtual Methods: Issues in Social Research on the Internet*. New York: Berg Publishers.

Hinsley, Curtis. 1983. Ethnographic charisma and scientific routine: Cushing and Fewkes in the American Southwest, 1879–1893. In *Observers Observed: Essays in Ethnographic Fieldwork*. G. W. Stocking, Jr., ed. 53–69. Madison: University of Wisconsin Press.

Holy, Ladislav. 1984. Theory methodology and the research process. In *Ethnographic Research: A Guide to General Conduct*. R. F. Ellen, ed. London: Academic Press.

Honigmann, John. 1970. Sampling in ethnographic fieldwork. In *Handbook of Method in Cultural Anthropology*. R. Naroll and R. Cohen, eds. 266–81. New York: Columbia University Press.

hooks, bell . 1989. *Talking Back: Thinking Feminist, Thinking Black*. Boston: South End.

————. 1990. *Yearning: Race, Gender, and Cultural Politics*. Boston: South End.

Horowitz, Irving, ed. 1967. *The Rise and Fall of Project Camelot*. Cambridge, MA: MIT Press.

Horowitz, Ruth. 1996. Getting in. In *In the Field: Readings on the Field Research Experience*, 2nd edition. C.D. Smith and W. Kornblum, eds. 41–50. Westport, CT: Praeger.

Howell, Nancy. 1990. *Surviving Fieldwork: A Report of the Advisory Panel on Health and Saftey in Fieldwork*. Special Publication of the American Anthropological Association 26.

Hugh-Jones, Christine. 1987. Children in the Amazon. In *Children in the Field*. J. Cassell, ed. 27–64. Philadelphia: Temple University Press.

Human Relations Area Files Inc. 2000. *Outline of Cultural Materials*, 5th edition. New Haven, CT: Human Relations Area Files.

————. 2010. Outline of Cultural Materials. www.yale.edu/hraf/ (accessed June 21, 2010).

Huntington, G. E. 1987. Order rules the world: Our children in the communal society of the Hutterites. In *Children and Anthropological Research*. B. Butler and D. M. Turner, eds. 53–71. New York: Plenum Press.

Jackson, Jean. 1986. On trying to be an Amazon. In *Self, Sex and Gender in Cross-Cultural Fieldwork*. T. L. Whitehead and M. E. Conaway, eds. 263–74. Urbana: University of Illinois Press.

————. 1990. I am a fieldnote: Fieldnotes as a symbol of professional identity. In *Fieldnotes: The Makings of Anthropology*. R. Sanjek, ed. 3–33. Ithaca, NY: Cornell University Press.

Johnson, Jeffrey C. 1983. Of strangers and outsiders: Ethnography and serendipity in coastal communities. In *Annual Meetings of the American Anthropological Association.*
———. 1990. *Selecting Ethnographic Informants.* Thousand Oaks, CA: Sage Publications, Inc.
———. 1998. Research design and research strategies. In *Handbook of Methods in Cultural Anthropology.* H. R. Bernard, ed. 131–70. Walnut Creek, CA: AltaMira Press.
Johnson, Jeffrey C., Christine Avenarius, and Jack Weatherford. 2006. The active participant-observer: Applying social role analysis to participant observation. *Field Methods* 18:111–34.
Jorgensen, Danny. 1989. *Participant Observation.* Newbury Park, CA: Sage Publications.
Katz, J. 1988. *Seductions to Crime: Moral and Sensual Attractions in Doing Evil.* New York: Basic Books.
Keiser, Lincoln R. 1970. Fieldwork among the Vice Lords of Chicago. In *Being an Anthropologist.* G. D. Spindler, ed. 220–37. New York: Holt, Rinehart, and Winston.
W. K. Kellogg Community Health Scholars Program. 2010. Community Based Participatory Research. wwkellogghealthscholars.org/about/community.cfm.
Kent1, Linda L. 1992. Fieldwork that failed. In *The Naked Anthropologist: Tales from Around the World.* P. R. DeVita, ed. 17–25. Belmont, CA: Wadsworth.
King, Storm A. 1996. Researching Internet communities: Proposed ethical guidelines for the reporting of research. *The Information Society* 12(2):119–27.
Kirk, Jerome, and Marc L. Miller. 1986. *Reliability and Validity in Qualitative Research.* Beverly Hills, CA: Sage Publications.
Klass, Morton, and Sheila Solomon Klass. 1987. Birthing in the bush. In *Children in the Field.* J. Cassell, ed. 121–48. Philadelphia: Temple University Press.
Kluckhohn, Florence R. 1940. The participant-observer technique in small communities. *American Journal of Sociology* 46(3):331–43.
Knoblauch, Hubert. 2005. Focused ethnography. In *Forum: Qualitative Social Research* 6(3): Art. 44.
Kornblum, William. 1996. Introduction. In *In the Field: Readings on the Field Research Experience,* 2nd edition. C. D. Smith and W. Kornblum, eds. 1–7. Westport, CT: Praeger.
Kottak, Conrad Phillip. 1994. *Cultural Anthropology.* New York: McGraw-Hill.
Kozinets, Robert V. 2010. *Netnography: Doing Ethnographic Research Online.* London, Thousand Oaks, CA: Sage Publications.
Kuhn, Thomas S. 1962. *The Structure of Scientific Revolutions.* Chicago: University of Chicago Press.
Kulick, Don. 1995. Introduction. In *Taboo: Sex, Identity, and Erotic Subjectivity in Anthropological Fieldwork.* D. Kulick and M. Willson, eds. 1–28. London: Routledge.
Kulick, Don, and Margaret Willson, eds. 1995. *Taboo: Sex, Identity, and Erotic Subjectivity in Anthropological Fieldwork.* London: Routledge.
Kumar, Krishna. 1993. *Rapid Appraisal Methods.* Washington, DC: World Bank.
Kuznar, Lawrence A., and Oswald Werner. 2001. Ethnographic mapmaking: Part 1: Principles. *Field Methods* 13(2):204–13.
Leach, Edmund. 1954. *Political Systems of Highland Burma.* Boston: Beacon Press.
———. 1957. The epistemological background to Malinowski's empiricism. In *Man and Culture: An Evaluation of the Work of Bronislaw Malinowski.* R. Firth, ed. 119–38. New York: Harper Torchbooks.

Leap, William. 1996. Studying gay English: How I got here from there. In *Out in the Field: Reflections of Lesbian and Gay Anthropologists.* E. Lewin and W. Leap, eds. 128–46. Urbana: University of Illinois Press.

LeCompte, Margaret D., and Jean J. Schensul. 1999. *Analyzing and Interpreting Ethnographic Data.* Volume 5 of *The Ethnographer's Toolkit.* Walnut Creek, CA: AltaMira Press.

Lederman, R. 1986. The return of Redwoman: Field work in highland New Guinea. In *Women in the Field: Anthropological Experiences,* 2nd edition. P. Golde, ed. 359–87. Berkeley: University of California Press.

Lee, Raymond. 1995. *Dangerous Fieldwork.* Thousand Oaks, CA: Sage Publications.

Lévi-Strauss, Claude. 1961. *Tristes Tropiques.* New York: Criterion Books.

Lewin, Ellen, and William Leap. 1996a. Introduction. In *Out in the Field: Reflections of Lesbian and Gay Anthropologists.* E. Lewin and W. Leap, eds. 1–28. Urbana: University of Illinois Press.

———. eds. 1996b. *Out in the Field: Reflections of Lesbian and Gay Anthropologists.* Urbana: University of Illinois Press.

Lewins, Ann, and Christina Silver. 2007. *Using Qualitaitve Software: A Step by Step Guide.* London: Sage Publications.

Lewis, Oscar. 1951. *Life in a Mexican Village: Tepoztlán Restudied.* Urbana: University of Illinois Press.

Lincoln, Y. S., and E. G. Guba. 1985. *Naturalistic Inquiry.* Newbury Park, CA: Sage Publications.

Lindeman, Eduard C. 1924. *Social Discovery: An Introduction to the Study of Functional Groups.* New York: Republic Publishing Company.

Lohman, Joseph D. 1937. Participant observation in community studies. *American Sociological Review* 2(6):890–97.

Lugosi, Peter. 2006. Between overt and covert research: concealment and disclosure in an ethnographic study of commercial hospitality. *Field Methods* 12:541–61.

Lundberg, George A. 1937. Census of current research. *American Sociological Review* 2(4):518–30.

Lunsing, Wim. 1999. Life on Mars: Love and sex in fieldwork on sexuality and gender in urban Japan. In *Sex, Sexuality, and the Anthropologist.* F. Markowitz and M. Ashkenazi, eds. 175–95. Urbana: University of Illinois Press.

Lutz, Katherine. 1988. *Unnatural Emotions: Everyday Sentiments in a Micronesian Atoll, Their Challenges to Western Theory.* Chicago: University of Chicago Press.

Magubane, Ben. 1971. A critical look at indices used in the study of social change in colonial Africa. *Current Anthropology* 12:419–66.

Malinowski, Bronislaw. 1961 [1922]. *Argonauts of the Western Pacific.* New York: Dutton.

———. 1967. *A Diary in the Strict Sense of the Term.* New York: Harcourt, Brace and World.

———. 1978 [1935]. *Coral Gardens and Their Magic.* New York: Dover.

Maman, Suzanne, et al. 2009. Using participatory mapping to inform a community-randomized trial of hiv counseling and testing. *Field Methods* 21(4):368–87.

Marcus, G. E., and M. J. Fischer. 1986. *Anthropology as Cultural Critique: An Experimental Moment in the Human Sciences.* Chicago: University of Chicago Press.

Markowitz, Fran, and Michael Ashkenazi, eds. 1999. *Sex, Sexuality, and the Anthropologist.* Urbana: University of Illinois Press.

Martin, David. 2000. Personal communication with the authors.

Martin, Judith N. 1984. The intercultural re-entry: Conceptualization and directions for future research. *International Journal of Intercultural Relations* 8:115–34.

Maybury-Lewis, David. 1965. *The Savage and the Innocent*. Boston: Beacon Press.

McCall, George G., and J. L. Simmons. 1969. *Issues in Participant Observation: A Text and Reader*. Reading, MA: Addison-Wesley.

Mead, Margaret. 1928. *Coming of Age in Samoa*. New York: William Morrow.

———. 1949. *Male and Female, A Study of the Sexes in a Changing World*. New York: W. Morrow.

———. 1953. National character. In *Anthropology Today*. A. L. Kroeber, ed. 642–67. Chicago: University of Chicago Press.

———. 1969 [1930]. *Social Organization of Manu'a*. Honolulu: Bernice P. Bishop Museum.

———. 1970a. The art and technology of fieldwork. In *Handbook of Method in Cultural Anthropology*. R. Naroll and R. Cohen, eds. 246–65. New York: Columbia University Press.

———. 1970b. Field work in the Pacific islands 1925–1967. In *Women in the Field: Anthropological Experiences*. P. Golde, ed. 293–331. Chicago: Aldine Press.

———. 1977. *Letters from the Field, 1925–1975*. New York: Harper and Row.

Michalski Turner, Diane. 1987. What happened when my daughter became Fijian. In *Children and Anthropological Research*. B. Butler and D. M. Turner, eds. 92–114. New York: Plenum Press.

Miles, Mathew B., and A. Michael Huberman. 1994a. *Qualitative Data Analysis*, 2nd edition. Thousand Oaks, CA: Sage Publications.

———. 1994b. *Data Management and Analysis Methods*. Thousand Oaks, CA: Sage Publications.

Minocha, Aneeta A. 1979. Varied roles in the field: A hospital in Delhi. In *The Fieldworker and the Field: Problems and Challenges in Sociological Investigation*. M. N. Srinivas, A. M. Shah, and E. A. Ramaswamy, eds. 201–15. Dehli: Oxford University Press.

Mishler, Elliot. 1986. *Research Interviewing: Context and Narrative*. Cambridge, MA: Harvard University Press.

Moreno, Eva. 1995. Rape in the field: Reflections from a survivor. In *Taboo: Sex Identity and Erotic Subjectivity in Anthropological Fieldwork*. D. Kulick and M. Wilson, eds. 219–50. London: Routledge.

Mukherjee, Amitava. 2004. *Participatory Rural Appraisal:Methods and Applications in Rural Planning*, 2nd edition. New Delhi: Concept Publishing Co. .

Muller, Kevin. 2009. Zuni-made man: Frank Hamilton Cushing and the power of Zuni material culture. In *Annual Meeting of the American Studies Association*.

Mullings, Leith. 2000. African-American women making themselves: Notes on the role of black feminist research. *Souls: A Critical Journal of Black Politics, Culture and Society* 2(4):18–29.

Mullings, Leith, and Alaka Wali. 2001. *Stress and Resilience: The Social Context of Reproduction in Central Harlem*. New York: Kluwer Academic/Plenum Publishers.

Mullings, Leith, Alaka Wali, Diane McLean, Janet Mitchell, Sabiyha Prince, Deborah Thomas, and Patricia Tovar. 2001. Qualitative methodologies and community participation in examining reproductive experiences: The Harlem Birth Right Project. *Maternal and Child Health Journal* 5(2):85–93.

Murphy, Yolanda, and Robert F. Murphy. 1974. *Women of the Forest*. New York: Columbia University Press.

Murray, Stephen O. 1991. Sleeping with the natives as a source of data. *Society of Gay and Lesbian Anthropologists Newsletter* 13:49–51.

———. 1996. Male homosexuality in Guatemala: Possible insights and certain confusions from sleeping with the natives. In *Out in the Field: Reflections of Lesbian and Gay Anthropologists*. E. Lewin and W. Leap, eds. 236–61. Urbana: University of Illinois Press.

Nader, Laura. 1986. From anguish to exultation. In *Women in the Field: Anthropological Experiences*. P. Golde, ed. 97–116. Berkeley: University of California Press.

Narayan, Kirin. 1995. Participant observation. In *Women Writing Culture*. R. Behar and D. A. Gordon, eds. 33–48. Berkeley: University of California Press.

Naroll, Raoul. 1962. *Data Quality Control: A New Research Technique*. New York: Free Press.

———. 1970. Data quality control in cross-cultural surveys. In *A Handbook of Method in Cultural Anthropology*. R. Naroll and R. Cohen, eds. 927–45. Garden City, NY: Natural History Press.

Nash, June. 1976. Ethnology in a revolutionary setting. In *Ethics and Anthropology: Dilemmas in Fieldwork*. M. A. Rynkiewich, M. A. James, and P. Spradley, eds. 148–66. New York: John Wiley and Sons.

Newton, Esther. 1993. My best informant's dress: The erotic equation in fieldwork. *Cultural Anthropology* 8(1):3–23.

Nichter, Mimi, and Mark Nichter. 1987. A tale of Simeon: reflections on raising a child while conducting fieldwork in rural South India. In *Children in the Field: Anthropological Experiences*. J. Cassell, ed. 65–90. Philadelphia: Temple University Press.

Nimuendaú, Curt. 1983. *Os Apinayé*. Belém-Pará: Museu Paraense Emílio Goeldi.

———. 1987. *As Lendas Da Criação E Distruição Do Mundo Como Fundamentos Da Religião Dos Apapocúva-Guaraní*. São Paulo: Editora da Universidade de São Paulo.

———. 1993. *Etnografia E Indigenismo: Sobre Os Kaingang, Os Ofaié-Xavante E Os Índios Do Pará*. Campinas, SP: Brasil Editora da Unicamp.

Oberg, Kalervo. 1954. Culture Shock. Lecture presented to the Women's Club of Rio de Janeiro, Brazil. www.smcm.edu/academics/internationaled/pdf/culture shockarticle.pdf.

Ottenberg, Simon. 1990. Thirty years of fieldnotes: Changing relationships to the text. In *Fieldnotes: The Makings of Anthropology*. R. Sanjek, ed. 139–60. Ithaca, NY: Cornell University Press.

Patton, Michael Q. 1987. *Qualitative Evaluation Methods*. Newbury Park, CA: Sage Publications.

Paul, Benjamin. 1953. Interview techniques and field relationships. In *Anthropology Today*. A. L. Kroeber, ed. 430–51. Chicago: University of Chicago Press.

Pelto, Pertti J. 1970. *Anthropological Research: The Structure of Inquiry*. New York: Harper and Row.

———. 2001 (January). Personal communication.

Pelto, Pertti J., and Gretel H. Pelto. 1978. *Anthropological Research: The Structure of Inquiry*, 2nd edition. New York: Harper and Row.

———. 1997. Studying knowledge, culture, and behavior in applied medical anthropology. *Medical Anthropology Quarterly* 11(2):147–63.

Picchi, Debra S. 1992. Lessons in introductory anthropology from the Bakairi Indians. In *The Naked Anthropologist: Tales from Around the World*. P.R. DeVita, ed.
144–55. Belmont, CA: Wadsworth Publishing.

Poats, Susan V., and Kathleen M. DeWalt. 1999. Examining the impact of "women's
projects": Does ten years of development have an impact? Paper presented in the
Symposium: Women's Associations, Social Power and Child Welfare in Manabi,
Ecuador.

Pratt, Mary Louise. 1986. Fieldwork in common places. In *Writing Culture: the Po-
etics and Politics of Ethnography*. J. Clifford and G. Marcus, eds. 27–50. Berkeley:
University of California Press.

Punch, Maurice. 1994. *Politics and Ethics in Qualitative Research*. Thousand Oaks, CA:
Sage Publications.

Quandt, Sara, Mara Vitolins, Kathleen DeWalt, and Gun Roos. 1997. Meal patterns
of older adults in rural communities: Life course analysis and implications for
undernutrition. *Journal of Applied Gerontology* 16(2):152–71.

Rabinow, Paul. 1977. *Reflections of Fieldwork in Morocco*. Berkeley: University of
California Press.

Rappaport, Roy. 1984. *Pigs for the Ancestors*, 2nd edition. New Haven, CT: Yale
University Press.

Reason, Peter, and Hilary Bradbury, eds. 2008. *The Sage Handbook of Action Research:
Participative Inquiry And Practice*. Los Angeles: Sage.

Redfield, Robert. 1930. *Tepoztlán*. Chicago: University of Chicago Press.

Reed-Danahay, Deborah. 1997. Introduction. In *Auto/Ethnography: Rewriting the Self
and the Social*. D. Reed-Danahay, ed. Oxford: Berg.

Reid, Elizabeth. 1996 Informed Consent in the study of online communities: A
reflection on the effects of computer-mediated social research. *The Information
Society: An International Journal* 12(2):169–74.

Riemer, Jeffrey W. 1977. Varieties of opportunistic research. *Urban Life and Culture*
5:467–78.

Robert Wood Johnson Foundation. 2010. Robert Wood Johnson Qualitaitive Research Project: Audit Trail. www.qualres.org/HomeAudi-3700.html (accessed
June 21, 2010).

Rohner, Ronald, Billie R. DeWalt, and Robert C. Ness. 1973. Ethnographer bias
in cross-cultural research: An empirical study. *Behavior Science Notes* 8:275–317.

Roper, J. Montgomery, John Frechione, and Billie R. DeWalt. 1997. *Indigenous People
and Development in Latin America: A Literature Survey and Recommendations*. Latin
American Monograph and Document Series 12.

Rynkiewich, Michael A., and James P. Spradley. 1976. *Ethics and Anthropology: Dilemmas in Fieldwork*. New York: John Wiley and Sons.

Saldaña, Johnny. 2009. *The Coding Manual for Qualitative Researchers*. Thousand
Oaks, CA: Sage Publications.

Sanders, Teela. 2005. Researching the online sex work community. In *Virtual Methods: Issues in Social Research on the Internet*. C. Hine, ed. 66–79. Oxford: Berg.

Sanjek, Roger. 1990a. The secret life of fieldnotes. In *Fieldnotes: The Makings of Anthropology*. R. Sanjek, ed. 187–270. Ithaca, NY: Cornell University Press.

———. 1990b. A vocabulary for fieldnotes. In *Fieldnotes: The Makings of Anthropology*.
R. Sanjek, ed. 92–121. Ithaca, NY: Cornell University Press.

———. ed. 1990c. *Fieldnotes: The Makings of Anthropology*. Ithaca, NY: Cornell University Press.

———. 1990d. *On Ethnographic Validity*. Ithaca, NY: Cornell University Press.

———. 1990e. *Fire, Loss, and the Sorcerer's Apprentice*. Ithaca, NY: Cornell University Press.

Schensul, Stephen, Jean J. Schensul, and Margaret D. LeCompte. 1999. *Essential Ethnographic Methods: Observations, Interviews, and Questionnaires*. Volume 2 of *The Ethnographer's Toolkit*. Walnut Creek, CA: AltaMira Press.

Scheper-Hughes, Nancy. 1987. A child's diary in the strict sense of the term: Managing culture shocked children in the field. In *Children in the Field*. J. Cassell, ed. 217–36. Philadelphia: Temple University Press.

———. 1992. *Death Without Weeping*. Berkeley: University of California Press.

———. 1996. The primacy of the ethical: propositions for a militant anthropology. *Current Anthropology* 36(3):409–40.

Scrimshaw, Nevin S., and Gary R. Gleason, eds. 1992. *RAP: Rapid Assessment Procedures*. Boston: International Nutrition Foundation for Developing Countries (INFDC).

Scrimshaw, Susan, and Elena Hurtado. 1987. *Rapid Assessement Procedures for Nutrition and Primary Health Care: Anthropological Approaches to Improving Programme Effectiveness*. Tokyo: The United Nations University.

Seligman, Brenda Z. 1951. *Notes and Queries on Anthropology*, 6th edition. London: Routledge & Kegan Paul.

Shankman, Paul. 1996. The history of Samoan sexual conduct and the Mead-Freeman controversy. *American Anthropologist* 98(3):555–67.

———. 2000. Culture, biology, and evolution: The Mead-Freeman controversy revisited. *Journal of Youth and Adolescence* 29(5):539–56.

SIL International. 2010. SIL International: Partners in Language Development. www.sil.org.

Singleton, John. 1989. Japanese folkcraft pottery apprenticeship. In *Apprenticeship: From Theory To Method And Back Again*. M. W. Coy, ed. 13–30. Albany: State University of New York Press.

Slim, Hugo, and John Mitchell. 1992. The application of RAP and RRA techniques in emergency relief programmes. In *RAP: Rapid Assessement Procedures*. N. S. Scrimshaw and G. R. Gleason, eds. 251–57. Boston: International Nutrition Foundation for Developing Countries.

Spier, Robert F. G. 1970. *Surveying and Mapping: A Manual of Simplified Techniques*. New York: Holt, Rinehart and Winston.

Spradley, James P. 1970. *You Owe Yourself a Drunk: An Ethnography of Urban Nomads*. Boston: Little, Brown.

———. 1979. *The Ethnographic Interview*. New York: Holt, Rinehart and Winston.

———. 1980. *Participant Observation*. New York: Holt, Rinehart and Winston.

Srinivas, Mysore N. 1976. *The Remembered Village*. Berkeley: University of California Press.

Stack, Carol. 1996. Doing research in the flats. In *In the Field: Readings on the Field Research Experience*, 2nd edition. C. D. Smith and W. Kornblum, eds. 21–25. Westport, CT: Praeger.

Sterk, Claire. 1996. *Prostitution, Drug Use and AIDS*. Westport, CT: Praeger.

Stocking Jr., George W. 1983. The ethnographer's magic: Fieldwork in British anthropology from Tylor to Malinowski. In *Observers Observed: Essays in Ethnographic Fieldwork.* G.W. Stocking Jr., ed. 70–120. Madison: University of Wisconsin Press.

Stone, Allucquère Roseanne. 1995. *The War of Desire and Technology at the Close of the Mechanical Age.* Cambridge, MA: MIT Press.

Strauss, Anselm. 1987. *Qualitative Analysis for Social Scientists.* New York: Cambridge University Press.

Strauss, Anselm L., and Juliet Corbin. 1990. *Basics of Qualitative Research: Grounded Theory Procedures And Techniques.* Newbury Park, CA: Sage Publications.

———. 1998. *Basics of Qualitative Research: Techniques And Procedures For Developing Grounded Theory.* Newbury Park, CA: Sage Publications.

Tedlock, Barbara. 1991. From participant observation to the observation of participation: The emergence of narrative ethnography. *Journal of Anthropological Research* 47(1):69–94.

Thomas, Jim. 1996. Introduction: A debate about the ethics of fair practices for collecting social science data in cyberspace. *The Information Society: An International Journal* 12(2):107–18.

Tonkin, Elizabeth. 1984. Participant observation. In *Ethnographic Research: A Guide to General Conduct.* R. F. Ellen, ed. 216–23. London: Academic Press.

Turnbull, Colin. 1986. Sex and gender: The role of subjectivity in field research. In *Self, Sex and Gender in Cross-Cultural Research.* T. L. Whitehead and M. E. Conaway, eds. 17–27. Urbana: University of Illinois Press.

Van Maanen, John. 1988. *Tales of the Field: On Writing Ethnography.* Chicago: University of Chicago Press.

van Schaik, Eileen. 1992. *Work, Gender, and Culture in the Jamaican Community Health Aide Program.* Dissertation for University of Kentucky. Ann Arbor, MI: University Microfilms.

van Willigen, John. 1989. Gettin' some age on me: Social organization of older people in a rural American community. Lexington: University of Kentucky Press.

van Willigen, John, and Billie R. DeWalt. 1985. *Training Manual In Policy Ethnography.* Washington, DC: American Anthropological Association.

Villa Rojas, Alfonso. 1979. Fieldwork in the Mayan Region of Mexico. In *Long-Term Field Research in Social Anthropology.* G. Foster, T. Scudder, E. Colson, and R. Kemper, eds. 45–64. New York: Academic Press.

Vogl, Christian R., Brigitte Vogl-Lukasser, and Rajindra K. Puri. 2004. Tools and methods for data collection in ethnobotanical studies of home gardens. *Field Methods* 16(3):285–306.

Ward, Colleen, Stephen Bochner, and Adrian Furnham. 2001. *The Psychology of Culture Shock.* Philadelphia: Routledge.

Warren, Carol A. B. 1988. *Gender Issues in Field Research.* Newbury Park, CA: Sage Publications.

Waskul, Dennis. 1996. Considering the electronic participant: Some polemical observations on the ethics of online research. *The Information Society: An International Journal* 12(2):129–40.

Wax, Rosalie H. 1971. *Doing Fieldwork.* Chicago: University of Chicago Press.

Weatherford, Jack M. 1986. *Porn Row.* New York: Arbor House.

Webb, Sidney, and Beatrice P. Webb. 1902. *Problems of Modern Industry*. London: Longmans, Green and Co.

Weiner, Annette B. 1988. *The Trobrianders of Papua New Guinea*. New York: Holt, Rinehart and Winston.

Weller, Susan C., and A. Kimball Romney. 1988. *Systematic Data Collection. Qualitative Research Methods Series, Volume 10*. Thousand Oaks, CA: Sage Publications.

Werner, Oswald, and Lawrence Kuznar. 2001. Ethnographic mapmaking: Part 2: Practical concerns and triangulation. *Field Methods* 13(3):291–96.

Werner, Oswald, and G. M. Schoepfle. 1987a. *Systematic Data Analysis*. Volume 1: *Foundations of Ethnography and Interviewing*. Newbury Park, CA: Sage Publications.

———. 1987b. *Systematic Data Analysis*. Volume 2: *Ethnographic Analysis and Data Management*. Newbury Park, CA: Sage Publications.

Whitehead, T. L., and M. E. Conaway, eds. 1986. *Self, Sex and Gender in Cross-Cultural Research*. Urbana: University of Illinois Press.

Whyte, William Foote. 1996a. Doing research in Cornerville. In *In the Field: Readings on the Field Research Experience*, 2nd edition. C. D. Smith and W. Kornblum, eds. 73–85. Westport, CT: Praeger.

———. 1996b. *On the Evolution of Street Corner Society*. Boulder, CO: Westview Press.

Whyte, William Foote, and Katherine King Whyte. 1984. *Learning from the Field: A Guide from Experience*. Beverly Hills, CA: Sage Publications.

Wiese, H. Jean. 1974. *Communication and Interviewing, a Self-Instructional Packet*. Lexington: University of Kentucky College of Medicine, Department of Behavioral Science.

Wilk, Richard R. 2001. The impossibility and necessity of re-inquiry: Finding middle ground in social science. *The Journal of Consumer Research* 28(2):308–12.

Wolcott, Harry. 1994. *Transforming Qualitative Data: Description, Analysis, and Interpretation*. Thousand Oaks, CA: Sage Publications.

———. 1999. *Ethnography: A Way of Seeing*. Walnut Creek, CA: AltaMira Press.

Wolf, Eric. 1982. *Europe and the People without History*. Berkeley: University of California Press.

Wycliffe Bible Translators. 2010. Wycliffe Bible Translators: World Missions for Unreached People Groups, www.wycliffe.org (accessed June 11, 2010).

Young, James C. 1980. *Medical Choice In A Mexican Village*. New Brunswick, NJ: Rutgers University Press.

Yow, Valerie Raleigh. 1994. *Recording Oral History: A Practical Guide for Social Scientists*. Thousand Oaks, CA: Sage Publications.

❧ Index ❧

AAA. *See* American Anthropological Association

abstraction, 200

acceptance: breakthrough moment of, 54–56; enhanced, 56; fear of non, 65

accuracy, 94; of information, 48, 205; of interpretation, 172; of observation, 89, 166

activism, ethnography and, 34, 53

adjustment, process of, 69

Adler, Patricia, 12, 22, 24–25, 27, 31, 39

Adler, Peter, 12, 22, 24–25, 27, 31, 39

Agar, Michael, 35, 44–45, 46–47, 94, 132, 204

age, 30, 94, 130

agriculture, 61–62; research on, 38, 51, 52, 128, 133

Allen, Katherine, 101

American Anthropological Association (AAA), 211, 213, 218, 223; code of ethics, 53, 215, 216, 219, 225

American Sociological Association (ASA), 211, 213

analysis, 21, 109, 110, 228; ability of, 5, 12, 17, 20, 26; field notes and, 159, 166, 170–71, 179; getting, done, 78; involvement and, 31;

notes, 170–71, 189, 190, 207; parts of, 188–89, 190, 200; process of, 209; quality of, 10–15; statistical, 195; of texts, 2, 22, 35, 207. *See also* data analysis

anger, 70

anonymity, 215, 218, 221, 222

Anthropological Research: The Structure of Inquiry (Pelto, P. and Pelto, G.), 158

anthropology, 2, 3, 5, 35, 126, 127, 157–58, 163; contemporary, 36, 39; controversies in, 94; interpretation and, 95; methods of, 19; nutritional, 91

anxiety, 68, 69, 70, 73

apprenticeship, 7, 11, 12

Argonauts of the Western Pacific (Malinowski), 7

Arhem, Kaj, 29

ASA. *See* American Sociological Association

Ashkenazi, Michael, 103

audit trail, 184, 185, 190, 205, 207, 210; defined, 206

Avenarius, 25–26, 224

Babbie, Earl R., 142

Bailey, Frederick G., 197

Baird, Spencer, 6

❧ About the Authors ❧

Kathleen M. DeWalt earned her Ph.D. in anthropology from the University of Connecticut (1980). She is a professor of anthropology and public health, and director of the Center for Latin American Studies at the University of Pittsburgh. From 1978 to 1993 she was a member of the Faculty of Medicine of the University of Kentucky College of Medicine. Since 1970 she has been carrying out research related to health and nutrition issues in Mexico, Brazil, Honduras, Ecuador, and rural Kentucky. Her primary research interests are in the impact of economic, agricultural, and health policy on the food security and health of families and individuals living in economically marginal rural communities. Her most recent research projects are on the impact of income-generating projects on women's social power and child welfare in several communities in Ecuador and the food systems and nutritional status of the Kichwa people of Napo Province, Ecuador. Her research has been funded by the National Science Foundation, National Heart Lung and Blood Institute, The National Institute on Aging, the National Institute for Nursing Research, the Mc Arthur Foundation, the U.S. Department of Agriculture, and the U.S. Agency for International Development. She is the author of five books and monographs and over seventy-five papers, chapters, and reports. She has served as the president of the Council for Nutritional Anthropology, Chair of the Committee on the Status of Women in Anthropology, and on the Nominations Committee of the American Anthropological Association.

Billie R. DeWalt is the founding president and director of the Musical Instrument Museum (MIM) in Phoenix, Arizona. He joined the museum in March 2007 with the responsibility for building a staff, assembling a globally comprehensive and renowned collection, fundraising, and coordinating with the building construction team. Prior to joining MIM, he served as the director of the Carnegie Museum of Natural History in Pittsburgh

About the Authors

from 2001 to 2007. At the University of Pittsburgh, he was director of the Center for Latin American Studies from 1993 to 2001 and distinguished service professor of public and international affairs from 1993 to 2007. He has a B.A. in sociology and anthropology (1969) and Ph.D. in cultural anthropology (1976), both from the University of Connecticut. He held teaching and administrative positions in anthropology at the University of Kentucky from 1977 to 1993. His extensive publications as an anthropologist focus on the human dimensions of natural resource and environmental policies, the cultures of Latin America, human ecology, and anthropological methods. He has received Fulbright awards for teaching and research in Ecuador and Argentina; overseen major international projects in Mexico, Honduras, and Ecuador; and supervised the work of doctoral students who have worked in many parts of the world. As a consultant on the human dimensions of agriculture, forestry, biodiversity, poverty, and aquaculture policy, he has served frequently as a consultant for such organizations as the World Wildlife Fund, World Bank, International Finance Corporation, Inter-American Development Bank, and the U.S. Agency for International Development.